Linkages between Land Management, Land Degradation, and Poverty in Sub-Saharan Africa

The Case of Uganda

Ephraim Nkonya, John Pender, Kayuki C. Kaizzi, Edward Kato, Samuel Mugarura, Henry Ssali, and James Muwonge

RESEARCH REPORT 159

INTERNATIONAL FOOD
POLICY RESEARCH INSTITUTE
sustainable solutions for ending hunger and poverty

IFPRI®

International Food Policy Research Institute
2033 K Street, NW
Washington, D.C. 20006-1002, U.S.A.
Telephone +1-202-862-5600
www.ifpri.org

DOI: 10.2499/9780896291683RR159

Library of Congress Cataloging-in-Publication Data

Linkages between land management, land degradation, and poverty in
   Sub-Saharan Africa : the case of Uganda / Ephraim Nkonya . . . [et al.].
      p.   cm. — (IFPRI research report ; 159)
   Includes bibliographical references.
   ISBN 978-0-89629-168-3 (alk. paper)
   1. Land use—Africa, Sub-Saharan. 2. Land use—Uganda. 3. Land
degradation—Africa, Sub-Saharan. 4. Land degradation—Uganda. 5.
Poverty—Africa, Sub-Saharan. 6. Poverty—Uganda. I. Nkonya, Ephraim.
II. International Food Policy Research Institute. III. Series: Research report
(International Food Policy Research Institute) ; 159.
HD966.L56   2008
333.73'1370967—dc22   2008039761

Contents

Tables

Figures

Foreword

A recent study by the Food and Agriculture Organization of the United Nations and World Soil Information revealed that about 24 percent of the world's land surface is degraded. The study also showed that about 1.5 billion people depend on that land. The area that is most affected is the part of Africa that is south of the equator—it accounts for 18 percent of the global degraded area. Given that the majority of the poor in Sub-Saharan Africa depend on agriculture for their livelihoods, efforts to address land degradation are crucial in achieving the Millennium Development Goals as well as national-level goals to significantly reduce poverty in the region.

Understanding the linkages between land degradation, land management, and poverty is essential for designing policies that simultaneously reduce poverty, reverse land degradation, and encourage the adoption of sustainable land management practices. This study uses carefully selected biophysical and socioeconomic variables to examine the case of Uganda, a country that has made significant progress in poverty reduction and is among the countries classified as experiencing severe land degradation.

Overall the results show a strong linkage between poverty and land degradation in Uganda and give credence to the land degradation–poverty trap, although some indicators did show a negative association with land degradation. The findings also indicate that investments in soil and water conservation and agroforestry simultaneously reduce land degradation and poverty and increase agricultural productivity. This underscores the importance of organic soil fertility-management practices in efforts to reduce land degradation and poverty in Sub-Saharan Africa.

The authors also found that strategies such as improving rural roads and access to rural finance are effective in reducing poverty, but their impact on the adoption of sustainable land management practices is generally not significant. Interestingly, nonfarm activities increase household income and are associated with lower soil erosion and higher soil nutrient balances. The results suggest that on their own investments in poverty reduction or agricultural modernization are not sufficient to address the problem of land degradation. What is required are complementary strategies that simultaneously reduce poverty and ensure sustainable land management in Uganda and Sub-Saharan Africa in general.

Joachim von Braun
Director General, IFPRI

Acknowledgments

The authors are grateful to the Trust Fund for Environmentally and Socially Sustainable Development for providing financial support to this research; to the World Bank, the Makerere University Institute of Statistics and Applied Economics, the Uganda Bureau of Statistics, the National Agricultural Research Organization of Uganda, and the Agricultural University of Norway for partnership with IFPRI in this project; and to the many farmers and community leaders who participated in the survey on which this study is based. Any errors or omissions are solely the responsibility of the authors.

Acronyms and Abbreviations

AEZ   agroecological zone

BNF   biological nitrogen fixation

CAADP   Comprehensive African Agricultural Development Program

CPR   common property resource

ENDR   economic nutrient depletion ratio

GDP   gross domestic product

GPS   global positioning system

IV   instrumental variables

K   potassium

LVCM   Lake Victoria crescent and Mbale

masl   meters above sea level

MFI   microfinance institution

N   nitrogen

NAADS   National Agricultural Advisory Services

NAP   National Action Plan

NEPAD   New Partnership for African Development

NGO   nongovernmental organization

NM   northern moist

NRM   natural resource management

NW   northwestern

OLS   ordinary least squares

P   phosphorus

PEAP   Poverty Eradication Action Plan

PMA   Plan for Modernization of Agriculture

PMI   potential market integration index

PRSP   Poverty Reduction Strategy Paper

RUSLE	revised universal soil loss equation
SIP	Strategic Investment Plan
SLM	sustainable land management
SSA	Sub-Saharan Africa
SUR	seemingly unrelated regression
SW	southwestern
SWC	soil and water conservation
SWH	southwestern highlands
3SLS	three-stage least square method
2SLS	two-stage least square method
TLU	tropical livestock units;
UBOS	Uganda Bureau of Statistics
UNCCD	United Nations Convention to Combat Desertification
UNHS	Uganda National Household Survey
Ush	Ugandan shillings
VIF	variance inflation factor
WNW	west Nile and northwestern

Summary

Poverty reduction and sustainable land management are two objectives that most African countries strive to achieve simultaneously. In designing policies to achieve these objectives concurrently a clear understanding of their linkage is crucial. Yet there is only limited empirical evidence to demonstrate the linkage between poverty and land management in Africa. Using Uganda as a case study, this analysis seeks to better understand this linkage. We used several poverty measures to demonstrate the linkage between poverty and a number of indicators of sustainable land management. In general we found a strong linkage. The results for many poverty indicators give credence to the land degradation–poverty trap, although some indicators showed negative association with land degradation.

These results suggest that certain poverty reduction strategies being implemented through agricultural modernization in Africa can achieve win-win-win outcomes, simultaneously increasing productivity, reducing poverty, and reducing land degradation. Examples of such strategies include promoting investments in soil and water conservation and agroforestry. Some strategies—such as road development, encouragement of nonfarm activities, and promotion of rural finance—appear to contribute to positive outcomes without significant trade-offs. Other strategies are likely to involve trade-offs among different objectives.

The presence of such trade-offs is not an argument for avoiding these strategies; rather it suggests the need to recognize and find ways to ameliorate such negative impacts where they occur. For example, incorporating teaching of the principles of sustainable agriculture and land management into educational curricula, and into the technical assistance approach of the National Agricultural Advisory Services and other organizations, is one important way of addressing such trade-offs. Investment in poverty reduction and agricultural modernization by itself is not sufficient to address the problem of land degradation in Uganda; it must be complemented by greater efforts to promote sustainable land management practices.

CHAPTER 1

Introduction

Problem and Background

Poverty and land degradation are major problems in Sub-Saharan Africa (SSA). About 41 percent of the population of SSA—more than 300 million people—lived on less than US$1 per day in 2005—the highest poverty rate of any region of the world (World Bank 2007). In recent years there has been some progress in reducing poverty in SSA, but the rate of progress falls far short of the Millennium Development Goal of cutting poverty in half by 2015.

Over 70 percent of the SSA population of over 750 million people live in rural areas, depending heavily on natural resources for their livelihoods (Thirtle, Lin, and Piesse 2003; UNDP 2004). Agriculture is the major sector on which two-thirds of the population depends (Diagana 2003; Thirtle, Lin, and Piesse 2003). Unfortunately agricultural productivity in most of the region has been stagnant or declining. SSA is the only region in the world where average cereal yields have not significantly increased and per capita food production has declined since the 1980s (Muchena et al. 2005).

Poor inherent soil fertility and other biophysical factors are important constraints to agricultural productivity in much of SSA (FAO 1995; Voortman, Sonneveld, and Keyzer 2000). However, land degradation is also a major cause of poor agricultural performance in the region. Nearly two-thirds of agricultural lands in Africa were estimated by one influential study to have degraded between 1945 and 1990, with serious degradation (involving major loss of productivity) on nearly one-fifth of agricultural land (Oldeman et al. 1991). Degradation is particularly severe in the drylands of SSA (Oldeman et al. 1991), with about half of these lands estimated to be severely degraded (Dregne and Chou 1992). The most important forms of degradation are soil erosion, caused by both water and wind, and soil nutrient depletion, caused by overgrazing, devegetation, crop production on fragile lands without sufficient soil cover or use of conservation measures, declining use of fallow, and limited application of soil nutrients.

Some of the areas experiencing the most rapid degradation are very densely populated areas with young and relatively fertile volcanic soils on steep mountain slopes, as in much of the highlands of eastern and central Africa (Smaling, Nandwa, and Janssen 1997; Voortman, Sonneveld, and Keyzer 2000; Henao and Baanante 2006). According to some experts, declining soil fertility (which includes the effects of soil erosion) is the root biophysical cause of stagnant and declining agricultural productivity in SSA (Sanchez et al. 1997; Lynam, Nandwa, and Smaling 1998), and it has particularly affected the land on which the poor depend (Sanchez 2002).

The severe land degradation in the region has threatened the agricultural productivity and livelihoods of the poor (Lufumpa 2005) and thereby efforts to reduce poverty. Estimates of cumulative productivity losses due to soil erosion in SSA range widely across countries and studies, from 2 to 40 percent (Scherr 2000). Bojö (1996) and Scherr (2000), citing case studies from several SSA countries, estimated gross annual immediate losses due to soil degradation (loss in productivity in the current year due to current degradation) to range from less than 1 percent (in most cases) to as high as 9 percent. However—considering that land degradation can cause permanent reductions in productivity, not just losses in the current year—the present value of expected future production losses due to current degradation (gross discounted future losses) should also be considered. Estimates of the value of these future losses range from less than 1 percent to as high as 18 percent (Bojö 1996; Scherr 2000). A more recent study by Jansky and Chandran (2004) estimated that land degradation reduces the annual agricultural gross domestic product (GDP) of Africa by 3 percent. Based on available literature, it appears that annualized current and future losses resulting from land degradation in SSA may average in the range of a few percent of agricultural GDP per year, with large variations across time and space (Yesuf et al. 2005).

In the past decade several critics have challenged the generality, methodology, accuracy, and motivations of many commonly cited studies concerning the extent and impacts of land degradation in Africa. Several question the extent of land degradation, providing examples of particular cases in which land conditions have improved in recent history (Tiffen, Mortimore, and Gichuki 1994; Fairhead and Leach 1996; Leach and Mearns 1996; McCann 1999) or evidence that earlier land conditions (for example, forest cover) were not as favorable as previously thought (McCann 1999). Some studies argue that land degradation is highly context specific, acknowledging that land degradation is a problem for some farmers in some places and times, but arguing that the problem is not as universal as is

sometimes claimed (for example, Elias and Scoones 1999). Some critique the methods used by agronomists and others to estimate land degradation as being conceptually flawed, subject to large errors, and driven by political motives (for example, Stocking 1996; Bassett and Crummey 2003; Keeley and Scoones 2003; Fairhead and Scoones 2005). For example, the common practice of scaling up estimates of soil erosion based on plot-level measurements and models to larger national or regional scales may overstate the impacts of erosion by orders of magnitude, since most of the soil eroded from particular plots is redeposited in nearby fields (Stocking 1996).

Some of these criticisms are well founded (Koning and Smaling 2005). Nevertheless many studies document serious degradation, and some of the studies questioning the importance of land degradation also suffer from methodological flaws, such as ignoring sources of soil nutrient outflows that are difficult to quantify (Koning and Smaling 2005). Regardless of the methodological and ideological debates and nuances, it seems clear that land degradation is a major problem confronting many (but not all) farmers in SSA, contributing to the problems of low agricultural productivity and poverty (Chen and Ravallion 2000; Dorward et al. 2004; Sachs et al. 2004; Lufumpa 2005).

Beyond its impacts on current agricultural production and poverty, land degradation represents a form of dis-saving in natural capital that will affect future production prospects and poverty, and that is not accounted for by traditional measures of income and savings. Even recent efforts to expand measures of wealth and savings to include changes in natural and human capital have not incorporated land degradation (Hamilton and Clemens 1999; World Bank 2006). The implications of this omission are likely to be substantial for SSA, for which estimates of "genuine savings" (which include depletion of exhaustible resources and deforestation as dis-saving, as well as investments in education as saving, but which exclude land degradation) averaged –2.8 percent in the early 1990s (Hamilton and Clemens 1999). Sachs et al. (2004) estimate that soil nutrient depletion represents an additional dis-saving of about 2 percent of Africa's gross national income; accounting for this would nearly double the estimated rate of dis-saving to –4.8 percent. Thus the negative impact of soil fertility depletion on the potential for sustainable economic growth and poverty reduction in Africa is substantial.[1]

At the regional and country levels, several strategies have been formulated to reduce poverty and land degradation (Anonymous 2007a). Of 49 African countries, 38 have developed National Action Plans (NAPs) under the United Nations Convention to Combat Desertification (UNCCD), and 18 countries have incorporated the NAPs into their Poverty Reduction Strategy Papers (PRSPs) (Anonymous 2007a; UNCCD 2007).[2] The Comprehensive African Agricultural Development Program (CAADP) of the New Partnership for African Development (NEPAD), in collaboration with African governments and donors, places high priority on promoting sustainable land management (SLM) in its investment plans. CAADP has emerged as one of the important programs for coordinating country- and regional-level agricultural and SLM investments in collaboration with international donors who are currently seeking to harmonize their support through the Paris Declaration. TerrAfrica, a global partnership to scale up, mainstream, and finance country-driven SLM approaches in Africa, is currently working in partnership with CAADP to coordinate country- and regional-level SLM investments.

These new initiatives to reduce poverty and land degradation have increased the need to understand the linkages between the two in order to implement policies appropriately. Many observers have hypothesized that a downward spiral of poverty and land degradation (or, more broadly, environmental degradation) exists in developing countries. Past studies have shown that the relationships between poverty and land management are complex, context specific, and resource specific.[3] More empirical evidence is needed to assess this complex relationship and to formulate policies for reducing poverty sustainably.

Objectives and Contributions of This Study

The main focus of this research is on how poverty—broadly defined to include limitations in physical, human, natural, and financial capital as well as limited access to infrastructure and services (Reardon and Vosti 1995)—influences land management practices, land degradation in the form of soil erosion and depletion of soil nutrients, crop productivity, and household incomes in Uganda. We investigate how policy-relevant factors—such as access to infrastructure, education, agricultural technical assistance, and credit—influence households'

---

[1]For example, Dasgupta (2000, 651)—using Hamilton and Clemens's (1999) estimates of the average dis-saving rate in SSA in the early 1990s (–2.8 percent), together with the estimated population growth rate of 2.7 percent and an assumed output/wealth ratio of 0.25—estimated the annual rate of change of per capita wealth in SSA to be –3.4 percent (–2.8 percent × 0.25 – 2.7 percent = –3.4 percent). Using the same method, but assuming a genuine dis-saving rate of –4.8 percent, based on the estimate of Sachs et al. (2004) for the effects of soil fertility depletion, results in a rate of change of per capita wealth of –3.9 percent. In other words, soil fertility depletion in SSA is estimated to reduce per capita wealth by 0.5 percent per year.

[2]These are Benin, Burkina Faso, Burundi, Cape Verde, Chad, Comoros, Djibouti, Ghana, Kenya, Lesotho, Madagascar, Mali, Mauritania, Niger, Senegal, Swaziland, Togo, and Uganda.

[3]The literature on these issues is reviewed in Chapter 2.

land management decisions and land degradation, thus providing information that can help prevent or reverse poverty and land degradation spirals where they occur. The results of this study will help the government of Uganda and its partners design policies for sustainable management and utilization of land for the present generation and future generations, as well as provide a case study of interest to researchers, development practitioners, and policymakers working in other countries of SSA.

We use Uganda as a case study because the country has been conducting ambitious poverty reduction efforts and has implemented ambitious conservation programs. Uganda is among the countries with the most severe soil nutrient depletion in Africa (Stoorvogel and Smaling 1990; Wortmann and Kaizzi 1998). For example, the estimated average depletion rates for nitrogen (N), phosphorus (P), and potassium (K) in SSA are –22, –2.5, and –15 kg/ha per year, respectively, while the equivalent rates in Uganda are –21, –8, and –43 kg/ha per year (Smaling, Nandwa, and Janssen 1997; Wortmann and Kaizzi 1998). Uganda also has numerous different agroecological zones (AEZs), which are representative of many of the biophysical features in which SSA farmers operate. These range from the zones in the north and northeastern parts of the country, characterized by dry unimodal rainfall and low agricultural potential, to the highlands and the southern region around Lake Victoria, characterized by bimodal rainfall and high agricultural potential. These heterogeneous biophysical characteristics make Uganda a good case study to represent the diverse biophysical characteristics of many countries in SSA.

One of the specific objectives of this study was to help the national statistical bureaus in SSA to establish a data collection module on land management and degradation that could be linked to their national income and expenditure surveys, to help develop the statistical basis for monitoring and assessing linkages between

changes in poverty and land degradation in the future. The Uganda Bureau of Statistics (UBOS) served as a good partner for this study because it has been conducting national household surveys on a regular basis since the early 1990s. The community and household survey conducted for this study in 2003 was therefore linked to the 2002–03 Uganda National Household Survey (UNHS), drawn from a subsample of the UNHS households. The analysis in this study draws from both the UNHS and the additional survey conducted for this study.

As noted in the literature review in Chapter 2, several studies have enabled investigation of some of the linkages between poverty and land management, and numerous studies have sought to estimate land degradation in SSA, but few have addressed the linkages between poverty and land degradation (taking into account the effects of poverty on land management and hence on degradation). In those that have, the coverage has generally been quite limited. This study seeks to address this information gap, analyzing data from a survey of 851 households in 123 communities representing six of the major seven AEZs of Uganda, conducted in 2003 at the community, household, and plot levels.

This report builds on earlier studies by Nkonya et al. (2004) and Pender et al. (2004b) in Uganda. The study by Pender et al. (2004b) assessed the household-level linkages between poverty and land management to the extent possible by analyzing available survey data from the 1999–2000 UNHS, which collected information on the use of inputs in crop production (for example, seeds and inorganic and organic fertilizer) and on crop production and income at the household level. Many, but not all, of the results in Pender et al. (2004b) support the idea that poverty, broadly defined, contributes to less intensive land management and lower productivity and income. However, several limitations of that study affected its ability to draw definitive conclusions about the linkages between poverty and land degradation. No land quality indicators were measured in the 1999–2000 UNHS, so estimated land value was used as a proxy; but land values may be poorly estimated and may reflect many factors other than land quality. The levels of use of inputs and of crop production were measured only at the household level, limiting the ability to take into account plot-specific characteristics that affect these responses. More importantly no indicators of land degradation were measured, so that the relationships of poverty with land degradation could not be directly assessed.

The analysis of the determinants of soil nutrient loss in this study builds on an approach pioneered in a small study of the determinants of household soil nutrient balances in eastern Uganda (Nkonya, Kaizzi, and Pender 2005). In this study the assessment of nutrient depletion is at the plot rather than the household level (which is the more relevant level for considering land degradation impacts), and this study has broader coverage with a much larger sample size, so that more robust conclusions can be drawn.

In the present study information on land quality indicators, land management, and land degradation was collected at the plot level, so that plot-specific characteristics and responses could be taken into account. Soil samples were used to quantify measures of soil fertility and as an input into the estimation of soil erosion and soil nutrient losses based on the survey data. Use of better soil quality indicators at the plot level (especially soil nutrient stock, plot slope, and topsoil depth) is one of the major contributions of this study. These indicators have not been used in many related studies (for example, Bhalla 1988; Barrett 1996; Lamb 2003). The availability of improved soil nutrient data helps us to better understand the relationship between land management and poverty.

The empirical analysis in this study focuses on linkages between poverty, land management, and land degradation at the household and plot levels in Uganda. There are many potentially important linkages between poverty and collective decisions affecting land management that are made at the level of farmer groups or communities, or at other decisionmaking levels beyond the individual household; these are not addressed in this study. We have recently published companion research in Uganda on some of these issues—for example, the impacts of poverty on communities' enactment of and compliance with bylaws and regulations related to natural resource management (NRM)—based on the community surveys used for this study (Nkonya, Pender, and Kato 2008).

As discussed in Chapter 4, we are limited in our ability to assert causal relationships between indicators of poverty, land management, and land degradation owing to the complex and multidirectional nature of the possible relationships and the cross-sectional nature of our data. Hence throughout the report we refer to observed statistical relationships as "associations" rather than using language implying causality, such as "determinants" of responses and outcomes or "impacts" of particular factors. The lack of causal certainty limits the policy implications that we are able to draw from the results, which are presented as potential implications deserving further analysis rather than as definitive implications or recommendations. Despite these limitations, we believe this study adds substantially to the existing literature on the linkages between poverty and land management in Africa because of the uniquely rich dataset used and our efforts to address potential confounding factors in these relationships using the best available statistical methods. It also establishes an important baseline on which future panel data collection efforts and dynamic analysis of these issues can build.

Organization of the Study

The rest of the report is organized as follows. The next chapter reviews the literature and presents the conceptual and empirical frameworks and hypotheses that guided this study. Chapter 3 discusses the agroecological, socioeconomic, and policy context of Uganda, and what situations the study may represent beyond Uganda. Chapter 4 discusses the research methodology, including data collection, soil nutrient balance computation, and analytical methods. Chapter 5 discusses the severity of land degradation and the factors associated with land degradation, focusing on soil erosion and soil nutrient depletion, which are the major forms of land degradation in SSA. The chapter also investigates the factors associated with variations in land management practices, purchased seeds, and the intensity of preharvest labor use. Chapter 6 assesses the factors associated with variations in crop productivity and household per capita income. Chapter 7 summarizes the results and evaluates their relevance to SSA. This chapter also discusses the weaknesses and gaps of the study and suggests future research to address them. Chapter 8 concludes the report and draws some potential policy implications of the findings.

CHAPTER 2

Linkages between Poverty
and Land Management

I n this chapter we review the literature on the linkages between poverty and land degradation, then present the conceptual framework and set of hypotheses, based on the literature
review and on our own reasoning, that guided this study. After defining concepts that are
used in the study and reviewing the literature, we present the specific empirical framework used
in analyzing the linkages between poverty, land management, agricultural productivity, land
degradation, and other causal and conditioning factors for the households in the study. We also
discuss the dynamic household model of livelihood and land management decisions.[1]

Definitions and Concepts: Poverty and Land Degradation

Poverty can be defined in many ways and has many dimensions. Typically economists study
income or consumption poverty, but poverty may also be measured by lack of assets, access
to infrastructure and services, education, or other factors that determine a household or community's livelihood status. Among the poor the meaning of poverty differs widely, depending
on their livelihoods and endowments of physical, human, natural, and financial capital. The
Uganda Participatory Poverty Assessment Process defines poverty as lack of basic needs
and services (food, clothing, and shelter), basic health care, education, and productive assets
(MFPED 2003). Poverty may also be considered to include lack of democracy or power to
make decisions that affect the livelihoods of the poor, and social exclusion. In the case of
farmers in northern Uganda, poverty also includes insecurity and internal displacement. In this
study we consider a broad definition of poverty, focusing on the impacts of limited endowments of physical, human, natural, and financial capital as well as poor access to services; on
land management; and on land degradation.

Reardon and Vosti (1995, 1498) define the concept of "investment poverty" as the
"(in)ability to make minimum investments in resource improvements to maintain or enhance
the quantity and quality of the resource base." They distinguish this concept from welfare
poverty as traditionally measured (based on benchmark income or consumption levels to attain minimum nutritional intake) and argue that people who are not welfare poor by traditional
definitions may be investment poor. They also argue that the threshold for investment poverty
is likely to be very context dependent, depending on local input costs and the types of investment needed for sustainable NRM. Consistent with Reardon and Vosti, and within the sustainable livelihoods framework (Carney 1998), in this study we consider poverty as a multi-

---

[1]Details of the empirical methods used are discussed in Chapter 4.

dimensional concept, involving limited access to many types of assets (for example, physical, human, natural, and financial capital), and not simply as a shortfall in current income or consumption. This approach is consistent with recent research on poverty dynamics and poverty traps, which emphasizes the importance of defining poverty in terms of asset levels (Carter and Barrett 2006).

The concepts of physical, human, natural, and financial capital draw on the sustainable livelihoods framework (Carney 1998; DFID 1999) and the substantial literature that informs that framework. Physical capital includes the stock of basic physical infrastructure and producer goods used to support livelihoods, such as roads, irrigation systems, buildings, tools, and equipment. As in Jansen et al. (2006), we include livestock in our classification of physical capital, since a household's ownership of livestock influences the productivity of both its land and its human resources in a way similar to ownership of production and transportation equipment.[2] Human capital reflects the stock of human skills, knowledge, and ability to provide labor in the household. Natural capital refers to access to and the quality of natural resources (for example, land, water, and forests) and the goods and ecosystem services that they provide. Financial capital refers to assets or access to financial flows that provide liquidity, such as savings (whether cash or stocks of readily marketable commodities) and access to credit. Investigation

of the impacts of other more political or social components of poverty—such as lack of democracy and power, social exclusion, insecurity, and internal displacement—was beyond the scope of this study.

Land degradation is the loss of productive and ecosystem services provided by land resources. For example, the UNCCD defines land degradation as "reduction or loss . . . of the biological or economic productivity and complexity of rainfed cropland, irrigated cropland, or range, pasture, forest and woodlands resulting from . . . processes . . . such as (i) soil erosion caused by wind and/or water; (ii) deterioration of the physical, biological or economic properties of the soil; and (iii) long-term loss of natural vegetation" (Pagiola 1999, 2).

Literature Review on Linkages between Poverty and Land Degradation

Interest in research on poverty and its linkage with NRM has grown enormously in the past few decades (Grepperud 1997).[3] There is as yet no consensus on the impact of poverty on land management and land degradation or vice versa. In part this is due to the complexity and context dependence of the linkages. It is also due to the lack of comparable empirical evidence on these issues, using a systematic approach to testing alternative hypotheses and dealing with the influences of confounding factors.

---

[2]For example, oxen or tractors may be used to provide draught power, and livestock provide transportation services just as do vehicles. Livestock are mentioned as a form of financial capital in the sustainable livelihoods guidance sheets of the Department for International Development (DFID 1999), since they are marketable and hence provide liquidity, but they also play the same role as other forms of physical capital. Some authors (for example, Quisumbing and Meinzen-Dick 2001) see livestock as part of natural capital, but unlike most forms of natural capital, they are produced and reproduced by people primarily for productive purposes. Regardless of the category in which one classifies particular assets, all of these types of capital, including livestock, are important determinants of livelihoods in rural areas of developing countries.

[3]We have not attempted to be and do not claim to have been exhaustive here in reviewing the vast literature related to poverty and environment linkages. We believe that the literature summarized is representative and that this review suffices to make the key points and to highlight important knowledge gaps.

The intersection of poverty, low agricultural productivity, land degradation (or more generally, natural resource or environmental degradation), and rapid population growth in SSA and some other developing regions has contributed to a commonly held hypothesis of a downward spiral of mutually reinforcing linkages among these factors (for example, WCED 1987; Durning 1989; Leonard 1989; World Bank 1992; Mink 1993; Pearce and Warford 1993; Cleaver and Schreiber 1994; Pinstrup-Andersen and Pandya-Lorch 1994). According to this hypothesis land degradation contributes to low and declining agricultural productivity, and this in turn contributes to continuing or worsening poverty. Land degradation can contribute directly to poverty, separately from its impact on agricultural productivity, by reducing the availability of other valuable goods and services important to poor households (for example, fuelwood, construction materials, wild foods, and medicinal plants) and by increasing the demands on labor needed to forage for such goods. Poverty in turn is hypothesized to contribute to land degradation as a result of poor households' presumed short-term perspective and inability to invest in natural resource conservation and improvement (Reardon and Vosti 1995).

Rapid population growth is seen by some as part of the engine driving these mechanisms, by contributing to both land degradation (for example, by causing expansion of agriculture into fragile areas and reduction of fallow periods) and poverty (for example, by reducing the stock of available assets per person and requiring high rates of savings and investment to keep pace). In some versions of the downward spiral hypothesis, poverty is also hypothesized to contribute to rapid population growth (for example, Cleaver and Schreiber 1994; Dasgupta 2000). These possible linkages between population growth, poverty, and land degradation are illustrated in Figure 2.1.

Figure 2.1 indicates possible linkages between poverty and land management, land degradation, and agricultural productivity, and the role of various factors affecting these linkages. There are 15 hypothesized linkages, labeled by number, with the direction of the hypothesized impact for each in parentheses.[4] The internal linkages (1–6) form the core of the "poverty–land degradation downward spiral" hypothesis: poverty causes poor land management, which causes land degradation and low agricultural productivity, which cause further impoverishment. The linkages between low agricultural productivity and poverty may operate in both directions, since poverty may reduce agricultural productivity separately from its impact on land management by affecting farmers' ability to use productive inputs (linkage 7) and may also be increased by declining productivity (linkage 6). This downward spiral hypothesis is often augmented by linkages with population pressure, which is asserted to cause both poor land management and poverty directly (linkages 8 and 9) and which in turn is exacerbated by poverty (linkage 10).

As is emphasized in much of the literature on poverty–environment linkages, this downward spiral is not inevitable, as it is influenced by many other factors, particularly policies, institutions, and technologies. Development and dissemination of improved land management technologies or changes in land policies and institutions may lead to improved land management (linkage 11), thus helping to break the spiral. Improved production technologies (for example, irrigation and improved seeds) may reverse de-

---

[4]In Figure 2.1 we specify hypothesized positive linkages (for example, poor land management causes land degradation) with a +, negative linkages (for example, improved production technologies reduce poor land management) with a –, and uncertain linkages (for example, poverty may or may not cause poor land management) with a ?.

Figure 2.1   Possible linkages between poverty and land management, land degradation, and agricultural productivity, with driving and conditioning factors

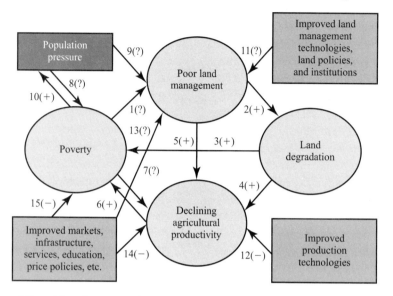

Note: Linkages followed by a ? are uncertain.

clining agricultural productivity and increase incentives to improve land management (linkage 12). Improved access to markets, infrastructure, and services, and changes in sectoral policies, may improve land managers' incentive and ability to manage land more sustainably (linkage 13). These factors are also likely to contribute directly to increased agricultural productivity, independent of impacts on land management, by increasing farmers' incentive and ability to use productivity-enhancing technologies (linkage 14). Finally, improved markets, infrastructure, and services and changes in policies may help to reduce poverty in other ways besides improving agricultural productivity (linkage 15), because they can encourage and enable people to shift into production of more profitable commodities or into profitable nonagricultural activities.

This downward spiral hypothesis has been challenged on both theoretical and empirical grounds. Theoretically there is no necessary causal link between resource degradation and worsening poverty. People may choose to degrade natural resources

while investing in other assets that yield higher returns. In this case resource degradation represents a process of substituting one type of capital for another, and it may be associated with overall improvement in incomes and welfare (Pender 1998). Of course private decisions to disinvest in natural capital may not be socially optimal if there are external benefits resulting from natural capital (for example, if conserving forests prevents sedimentation of streams and flooding and reduces atmospheric CO_2) or external costs of other forms of capital (for example, negative effects of agrochemical use on water quality). But the implications of such externalities do not necessarily depend on whether people are poor.

There is no necessary causal link between poverty and resource degradation. If markets and institutions are "perfect" (that is, they provide clear and secure access to assets, goods, and services, and they allow costless transactions among all assets, goods, and services, with perfect information), land and other resources will be allocated to their most profitable uses, and all investments yielding a positive net present value will be made (Singh, Squire, and Strauss 1986; de Janvry, Fafchamps, and Sadoulet 1991). In this (unrealistic) case, resource management and investment decisions will be independent of the characteristics of the owners of resources, including their level of poverty. Even with one missing market, resources may be efficiently allocated if all other markets are functioning competitively. For example, households facing binding cash or labor constraints may lease their land out to other households with more cash or family labor, who are thus able to farm the land more profitably and better able to make investments in the land. Thus it requires at least two market failures for household characteristics such as poverty to influence private resource management decisions.

In the more realistic case in which transaction costs, imperfect and asymmetric information, uncertainty, and other problems cause market and institutional failures, there may indeed be linkages between poverty and land degradation as illustrated in Figure 2.1. However, the possible relationships are complex, depending on the nature of the market failures, the nature of poverty, and the type of resource management and resource degradation considered. For example, if there is no land or credit market, but all other markets function perfectly, households with less wealth or income will be less able than wealthier households to invest in soil and water conservation (SWC) measures (since wealthier households can more readily hire labor or purchase other required inputs for such investments), other factors being equal. Thus households with less wealth or income may suffer greater land degradation (Pender and Kerr 1998). On the other hand wealthier households are also better able to invest in livestock, mechanical equipment, or other assets that may contribute to erosion or other forms of land degradation. Furthermore the land management practices pursued by wealthier households may increase some forms of resource degradation (for example, more erosion due

to use of mechanical equipment, or more damage to water resources and biodiversity due to greater use of agrochemicals) while reducing other forms of resource degradation (for example, less soil nutrient depletion as a result of greater ability to purchase fertilizers or greater ownership of livestock and recycling of manure) (Swinton, Escobar, and Reardon 2003).

If there are imperfect labor and land markets, households with access to more family labor relative to their land are likely to use more labor-intensive and less land-intensive farming practices—such as fallowing less or not at all, farming on steep slopes, tilling more frequently, applying manure or mulch, or investing in SWC measures—as argued by Boserup (1965) and others. Such intensification of labor may have mixed impacts on land degradation, potentially increasing soil fertility depletion as a result of declining fallow use or increasing erosion as a result of farming on steep slopes, or restoring soil fertility and reducing erosion as a result of adoption of labor-intensive soil fertility management techniques and SWC measures.

In an imperfect markets setting, the nature of poverty may be important in determining the impacts on NRM and degradation. Households that are not poor by welfare criteria such as minimum levels of consumption may nevertheless face "investment poverty" that prevents them from making profitable investments in resource conservation and improvement (Reardon and Vosti 1995). Households that lack access to roads and markets, or that own little land, may deplete soil nutrients less rapidly since they are subsistence oriented and thus export fewer soil nutrients in the form of crop sales. On the other hand households that are livestock poor may deplete soil nutrients more rapidly because they lack access to manure. A study of determinants of soil nutrient depletion in eastern Uganda found support for these hypotheses of divergent effects of different types of assets (Nkonya et al. 2004).

Empirically some of the linkages in this hypothesis are fairly noncontroversial, while others are subject to considerable debate. Next we consider some of the evidence available in the literature on the hypothesized linkages illustrated in Figure 2.1.

Impacts of Land Degradation on Agricultural Productivity and Poverty

The link between land degradation and reduced agricultural productivity holds almost by definition, although degradation may not imply an immediate loss of agricultural productivity since it may involve loss of other ecosystem services, and other factors such as improved technologies may outweigh any productivity effect. The extent to which land degradation is occurring in SSA and the magnitude, location, and time frame of productivity impacts are much debated in the literature. A wide range of productivity impacts of land degradation have been estimated in different contexts, as discussed in Chapter 1.

That reduced agricultural productivity will lead to worsening poverty is quite plausible, especially among people heavily dependent on agriculture for their livelihoods, although direct evidence on impacts of productivity changes on poverty in SSA is limited. Such a negative impact is not automatic, since people may compensate for declining agricultural productivity by increasing nonagricultural income. In rural Africa nonfarm activities often account for 40 percent or more of household income, and these appear to be growing in importance (Reardon 1997; Barrett, Reardon, and Webb 2001). Nevertheless nonfarm opportunities in rural areas are usually linked to the development and dynamism of the agricultural sector (Haggblade, Hazell, and Brown 1989; Reardon 1997), so such opportunities may be undermined by land degradation and low agricultural productivity.

Earlier research in India by Jodha (1986) and more recent research in Zimbabwe (Cavendish 2000), India (Reddy and Chakravarty 1999; Narain, Gupta, and van't Veld 2005), and Nepal (Adhikari 2003) have shown that poor households in rural areas of these countries depend heavily on common pool resources for consumption and income, and are in most cases more dependent on this income than wealthier households.[5] This does not necessarily mean that poorer households are larger users of common pool resources in total. For example, Cavendish (2000) and Adhikari (2003) found that the total value of resources taken from the commons was greater among wealthier households. Hence, while the poor may be more dependent on common pool resources and more negatively affected by degradation of these resources in most cases, this does not mean that they are always or usually the main cause of such degradation.

---

[5]In a study of 502 households in 21 villages of India Jodha (1986) found that among the poorest families the proportion of household income based directly on the local commons was in the range of 9–26 percent, while wealthier (although still absolutely poor) households derived only 1–4 percent of their income from local commons. Based on data from 232 households in 12 Himalayan villages in India, Reddy and Chakravarty (1999) found that dependence on local forest resources decreases from 23 percent for the poorest households to 4 percent for the richest. In a study of 197 households in 29 villages in rural Zimbabwe, Cavendish (2000) found that the average share of income based on the local commons was 35 percent, with the poorest quintile having the highest dependence on the local commons (about 40 percent) and the richest quintile having the lowest dependence (about 30 percent). In contrast to these findings, in a study of 537 households in 60 villages of India, Narain, Gupta, and van't Veld (2005) found a U-shaped relationship between income and dependence among common pool resource users, with dependence on income from common pool resources higher among both the poorest and the richest households than among those with intermediate income. Adhikari (2003), based on data from 330 households in eight forest user groups in Nepal, found that dependence on forest resources increases with wealth, from 14 percent for the poorest to 22 percent for the richest households.

Impacts of Poverty on Land Management and Land Degradation

Whether poverty causes people to degrade land or initiate other forms of environmental degradation is highly contested. Consistent with the hypothesis that poverty causes degradation, there is evidence from several studies in developing countries that poor rural households discount the future heavily, at higher rates than wealthier ones. These studies include those of Pender (1996) in rural India; Cuesta, Carlson, and Lutz (1997) in rural Costa Rica; Holden, Shiferaw, and Wik (1998) in rural Ethiopia, Zambia, and Indonesia; Nielsen (2001) in Madagascar; Kirby et al. (2002) in rural Bolivia; and Yesuf (2004) in rural Ethiopia. By contrast Anderson et al. (2004) did not find that private discount rates were correlated with income in Vietnam, but they did find that rural households had higher discount rates than urban ones. Several studies conducted in Ethiopia have shown that higher discount rates are associated with lower willingness to pay for conservation measures (Shiferaw and Holden 1998; Holden and Shiferaw 2002) or with less actual investment in SWC measures (Teklewold 2004; Yesuf 2004). These findings are consistent with the predictions of bioeconomic models developed for Ethiopian settings (Shiferaw and Holden 2000, 2001; Bekele 2004). Such findings are not universal, however. For example, Hagos and Holden (2006) found statistically insignificant impacts of measured discount rates on SWC investments in their study in northern Ethiopia.

Contrary to this evidence, some have argued that the view that poor people have a short-term perspective is belied by evidence from many case studies that the poor will often act to reduce consumption and preserve their assets in the face of drought and famine (Moseley 2001; Gray and Moseley 2005). Recent theoretical models have explained this phenomenon of "asset smoothing" (as opposed to the more commonly understood phenomenon of consumption smoothing) as resulting from disaster avoidance by very poor households facing survival risks (Fafchamps and Pender 1997; Dercon 1998; Zimmerman and Carter 2003). To avoid disasters such households choose to preserve assets essential to future consumption (precautionary savings), even if this means forgoing present consumption or opportunities to invest in higher-return assets. This behavior contributes to the possibility of a poverty trap, with poorer households remaining poor because they are unable to make risky investments that have higher returns, even though they demonstrate a willingness to preserve essential subsistence assets. The implications of this theory for land management decisions are not clear. To the extent that the poor recognize land quality as an essential asset to their survival, this may cause them to invest substantial effort to protect this asset. However, they may view other assets (such as their oxen and cereal seeds) as more critical to their near-term survival.

High discount rates are not the only mechanism by which poverty may influence land improvement or degradation. For example, to the extent that poverty affects households' attitudes toward or exposure to risk (as noted previously), this may also influence their decisions concerning land investments and degradation (Ekbom and Bojö 1999). The likely impact of differences in risk aversion on land investments will depend on whether such investments are risk increasing or risk reducing, with greater risk aversion expected to reduce incentives to make risk-increasing investments but expected to increase risk-reducing investments.

Evidence is mixed on whether poverty causes people to be more risk averse. In his seminal study of risk aversion among peasant farmers in India, Binswanger (1980) found no relationship between households' degree of partial risk aversion and their wealth. Similar insignificant associations between wealth and risk aversion have been observed in numerous other experimental studies of risk aversion (Cardenas and Carpenter 2005). However, one recent study in northern Ethiopia determined, using Binswanger's method, that poorer households have higher risk aversion and that higher risk aversion reduces the adoption of inorganic fertilizer (Yesuf 2004). Hagos and Holden (2006) found that poorer households in northern Ethiopia have higher risk aversion and that higher risk aversion is associated with less investment in SWC measures. By contrast Teklewold (2004) noted that greater risk aversion was associated with more investment in SWC in Ethiopia, suggesting that such investments are risk reducing in his study context. Hence the impact of poverty on land management via its impacts on risk aversion appears to be quite context dependent.

The impacts of poverty on the risk exposure of households are subject to debate. It is often argued that the poor are forced to live in marginal environments, where their exposure to risks is greater. Although there is certainly evidence that many poor people live in less-favored environments (Fan and Chan-Kang 2004), whether the incidence or depth of poverty is greater in such environments is not clear (Renkow 2000). In a rare study of determinants of peasant households' perceptions of production risk exposure, Tesfay (2006) found that wealthier households in Ethiopia were exposed to more risk, possibly because they are better able to bear risks than poorer ones (consistent with the theories of asset smoothing discussed previously). The generality of this finding is not yet clear.

Poverty may affect land management by influencing households' labor opportunity costs. If poorer households have lower labor opportunity costs than wealthier ones, due to smaller endowments of land or human capital, barriers to entry to higher-return activities, or other labor market imperfections, they may be more likely to undertake labor-intensive land management, such as implementing SWC measures (Pender and Kerr

1998) or applying organic materials to their land (Nkonya et al. 2004). In several studies conducted in different locations, households with smaller endowments of land were found to invest more per hectare in labor-intensive land improvements (for example, Clay, Reardon, and Kangasniemi 1998 for Rwanda; Pender and Kerr 1998 for India; Bekele and Drake 2003 for Ethiopia; Nkonya et al. 2004 and Pender et al. 2004b for Uganda; Hagos and Holden 2006 for Ethiopia; Jagger and Pender 2006 for Uganda; Jansen et al. 2006 for Honduras), although this finding is not universal (for example, Kazianga and Masters 2002 for Burkina Faso).

Land endowments can affect use of purchased inputs, such as inorganic fertilizer, by affecting labor opportunity costs, access to finance to purchase inputs, or the ability to fallow. Larger farms are more likely to use inorganic fertilizer in some contexts, including higher-rainfall areas of the Amhara region of Ethiopia (Benin 2006), but less likely to do so in others, such as the lower-rainfall area of Tigray (Pender and Gebremedhin 2006). Croppenstedt, Demeke, and Meschi (2003) established that larger farms in Ethiopia used less fertilizer per hectare. Different impacts of farm size on fertilizer use have been reported in Uganda (Nkonya et al. 2004; Pender et al. 2004b).

Education can influence land management decisions in complex ways by affecting labor opportunity costs; farmers' access to credit, information, and technical assistance; or ability to use modern inputs. In some contexts households with more education invest less in labor-intensive land management measures, probably because this increases labor opportunity costs (Shiferaw and Holden 1998, Gebremedhin and Swinton 2002, and Benin 2006 for Ethiopia; Place et al. 2002 for western Kenya; Nkonya et al. 2004 and Jagger and Pender 2006 for Uganda; Jansen et al. 2006 for Honduras). However, in other contexts education increases such investments, possibly because education increases awareness and access to technical assistance or relaxes credit constraints or other limitations on adoption (for example, Clay et al. 1998; Pender and Kerr 1998; Mekuria and Waddington 2002; Pender et al. 2004b).[6] Education has been observed to contribute to greater use of fertilizer in Ethiopia (Croppenstedt et al. 2003; Benin 2006), Uganda (Nkonya et al. 2004; Pender et al. 2004b), eastern Kenya (Freeman and Coe 2002), and Honduras (Jansen et al. 2006). The effects of education on land management differed between males and females in one study in Uganda, with education of males contributing to more intensive land management (Pender et al. 2004b).

Nonfarm and off-farm activities can affect land management in ambiguous ways by affecting labor opportunity costs or the ability to finance purchase of inputs and investments. Nonfarm and off-farm income have negative impacts on labor-intensive land management practices in many contexts (for example, Clay et al. 1998, Shiferaw and Holden 1998, Alemu 1999, Ersado et al. 2003, Holden et al. 2004, Hagos and Holden 2006, and Pender and Gebremedhin 2006, all for northern Ethiopia; Jagger et al. 2006; Jansen et al. 2006), but they have positive impacts in some contexts (Pender and Kerr 1998; Kazianga and Masters 2002).

Poverty—to the extent it is associated with limited access to land, education, and off-farm employment relative to household labor endowments—appears to contribute to more labor-intensive land management in many, but not all, cases. Conversely household labor constraints—another dimension of poverty—reduce the adoption of such practices in many cases (for example, Pender and Kerr 1998; Gebremedhin and Swinton 2002; Place et al. 2002; Nkonya et al. 2004; Benin 2006; Jagger and Pender 2006; Jansen et al. 2006). By contrast labor constraints are associated with greater use

of inorganic fertilizer in some cases (Freeman and Coe 2002; Pender et al. 2004b) but less in others (Croppenstedt, Demeke, and Meschi 2003; Benin 2006).

The gender composition of the household's labor endowment, which may be related to poverty, has been shown in several studies to affect land management. For example, Pender and Kerr (1998) observed that male labor supply was associated with greater investment in SWC in one of their study villages in India, while female labor supply was associated with less investment. Jagger and Pender (2006) found that increased male labor endowment contributed to greater use of some labor-intensive practices in Uganda, while female labor was associated with decreased use of some labor-intensive practices and greater use of inorganic fertilizer. Similarly Kazianga and Masters (2002) reported that female labor supply was associated with decreased adoption of labor-intensive soil conservation measures in Burkina Faso, while male labor supply was associated with greater adoption. By contrast Benin (2006) found decreased use of some conservation practices, inorganic fertilizer, and improved seeds among Ethiopian households with a larger share of male labor. Place et al. (2002) observed in western Kenya that female-headed households, from which the husbands were absent, were less likely to use chemical fertilizer but more likely to use compost than married male-headed households. Hence the balance between labor and other constraints (such as the availability of cash) is influenced by the gender composition of the household and can lead to different impacts of particular dimensions of poverty in particular contexts.

Lack of access to livestock influences land management in complex and context-dependent ways. Several studies have deter-

---

[6]Hagos and Holden (2006) found different effects of education in the Tigray region of Ethiopia depending on the type of investment: a positive impact on soil bund investment, which is less labor intensive, and a negative impact on stone terrace investment, which is more labor intensive.

mined that ownership of livestock contributes to use of manure (Clay, Reardon, and Kangasniemi 1998; Freeman and Coe 2002; Mekuria and Waddington 2002; Pender et al. 2004b; Pender and Gebremedhin 2006), as one would expect. Livestock ownership can affect other land management practices, owing to, for example, complementarity or substitution between organic inputs and other land management practices, demand for fodder for livestock, and use of animal power for traction or to transport bulky organic inputs. These factors have the potential to affect land management practices and household liquidity.

Several studies have found that greater livestock ownership is associated with greater use of inorganic fertilizer (Freeman and Coe 2002; Mekuria and Waddington 2002; Benin 2006). Jagger and Pender (2006) reported that livestock ownership is associated with greater use of inorganic fertilizer in Ethiopia, while Jansen et al. (2006) found the opposite result in Honduras. Clay, Reardon, and Kangasniemi (1998) found that livestock are associated with more erosive land uses in Rwanda. Pender and Gebremedhin (2006) observed that livestock contribute to increased use of contour plowing but decreased use of reduced tillage in Tigray, while Benin (2006) reported mixed impacts of different types of livestock (oxen versus other cattle) on land management practices in various zones of Amhara. Kazianga and Masters (2002) found that livestock intensification (that is, more involvement in intensive feeding on farms) was associated with greater adoption of SWC measures in Burkina Faso. Hence, although livestock ownership may have complex impacts on land management, in most of the studies reviewed it appears to promote more intensive land management.

Lack of access to other forms of physical capital, such as irrigation and farm equipment, can influence land management. Pender and Kerr (1998) found greater investment in SWC measures to be strongly associated with irrigation. According to

Hagos and Holden (2006) the probability of farmers' investing in stone terraces in Tigray was lower on irrigated plots, but when investments were made, the intensity of investment was greater on irrigated plots. Benin (2006) found that irrigation was associated with greater application of household refuse to farmers' plots in Amhara but with decreased use of inorganic fertilizer. Kazianga and Masters (2002) observed that ownership of agricultural equipment contributed to adoption of SWC measures in Burkina Faso. Pender et al. (2004b) found that ownership of farm equipment contributes to use of both organic and inorganic fertilizer in Uganda. In contrast, Nkonya et al. (2004) noted that ownership of farm equipment was associated with decreased use of fertilizer, slash and burn, and mulching in southern, western, and eastern Uganda. Jansen et al. (2006) observed that ownership of farm equipment was associated with decreased use of zero or minimum tillage. Overall, ownership of equipment is associated with more intensive land management practices in most of the cases reviewed.

Impacts of Population Pressure on Land Management and Land Degradation

Concerning population pressure, there is substantial evidence that poverty is a cause as well as a consequence of rapid population growth (Dasgupta 2000; Birdsall and Sinding 2001). However, as argued by Boserup (1965) and her followers, population growth can induce responses, in terms of agricultural intensification and technological and institutional innovation, that act to reduce poverty and natural resource degradation. There are many examples of such induced intensification and innovation leading to improved welfare and NRM (for example, Tiffen, Mortimore, and Gichuki 1994; Leach and Mearns 1996; Templeton and Scherr 1999). However, there is also much evidence that such Boserupian responses have not occurred to a substantial extent in the wake of rapid population growth in many developing countries, especially in SSA (Kates and Haarmann 1992; Grepperud 1996; López 1998; Pender et al. 2001a). Hence population pressure and its linkages to poverty remain major concerns in the effort to promote sustainable development in SSA, although their importance varies considerably across contexts.

Impacts of Property Rights and Land Tenure

Lack of secure access to private property is commonly viewed as a major constraint to SLM and improved livelihoods of the poor in developing countries. To some, formalization of land rights is a prerequisite for enabling productive use of the large amount of "dead capital" in many poor countries (for example, De Soto 2000). There have been several studies demonstrating that insecure private tenure is a problem for poor people in developing countries and that land titling can help address the problem (for example, Feder et al. 1988 for Thailand; Alston, Libecap, and Schneider 1996 for Brazil; López 1997 for Honduras; and Deininger and Chamorro 2004 for Nicaragua). Yet there are even more studies showing that customary land tenure systems in SSA provide sufficient tenure security to promote SLM and that land titling efforts in this context have often been ineffective or, even worse, have undermined the tenure security of the poor (for example, Atwood 1990; Migot-Adholla et al. 1991; Place and Hazell 1993; Platteau 1996; Toulmin and Quan 2000; Deininger 2003). This does not mean that land tenure security is not a problem in SSA or that formalization efforts are never warranted or effective (for example, Deininger et al. 2003, 2007). But such efforts must be tailored to the particular local context, and the general presumption that insecure private land tenure is a major constraint to sustainable rural development is false. Evidence on the context-specific nature of land tenure insecurity and its relationship to poverty and land degradation is needed to guide policies.

Unrestricted access to common pool resources has long been seen as a major cause of resource degradation and impoverishment in developing countries, at least since the time of Olson's (1965) seminal work on collective action and Hardin's (1968) influential essay on the "tragedy of the commons." In contrast to the pessimistic predictions of Olson and Hardin about the possibility of effective local collective action to manage commons, research on common property resource (CPR) management in the past two decades has established that effective and sustainable institutions for CPR management exist in many environments of the developing world and has identified some of the conditions that contribute to the emergence and effectiveness of these institutions (for example, Wade 1987; Ostrom 1990; Baland and Platteau 1996; Agrawal 2001). Many factors have been identified (or hypothesized, based on theory and case study evidence) in this literature as contributing to the emergence and sustainable management of CPRs (Agrawal 2001). Most of them are relevant to the relationships between poverty and common land management. Examples of such factors are shared norms and prior successful experience of the resource users in collective action (that is, social capital), interdependence among group members, heterogeneity of the endowments of group members but homogeneity of their interests and identities, low poverty and low discount rates of resource users, high dependence of group members on the resource, a low level of and gradual change in user demands for the resource, ease of rule enforcement, low levels of articulation with external markets, and a supportive role of state institutions.

This extensive list of factors includes many that may be undermined by poverty, as well as others that may be more common in poor communities. For example, poverty is hypothesized by Agrawal (2001) to undermine CPR management to the extent that poorer people consume more resources per person from the commons than wealthier households, as found by Jodha (1986). However, as we have seen, there is evidence from several more recent studies that wealthier households in some cases consume more from the commons per household, even when the share of income earned from the commons is greater for the poor. Hence poverty may favor less total exploitation of the commons, and it may be associated with greater dependence on the resource—another factor that, Agrawal (2001) hypothesizes, enables better CPR management. Other positive factors associated with poverty that enable effective CPR management include the observations that poor communities are often quite interdependent, that they may be (but are not necessarily) more homogeneous in their interests and endowments than wealthier communities, that they are often more remote from markets, and that it may be easier to impose penalties on poor individuals than on wealthier ones, as the poor may have less political power or ability to leave the community.

On the negative side, poorer people often tend to have higher discount rates, which are argued by Ostrom (1990, 8–45) to undermine the emergence of CPR institutions, since the present value of future costs that can be imposed on rule violators declines with higher discount rates. Poor people may be relatively well endowed with social capital, although there is substantial evidence that many poor people have limited capital, social and otherwise (Tripp 2006). To the extent that poverty is associated with more rapid population growth, poverty may contribute to a rapidly growing demand for common pool resources, tending to undermine CPR management. The role of state institutions is not necessarily determined by poverty, although in many cases state policies toward people in poor areas are top-down and paternalistic rather than supportive of local institutional devel-

opment, due in part to the limited political influence of poor communities and in part to the belief that poverty causes poor people to degrade resources and therefore that they cannot be trusted to manage them sustainably (Moseley 2001; Ravnborg 2003).

Impacts of Access to Markets, Infrastructure, and Services

The effects of limitations in access to markets, infrastructure, and services on land management, at either the household or the community level, are ambiguous and context dependent. Households with better access to markets and infrastructure will tend to receive higher prices for their outputs and pay lower prices for purchased inputs, stimulating more profitable production and greater incentive and ability to produce higher-value products and use inputs more intensively (Binswanger and McIntire 1987; Pender, Ehui, and Place 2006). This will tend to increase the use of purchased inputs, but it may have ambiguous impacts on labor-intensive practices, since labor opportunity costs also tend to be higher where access is greater. The impacts of more profitable agricultural opportunities on incentives to invest in SWC or to degrade land are ambiguous, as greater profits increase the incentive to degrade as well as to conserve land (LaFrance 1992; Pagiola 1996). This is true with respect to management of common pool resources as well (McCarthy, Sadoulet, and de Janvry 2001; Benin and Pender 2006). Where open-access resources are available, investments in infrastructure and market access tend to lead to overexploitation (Chomitz and Gray 1996; Mertens and Lambin 1997; Nelson and Hellerstein 1997). Evidence from several studies in the East African highlands indicates that better access to markets and roads generally increases farmers' use of purchased inputs but has more negative impacts on labor-intensive land management practices and on collective action to manage common pool resources (woodlots and grazing lands) (Pender, Place, and Ehui 2006).

Summary of the Literature and the Need for Further Research on Poverty and Land Degradation

The preceding summary of the arguments and evidence from the literature emphasizes that the impacts of poverty on land management are conditioned by many factors and complex influences, are highly context dependent, and are far from certain. Substantial evidence supports the view that poverty (broadly defined) contributes to higher discount rates and thereby reduces incentives to invest in land improvement. Poverty also reduces households' ability to invest in land management practices that require cash, such as the use of inorganic fertilizer, and limits their access to livestock, irrigation, and farm equipment, which in many cases contribute to more intensive land management practices. Poverty contributes to high fertility rates and rapid population growth, which, despite Boserupian responses in some places, appear to be contributing to unsustainable land management in many parts of SSA. On the other hand, many poor households tend to have lower opportunity costs of their time and are therefore more prone to invest in labor-intensive land management practices that wealthier households do not find sufficiently remunerative. Poorer households in some cases consume less of the commons than wealthier households. Poorer communities may be better able than wealthier ones to take effective collective action to manage common pool resources because of their ability to sanction violators of rules or their poorer market access (although the evidence on the impacts of poverty on common pool resource management is generally limited).

The net effects of poverty on land degradation depend on local biophysical and socioeconomic factors that influence the risks, costs, and benefits of land management investments relative to alternatives, as well as the policy, market, and institutional environment that influences both these incentives and the capacities of households and communities to respond to the incentives. Several studies have assessed the impacts of such factors on particular land management practices, agricultural productivity, and household incomes in parts of SSA (for example, see Barrett, Place, and Aboud 2002; Pender, Place, and Ehui 2006; and other references cited earlier), and many others have measured land degradation in various parts of SSA. Yet few studies have linked these types of analyses to be able to explain the impacts of the underlying biophysical, socioeconomic, policy, market, and institutional factors on land degradation, via their impacts on livelihood activities and land use and land management practices.[7] Of the studies that have been carried out, nearly all are highly localized in nature or address only partial measures of land degradation, such as soil erosion (for example, Nkonya et al. 2004). The present study seeks to build on and add value to this literature by assessing the impacts of the multidimensional aspects of poverty on land management, land degradation (including both soil nutrient depletion and soil erosion), agricultural production, and income for a large sample of households representative of most of the major farming systems of Uganda.

To help inform policymakers' decisions on how to prevent or reverse poverty and land degradation spirals, research is espe-

---

[7]Exceptions to this generalization include the studies of Nkonya, Kaizzi, and Pender (2005), who estimated the determinants of soil nutrient balances in eastern Uganda based on an econometric analysis of household survey data together with a household-level analysis of soil nutrient balances; Nkonya et al. (2004), who estimated the determinants of soil erosion losses in Uganda using household survey and plot-level estimates of erosion; Woelcke (2003), who estimated the impacts of various policy and market options on farmers' incomes and soil nutrient depletion, based on a bioeconomic model developed for a community in eastern Uganda; and Holden, Shiferaw, and Pender (2005), who estimated the impacts of various policy, market, and institutional options on farmers' incomes and soil erosion, based on a bioeconomic model of a community in north-central Ethiopia.

cially needed on the impacts on land management and land degradation of the interventions highlighted in the corners of Figure 2.1, such as agricultural research and technical assistance programs, changes in land policies and institutions, and investments in improved markets, infrastructure, education, and agricultural services in rural areas of developing countries, where problems of land degradation and poverty are severe. The present study seeks to address this information gap.

In the remainder of this chapter we present a theoretical and empirical model of households' livelihood and land management decisions. We also discuss hypotheses on the impacts of various policy-relevant factors on these decisions, based on the literature reviewed and the models developed.

A Dynamic Household Model of Livelihood and Land Management Decisions

In this section we develop a dynamic household model of livelihood strategies and land management decisions, which is used as the basis for the empirical model used in this study.[8] The model incorporates household investment decisions—with investments broadly defined to include investments in physical, human, natural, and financial capital—as well as annual decisions regarding crop choice, labor allocation, and adoption of land management practices.

Consider a household that seeks to maximize its lifetime welfare:

$$Mx \, E_0[\sum_{t=0}^{T} u_t(c_t)], \qquad (1)$$

where c_t is the value of consumption in year t, $u_t(\cdot)$ is the single-period consumption utility, and the expectation (E_0) is taken with respect to uncertain factors influencing future income at the beginning of year $t = 0$.[9] Consumption in year t is given by

$$c_t = I_{lt} + I_{wt} + I_{nt} + p_{wt} INV_{wt}, \qquad (2)$$

where I_{ct} is gross crop income, I_{lt} is gross livestock income, I_{wt} is net wage income, and I_{nt} is income from nonfarm activities and transfers in year t.[10] p_{wt} is the price of marketed assets; in the case of non-marketed assets (for example, experience), we interpret p_{wt} as the cost of acquiring an additional unit of these assets. INV_{wt} is a vector of investments (or disinvestments) in assets during year t, including investments in physical capital (PC_t; livestock, equipment), human capital (HC_t; education, experience, training), "natural capital" (NC_t; assets embodied in natural resources, including land quantity and quality, and land-improving investments), and financial capital (FC_t; access to liquid financial assets). w_t is the vector of stocks of these endowments.

Household gross crop income is given by

$$S_{ct} = y(L_{ct}, LM_t, NC_t, T_t, PC_t,$$
$$HC_t, FC_t, AS_t, BP_t, X_{vt})A_t, \qquad (3)$$

where $y(\times)$ represents the value of production per acre farmed, L_{ct} is the amount of labor applied per acre; LM_t is a vector of land management practices and input use (for example, use of fallow, crop residues, or fertilizer); T_t represents the tenure char-

---

[8]This section is adapted from the theoretical model developed in Nkonya et al. (2004).

[9]The function $u_t(\cdot)$ is a generalization of the commonly used discounted utility formulation $u_t(c_t) = \beta^t u(c_t)$ (for example, see Stokey and Lucas 1989).

[10]The value of hired labor used in crop and livestock production is subtracted from net wage income. Costs of other purchased inputs used in agricultural production can be treated in exactly the same way. For simplicity of exposition, we treat labor as the only variable input in agricultural production (it is by far the most important for small farmers in Uganda).

acteristics of the land; AS_t represents household access to information and services (for example, agricultural extension); BP_t are biophysical factors affecting the quantity of crop production (for example, rainfall and temperature); X_{vt} are village-level factors determining local input and output prices, including agroecological conditions, access to markets and infrastructure, and population density; A_t is the area farmed in year t (part of NC_t); and other variables (NC_t, PC_t, HC_t, FC_t) are as defined previously. The physical, human, and financial capital of the household is included as possible determinants of crop production because these assets may affect agricultural productivity if there are imperfect factor markets (de Janvry, Fafchamps, and Sadoulet 1991).

We model biophysical conditions in a given year (BP_t) as dependent on observable agroecological conditions (a subcomponent of X_{vt}) and random factors (u_{bt}):

$$BP_t = BP(X_{vt}, u_{bt}), \qquad (4)$$

where X_{vt} is as defined above and u_{bt} represents unobserved random factors affecting crop production.

Substituting equation (4) into equation (3), we redefine the value of crop production per acre function:

$$y \equiv y'(L_{ct}, LM_t, NC_t, T_t, PC_t, \\ HC_t, FC_t, AS_t, X_{vt}, U_{bt}). \qquad (5)$$

In a similar way, livestock income is determined by labor allocated to livestock activities (L_{lt}); ownership of land, livestock, and other physical assets; the human and financial capital of the household; access to information and services; biophysical conditions; and village-level factors, which include access to markets and infrastructure, and population density:

$$I_{lt} = I_l(L_{lt}, PC_t, NC_t, HC_t, FC_t, \\ AS_t, T_t, BP_t, X_{vt}, u_{lt}). \qquad (6)$$

Net wage income is given by

$$I_{wt} = w_{ot}(X_{vt}, HC_t, u_{wot})L_{ot} \\ - w_{it}(X_{vt}, HC_t, u_{wit})L_{it}, \qquad (7)$$

where L_{ot} and L_{it} are the amounts of labor hired out and in by the household, respectively, and w_{ot} and w_{it} are the wage rates paid for hired labor. We assume that wages may be affected by village-level factors, such as agroecological conditions, market access, and population density (X_{vt}), that influence the local supply and demand for labor; by household-level human capital; and by other random factors (u_{wot}, u_{wit}).

Nonfarm income is determined by the labor allocated to nonfarm activities; the physical, human, and financial capital of the household; access to information and services; the local demand for nonfarm activities as determined by X_{vt}; and random factors:

$$S_{nt} = I_n(L_{nt}, PC_t, HC_t, FC_t, \\ AS_t, X_{vt}, u_{nt}). \qquad (8)$$

Labor demand by the household must be no greater than labor supply:

$$L_{ct} + L_{lt} + L_{ot} + L_{nt} \le L_{ft} + L_{it}, \qquad (9)$$

where L_{ft} is the supply of household family labor.

Most forms of capital must be nonnegative:

$$PC_t \ge 0, HC_t \ge 0, NC_t \ge 0. \qquad (10)$$

Financial capital may be negative, however, if borrowing occurs. We assume that the household's access to credit is determined by its stocks of nonfinancial capital (which determine the household's collateral, potential for profitable investments, and transaction costs of monitoring and enforcing credit contracts):

$$FC_{t+1} \ge -B(PC_t, HC_t, NC_t), \qquad (11)$$

where B is the maximum credit obtainable. Financial assets (or liabilities) grow at the household-specific rate of interest r, which may be influenced by the same factors affecting prices and wages, as well as factors affecting the borrowing constraint:

$$FC_{t+1} = (1 + r(X_{vt}, PC_t, HC_t,$$
$$NC_t, u_{Ft}))FC_t + INV_{FCt}, \qquad (12)$$

where INV_{FCt} is investment (or disinvestment) in financial capital in year t, a subvector of INV_{wt} in equation (2).

Physical capital may grow or depreciate over time, in addition to changes in stocks resulting from investments:

$$PC_{t+1} = (1 + g)PC_t + INV_{PCt}, \qquad (13)$$

where g is a vector of asset-specific growth (or depreciation if negative) rates and INV_{PCt} is investment in physical capital in year t.

Natural capital may depreciate (degrade) over time as a result of unsustainable resource management practices, as well as being improved by investment. For example, if we think of soil depth as one component of natural capital, this may be depleted by soil erosion as well as restored by investments in soil conservation:

$$NC_{t+1}^p = (1 - E(LM_t^p, L_t, NC_t^p,$$
$$X_{vt}, u_{et}))NC_t^p + INV_{NCt}, \qquad (14)$$

where NC_t^p is taken here to represent soil depth on plot p, LM_t^p is a vector of land management practices on plot p, E is the rate of erosion (net of the rate of soil formation), u_{et} are random factors affecting erosion, and INV_{NCt} is investment in increasing soil depth in year t. A similar relation for change in soil nutrient stocks also holds.

We assume that human capital does not depreciate or grow without investment. Since these are also nonmarketed assets, they are subject to irreversibility constraints:

$$HC_{t+1} = HC_t + INV_{HCt} \geq HC_t. \qquad (15)$$

Maximization of equation (1) subject to the constraints defined by equations (2), (3),

and (5)–(15) defines the household optimization problem. If we define the optimized value of (1) (the "value function") as V_0 and notice that this is determined by the value of the state variables at the beginning of period 0 (PC_0, HC_0, NC_0, FC_0), and by the other exogenous variables in this system that are determined at the beginning of period 0 ($X_{v0}, T_0, AS_0, L_{f0}$), then we have that

$$V_0(PC_0, HC_0, NC_0, FC_0, T_0, AS0, _{Xv0}, L_{f0})$$

$$\equiv \max E_0 \left[\sum_{t=0}^{T} u_t(c_t) \right] \text{ subject to equations (2),}$$

(3), and (5)–(15). $\qquad (16)$

Defining $W_t = (PC_t, HC_t, NC_t, FC_t)$ and defining V_1 as the value function for the same problem as in equation (1), but beginning in year $t = 1$, we can write the Bellman equation determining the solution in the first period:

$$V_0(W_0, X_{v0}, T_0, AS_0, L_{f0}) = \max_{L_0, LM_0, INV_{W0}}$$
$$E_0[u(c_0)] + E_0V_1(W_0, X_{v1}, T_1, AS_1, L_{f1}),$$
$$\qquad (17)$$

where L_0 is a vector of all labor allocation decisions in year 0, INV_0 is a vector of land management choices on all plots in year 0, and INV_{W0} is the vector of investments in different forms of capital in year 0.

Solution of the maximization in equation (17) implicitly defines the optimal choices of $L_0, LM_0,$ and INV_{W0}:

$$L_0^* = L_0(W_0, X_{v0}, T_0, AS_0, L_{f0}) \qquad (18)$$

$$LM_0^* = LM_0(W_0, Xv_0, T_0, AS_0, L_{f0}) \qquad (19)$$

$$INV_{W0}^* = INV_0(W_0, X_{v0}, T_0, AS_0, L_{f0}). \qquad (20)$$

The optimal solutions for labor allocation and land management determine the optimized value of production, land degradation, and household income. Substituting equations (18) and (19) into equation (5), we obtain the optimal value of crop production per acre:

$$y_0^* = y'(L_{c0}(W_0, X_{v0}, T_0, AS_0, L_{f0}), LM_0$$
$$(W_0, X_{v0}, T_0, AS_0, L_{f0}), NC_0, T_0,$$
$$PC_0, HC_0, FC_0, AS_0, X_{v0}, u_0). \qquad (21)$$

Equation (21) forms the basis for empirical estimation of the determinants of the value of crop production. It will be estimated in structural form, including the impacts of the endogenous variables (L_0^p, LM_0^p). The model will also be estimated in reduced form:

$$y_0^* = y''(W_0, X_{v0}, T_0, AS_0, L_{f0}, u_0). \qquad (22)$$

The reduced-form income function is derived by substituting the crop value of production function from equation (22) into crop income equation (3), substituting the labor allocation functions in equation (18) into the other income equations (6)–(8), and then summing up total household income:[11]

$$I_0^* = y''(W_0, X_{v0}, T_0, AS_0, L_{f0}, u_0)A_0$$
$$+ I_l(L_{l0}(W_0, X_{v0}, T_0, AS_0, L_{f0}),$$
$$PC_0, NC_0, HC_0, FC_0, AS_0, X_{v0},$$
$$u_{l0}) + w_{o0}(X_{v0}, HC_0, u_{wo0})L_{o0}$$
$$(W_0, X_{v0}, AS_0, L_{f0}) - w_{i0}(X_{v0},$$
$$HC_0, u_{wi0})L_{i0}(W_0, X_{v0}, AS_0,$$
$$L_{f0}) + I_n(L_{n0}(W_0, X_{v0}, AS_0, L_{f0}),$$
$$PC_0, HC_0, FC_0, AS_0, X_{v0}, u_{n0})$$
$$= I_0(W_0, X_{v0}, T_0, AS_0, L_{f0}, u_{I0}). \qquad (23)$$

Equations (18)–(23) are the basis of the empirical work.

Empirical Framework

Figure 2.2 illustrates the empirical framework for the study, drawing from the dynamic household model presented earlier.[12] This framework assumes that land management decisions are determined by the quantity and quality of assets to which households have access (natural, physical, and human capital); the security of tenure to land; households' access to relevant services, such as agricultural technical assistance; the biophysical and socioeconomic endowments of the village (agroecological potential, access to markets and infrastructure, and resource scarcity); the opportunity cost of labor in the village; and local institutions for NRM, such as locally enacted community bylaws related to land management.[13]

Households' land management and input use decisions affect both agricultural production and land degradation in the current year. In addition agricultural production may be affected by the household and village endowments to the extent that these affect the productivity with which inputs and land management practices are used. For example, ownership of farm equipment or draught animals, education, land quality, land tenure, access to agricultural extension, and climate may all affect agricultural productivity, apart from their impacts on land management practices and input use.[14] Agricultural production in the current year affects land degradation in the cur-

---

[11]In the last part of equation (23), u_{I0} combines the effects of the different random factors included in the middle expression ($u_0, u_{l0}, u_{wo0}, u_{wi0}, u_{n0}$).

[12]Figure 2.2 is adapted from the framework developed by Pender, Ehui, and Place (2006) for their study of determinants of livelihoods and land management and its impacts in the East African highlands.

[13]We do not include village-level prices of commodities because of the many different commodities produced in the study regions of Uganda, incorporation of which would lead to many missing observations for most commodities. Since cross-sectional variation in commodity prices is expected to be largely determined by variations in access to markets and infrastructure (as determinants of transaction costs), agroecological characteristics, and resource scarcity (as determinants of local supply and demand), we expect that much of the variation in such prices will be reflected by the other village-level factors in the model.

[14]If not all inputs and practices are completely measured (for example, inputs of management expertise), factors such as access to markets and infrastructure (and therefore information), resource scarcity, and labor opportunity costs may also indirectly affect productivity via their effects on such incompletely measured factors.

Figure 2.2 Empirical framework

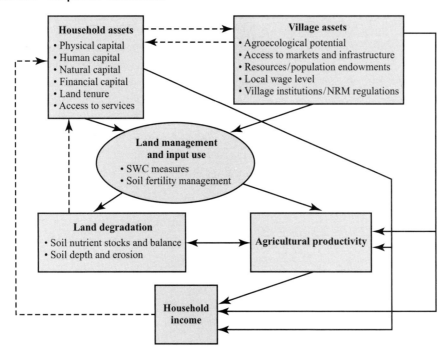

Note: NRM—natural resource management; SWC—soil and water conservation.

rent year (for example, by influencing soil nutrient outflows), while past land degradation, as reflected in initial soil nutrient stocks and depth, affects agricultural production in the current year. Agricultural production also affects household income. Land degradation (on the farmers' own plots) affects household income through its impact on agricultural production.[15] Household- and village-level assets can influence household income independently of their influence on agricultural production, by affecting nonagricultural opportunities and income.

There are several feedback effects in this system, which we indicate in Figure 2.2 as dashed arrows, but which we are not able to investigate with our cross-sectional data.

Land degradation has a feedback impact on households' future stock of natural capital, shown by a dashed arrow from land degradation to household assets in Figure 2.2. Household income has feedback effects on household assets via its effect on household savings and investment decisions. There are also potential feedback effects between changes in household and village endowments. For example, changes in village population pressure or NRM regulations may lead to changes in the land tenure security of households. Conversely changes in household level assets may lead to changes in local wage levels, village institutions, or resource scarcity at the village level. Understanding the nature and magnitude of such feedback effects is important to a full

---

[15]Here we are ignoring the value of nonagricultural goods and services taken from farmers' own plots, which may be affected by land degradation and which can influence income separately from agricultural production. The value of such goods and services is quite small compared to the value of agricultural production from farmers' plots in our data.

understanding of the dynamics of poverty and land degradation in the village and household economy, but they are beyond the scope of this study.

Next we consider some of the specific hypotheses that have been tested regarding the linkages in Figure 2.2.

Factors Associated with Household-Level Response and Outcomes

We are particularly interested in knowing how different types of capital and access constraints (as measures of different types of poverty) influence household decisions on labor use, land management practices, and use of agricultural inputs, and the implications for agricultural productivity, income, and land degradation. Households make decisions on these farm management variables subject to a set of constraints, including household capital endowments and village-, national-, and higher-scale factors, such as market access, prices, institutions, services, and agricultural potential in the community.

The major land management practices and inputs that we analyze are those that are sufficiently common among survey respondents to be investigated empirically. These include application of organic matter (plant residues and animal manure) and inorganic fertilizer, use of short-term SWC practices, crop rotation, slash and burn, fallow, and use of purchased seeds. The short-term SWC practices include trash lines, deep tillage, zero tillage, and plowing and planting along contour lines.[16]

We investigate the associations of land management decisions with crop productivity, which we measure using the value of crops produced per acre (and hence indirectly linked to income), thus quantifying some of the linkages from land management

to poverty. We also investigate the relationships of endowments to crop production per acre and household income per capita in reduced form, through which the total effects of asset holdings on income poverty (via relationships with labor use, land management, and input use) can be assessed.

As indicators of land degradation, we focus on soil erosion and soil nutrient depletion, which are among the most severe forms of land degradation in Uganda. We analyze the severity of estimated soil erosion using the revised universal soil loss equation (RUSLE) (Renard et al. 1991), and we analyze soil nutrient depletion by computing the soil nutrient inflows, outflows, and balances (Smaling, Stoorvogel, and Windmeijer 1993). We define soil nutrient flow as the amount of plant nutrients that flow into or out of a system or area during a specified time period (one year in this case). The difference between soil nutrient inflow and outflow is referred to as "nutrient balance." Nutrient flows and balances may be measured at different scales, such as at the plant, plot, household, water catchment, village, district, national, or higher level (Smaling et al. 1993). Our study measures soil nutrient flows and balances at the plot level since there are wide variations across plots in soil nutrient balances, and it is at this level that actual impacts of land use on sustainability will be most evident. The RUSLE estimate of soil erosion does not account for flow accumulation from rill and inter-rill soil relocation (Meyer, Dabney, and Kemper 2001). To address these weaknesses we used the RUSLE-Bernie method, which addresses the accumulation of rill erosion (Meyer et al. 2001). The RUSLE model has been calibrated for use on soils in Uganda by Tukahirwa (1996), Lufafa et al. (2003), Majaliwa (2003), and Mulebeke (2003).

---

[16]The long-term SWC measures analyzed in this research are long-term structures, such as bench terraces, stone walls, drainage ditches, and soil bunds. These are land investments made in the past and likely to be present in the future.

Hypotheses on the Determinants of Household-Level Responses and Outcomes

Our household- and plot-level analysis is centered on land management since land is the major resource for the livelihoods of the poor. A large body of past research shows that the major determinants of land management include households' endowments of different types of capital, land tenure, and the biophysical and socioeconomic environment in which rural households live (for example, see Reardon and Vosti 1995; Barrett, Place, and Aboud 2002; Nkonya et al. 2004). We have discussed most of the determinants of the response and outcome variables previously. Here we briefly discuss the relevant determinants, elaborating their influence on the household-level response and outcome variables. Table 2.1 summarizes these specific hypotheses.

As noted earlier, because of imperfect or missing markets for capital goods and services, household land management decisions may differ depending on the levels of the households' capital endowments. For instance, holding all else constant, households with abundant labor but with land scarcity are likely to invest more labor in their small land parcels than households with large farms, if land and labor markets do not function perfectly (for example, see Feder 1985). Specifically the capital endowments that may influence land management practices (depending on the nature of markets) include the following:

1. *Natural capital.* The household natural capital endowment that we consider in this research is mainly land, which includes the amount of land owned and the quality of the land, measured in this study as topsoil depth, the stock of macronutrients (N, P, and K) in the topsoil, average slope, and the presence of prior land investments on the plot. Most past studies consider land endowment as only farm size, since it is difficult and expensive to measure

quality of land. As noted earlier, one of the contributions of this study to the literature is its use of better data on land quality indicators. The topsoil is a storehouse of plant nutrients (Sanchez et al. 1997). Hence in farming systems where farmers apply a limited amount of inorganic fertilizer—as is the case in Uganda—topsoil depth largely determines soil quality (Ssali 2002). We enrich the measure of land quality by including the stock of macronutrients, which is a more specific measure of soil fertility. We also include the slope of the plot since it measures the potential for soil erosion, which accounts for a large share of nutrient loss (Wortmann and Kaizzi 1998). Land investments—such as SWC structures and agroforestry—can also improve soil moisture holding capacity and fertility (Sanchez et al. 1997), thus increasing land quality.

The impacts of natural capital on land management decisions may be mixed. As noted earlier, farmers who own more land may farm the land that they own less intensively if factor markets are imperfect, and hence may be less prone to invest in labor- and input-intensive land management practices. On the other hand, greater land ownership may increase households' ability to hire labor or purchase inputs by increasing their access to credit (Pender and Kerr 1998). The need to invest in intensive SWC practices will be greater on steeper soils, but the costs of such investments may be higher or the returns lower if slopes are very steep. The benefits of investing in fertilizer may be lower on more fertile soils, unless there are complementarities between different types of nutrients or between organic practices and the use of inorganic fertilizer (Palm, Myers, and Nandwa 1997). The presence of land investments, such as SWC structures, may promote greater use of

Table 2.1 Summary of hypotheses and the expected signs of the independent variables

Variable	Land management	Land degradation	Intensity of labor	Purchased seeds	Crop productivity	Household per capita income
Land management practices and use of inputs						
Land management practices and use of inputs					+	
Use purchased seed? (yes = 1, no = 0)					+	
Use inorganic fertilizer? (yes = 1, no = 0)					+	
Use organic fertilizer? (yes = 1, no = 0)					+	
Pre-harvest labor (days)					+	
Crop residue incorporated? (yes = 1, no = 0)					+	
Natural capital						
Plot slope (%)	–/+	–	–/+	–/+	–/+	–/+
Topsoil depth (cm)	–/+	–/+	–/+	+	+	+
Nitrogen (kg/ha)					+	+
Phosphorus stock (kg/ha)					+	+
Potassium stock (kg/ha)					+	+
Percentage of sand	–	–	–	–/+	–	–
Practice agroforestry?						
(yes = 1, no = 0)	+	–	+	+	+	+
Have SWC structures? (yes = 1, no = 0)	+	–	+	+	+	+
Perennial crops (cf. annual crops)	–/+	–/+	+	–	+	+
Have other NRM investments? (yes = 1, no = 0)	–/+	–/+	–/+	–/+	–/+	+
Physical capital						
Plot area (acres)	–/+	–/+	–/+	–/+	–/+	–/+
Farm area (acres)	–/+	–/+	–	–/+	–	–
TLU	–/+	–/+	–/+	–/+	–/+	+
Value of equipment (thousand Ush)	–/+	–/+	–/+	–/+	+	+
Human capital						
Share of female household members with:						
(cf. no formal education)						
Primary education	–/+	–/+	–/+	–/+	–/+	–/+
Secondary education	–/+	–/+	–/+	–/+	–/+	–/+
Postsecondary education	–/+	–/+	–/+	–/+	–/+	–/+
Share of male household members with:						
(cf. no formal education)						
Primary education	–/+	–/+	–/+	–/+	–/+	+
Secondary education	–/+	–/+	–/+	–/+	–/+	+
Postsecondary education	–/+	–/+	–/+	–/+	–/+	+
Male household head	+	–/+	+	+	+	+
Household size	+	–/+	+	–/+	+	–
Share of farm owned by women	–	–/+	–/+	–	–	–
Primary activity of household head (cf. crop production)						
Nonfarm activity	–/+	–/+	–	–/+	–/+	–/+
Livestock	–	–/+	–	–	–	–
Access to markets and services						
Distance from plot to residence (km)	–	+	–	–	–	–
PMI	+	+	–/+	–/+	+	+
Distance to all-weather road (km)	–	–/+	–/+	–/+	–	–
Contact hours with extension agent	+	–/+	–/+	+	+	+
Participate in NAADS? (yes = 1, no = 0)	+	–/+	–/+	+	+	+
Have access to credit? (yes = 1, no = 0)	–/+	–/+	–/+	–/+	–/+	+

(continued)

Table 2.1　Continued

Variable	Land management	Land degradation	Intensity of labor	Purchased seeds	Crop productivity	Household per capita income
Land tenure						
Land tenure of plot (cf. freehold and leasehold)						
Customary	–	–/+	–/+	–/+	–/+	–/+
Mailo	+	–/+	–/+	–/+	–/+	–/+
Village-level factors						
Community NRM regulations	+	–	+	–/+		
Population density (persons/km^2)	–/+	–/+	+	+	–/+	–/+
Village wage rate (Ush/day)	–	–/+	–	–/+	–/+	–/+
Agroecological zone (cf. LVCM)						
NW moist farmlands	–/+	–/+	–/+	–/+	–	–
NM farmlands	–/+	–/+	–/+	–/+	–	–
Mt. Elgon farmlands	–/+	–	+	–/+	–/+	–/+
SW grass-farmlands	–/+	–/+	–/+	–/+	–	–
SWH	–/+	–	–/+	–/+	–/+	–/+

Note: LVCM—Lake Victoria crescent and Mbale; NAADS—National Agricultural Advisory Services; NM—northern moist; NRM—natural resource management; NW—northwestern; PMI—potential market integration; SW—southwestern; SWC—soil and water conservation; SWH—southwestern highlands; TLU—tropical livestock units; Ush—Ugandan shillings.

inputs, such as fertilizer, by increasing the return to such inputs. For example, plot terraces may conserve soil moisture, which may be complementary to fertilizer, seeds, or other inputs. On the other hand, such structures may reduce the need for inputs (since less may be lost through erosion). Other types of land investments may be oriented more to livestock or other production (for example, paddocks and fish ponds) and thus may tend to reduce farmers' use of crop inputs. Some land investments, such as bench terraces, may also compete for space and other household factor inputs.

Clearly the theoretical impacts of natural capital endowments on land management practices are ambiguous, and empirical research is needed to identify the actual impacts in a particular context. Prior land investment is expected to make the plot (eventually) more productive, since otherwise farmers would have had little incentive to invest. Since the impacts of natural

capital on land management are theoretically ambiguous, impacts on land degradation will also be ambiguous. The same can be said regarding the impacts of most other endowments.

2. *Physical capital* includes the value of farm equipment and buildings and other durable goods, and number of livestock. As with natural capital, these assets may have mixed impacts on land management. Ownership of physical assets in general increases the household's ability to finance investments and purchase inputs, which may favor the use of purchased inputs such as inorganic fertilizer. On the other hand, ownership of livestock may increase the importation of nutrients (feeds, external grazing) and will increase the supply of manure available to the household, which may substitute for purchased inorganic fertilizer. Farm equipment may increase the productivity of labor in crop production, thus increasing the demand for labor, or it may substitute for labor. Farm equip-

ment and durable goods, such as an ox cart, bicycle, or motorcycle, may promote the use of bulky organic inputs by making them easier to transport and incorporate into the soil, or they may reduce the use of such inputs by increasing the opportunity cost of the farmer's labor.

3. *Human capital* variables affect farmers' ability to make land management decisions. For example, because of imperfect labor markets, households that are well endowed with family labor are more likely to use labor-intensive land management practices. Likewise an experienced farmer will know the biophysical and socioeconomic environment well and thus be able to make informed decisions on land management. Holding all else constant, a better-educated household head is likely to collect and interpret extension messages better, hence be more likely to adopt improved land management practices where these are being promoted by extension and are suitable to the farmer's needs. On the other hand and as discussed earlier, education offers alternative livelihood strategies, which may increase labor opportunity costs and compete with agricultural production (Scherr and Hazell 1994). Since education of all household members may matter, not only the education of the household head (Joliffe 1997), and since there may be differences in impacts of female versus male education on agricultural activities (Pender et al. 2004b), we represent education using the level of education of men and women in the household separately.

4. *Financial capital* includes household liquid financial assets and access to credit. We measure access to financial capital by whether farmers participate in rural credit and savings organizations. Access to financial capital may have mixed impacts on land management, crop production, and land degradation. It may increase the use of purchased inputs or hired labor in crop production where these are profitable and limited by liquidity constraints. On the other hand, financial capital is fungible and may increase investments and labor allocation to higher-return nonfarm activities, thus possibly reducing investments and inputs in land management and crop production. Since the impacts of financial capital on land management and input use are ambiguous, so is the impact on crop production and land degradation. Nevertheless we expect access to financial capital to increase household income to the extent that liquidity is a binding constraint limiting any type of remunerative activity, whether in agriculture or otherwise.

In general household capital endowments have ambiguous impacts on land management, crop productivity, and land degradation, depending on the nature of market imperfections, as discussed in the previous section. However, most endowments that require household investment are expected to contribute to higher household income (since this is part of the reason why households invest in them), although larger household size may lead to lower income per capita if there are diminishing returns to additional labor in the household, or because larger households tend to have a larger share of dependents.

Land tenure relationships can have an important influence on land management decisions and agricultural productivity. As discussed earlier, insecure land tenure is likely to reduce farmers' incentive to invest in land conservation and improvement, since the returns to such investments will be at risk. Tenure insecurity can also reduce farmers' ability to invest in land improvement and inputs, since it reduces the collateral value of land and thus farmers' access to credit. The collateral value of land will also be reduced or even eliminated if there are restrictions on the transferability of land (Pender and Kerr 1999).

Access to agricultural technical assistance services can increase the adoption of inputs and land management practices by increasing farmers' awareness of and ability to effectively use new agricultural inputs and practices. The impacts of extension will depend on the type of enterprises and technologies that are promoted, as well as the suitability of these to the farmers' conditions. Thus extension may have mixed impacts on agricultural production and land management practices, depending on the approach and emphasis of the program. In this study we distinguish households participating in the traditional government agricultural extension programs from those participating in the new extension program, the National Agricultural Advisory Services (NAADS).[17] The new extension approach is more demand driven than the traditional approach. It emphasizes the development of farmer organizations and the promotion of new commercial agricultural enterprises that are expected to be more profitable for farmers than traditional production. The expected impacts on land management are not clear, since land management is not a major emphasis of the program. Yet to the extent that more profitable cash crops are adopted, one could expect this to promote greater adoption of purchased inputs, such as seeds and fertilizer, and greater labor intensity in crop production, since the returns to use of such inputs are likely to be increased.

In addition to household-level capital endowments, land tenure, and participation in technical assistance programs, other village- or higher-level factors affect land management. Factors that determine local comparative advantages and hence the profitability of labor use, land management, and input use include AEZs (see Chapter 3 for a discussion of the AEZs of Uganda), ac-

cess to markets, roads, population density, local wages, and NRM regulations. Rainfall regimes, topography, and other biophysical factors greatly influence farming systems and land management practices. Rainfall patterns influence the type of crops that can be grown in a given AEZ. The choice of crops in turn influences land management practices. For example, bananas are a perennial crop that needs long, well-distributed rains. Among banana growers in Uganda, mulching and application of organic fertilizers are more common than for cereals and other annual crops (Nkonya et al. 2004). Slash and burn may also not be possible for plots that have perennial crops.

Access to markets and roads heavily influences farmer decisions on land management since it affects local prices, availability of inputs and market information, and other socioeconomic aspects. Access to roads was classified based on information from the community survey on the distance between the community and an all-weather road. Better access to markets and roads is expected to favor adoption of purchased inputs, by increasing their availability and reducing their costs relative to farm-level commodity prices, and by favoring commercial production of higher-value crops. Access to markets and roads is also expected to contribute to production of higher-value crops and higher per capita incomes, the latter through the increased value of crop production as well as increased opportunities for other sources of income (for example, nonfarm activities and livestock production). The impacts on adoption of labor or land-intensive management practices are ambiguous, since market and road access can increase the opportunity costs of labor and land, as well as increase the marginal returns to investments in land management. The impacts on land degradation are also, therefore, theoretically ambiguous.

---

[17]The old approach used extension workers employed by local governments, who are still active in the non-NAADS subcounties and to some extent in the NAADS subcounties.

Population density reflects community-level scarcity of natural resources, since we are also controlling for household endowments. Greater scarcity of resources may constrain households from using some organic land management practices, but it may also promote greater investment in resource improvement at the household level. The local average agricultural wage rate variable is an indicator of the scarcity of unskilled casual labor. We expect higher local wages to contribute to lower labor intensity and decreased adoption of labor-intensive land management practices, while they may promote greater use of purchased inputs by increasing households' access to cash.

NRM regulations could affect adoption of land management practices, severity of land degradation, and consequently crop productivity. Studies have shown the key role that community NRM regulations play in management of both community- and privately owned natural resources (Ostrom 1990; Hanna 1995; Varugheese and Ostrom 2001; Nkonya, Pender, and Kato 2008). Programs and organizations focused on NRM positively influence the management of natural resources by facilitating collective action and the enactment of NRM regulations (Pender and Scherr 2002; Nkonya, Pender, and Kato 2008). Community participation in the enactment and enforcement of NRM regulations has been shown to improve NRM (Pender and Scherr 2002; Nkonya, Pender, and Kato 2008). Ostrom (1990) and Hanna (1995) show that participation of local institutions in the enactment and enforcement of NRM regulations improves NRM compared to management by regional-, national-, or higher-level institutions. Nkonya et al. (2008) demonstrated that compliance with requirements to plant trees and restrictions on bush burning on private farms is higher for NRM regulations enacted by the local council than for similar regulations enacted by higher authorities.

CHAPTER 3

Policy, Socioeconomic, and Biophysical Context for Poverty Reduction and Sustainable Land Management in Uganda

To understand the case study country, we briefly discuss the socioeconomic contexts, major poverty reduction strategies, and severity of land degradation in Uganda. We then discuss the Land Act, which is the major statute for improving land management in Uganda. This background will help relate our results to these strategies and to the statute. In particular, discussion of the Land Act will clarify some of the variables included in the econometric models. We also discuss the major biophysical characteristics of Uganda and show that these characteristics are representative of most of SSA.

Poverty Reduction Strategies and Severity of Land Degradation in Uganda

Uganda is a poor country that has achieved remarkable economic growth and poverty reduction in the past decade. Absolute poverty declined from 56 percent of the population in 1992 to 34 percent in 1999–2000 (Appleton 2001a). This significant economic growth was a result of the expanding service and manufacturing sectors in urban areas and, to some extent, the agricultural export sector. Yet there is concern over whether this trend is reflected in an improvement of the living standards for the majority of the people, particularly in rural areas, where 96 percent of the poor live.

Agricultural productivity in general has stagnated or declined for most farmers (Deininger and Okidi 2001). During the 1990s the agricultural sector grew at an annual rate of 4.4 percent while the overall economy grew at an average of 7.4 percent per year. Consequently, by 2000, agriculture's share of total GDP had dropped to around 42 percent (UBOS 1999, 2002, 2005). In responding to a participatory poverty assessment (UPPAP 2002), many people felt that poverty was worsening in their communities, and respondents reported more movement into poverty than out of it. The 2002–03 UNHS showed a significant increase in the incidence of poverty, from 34 percent (7.2 million people) in 1999–2000 to 38 percent (8.9 million people) in 2002–03 (UBOS 2003a), although the poverty rate has since declined to 31 percent in 2005–06 (UBOS 2006). Poverty reduction in the northern region has been much less than that in the rest of the country.

In all regions of the country income is growing at a slower rate in rural areas than in urban areas, and both areas are experiencing growing inequality between the top and bottom income quintiles (Appleton and Ssewanyana 2003). Income inequality, as measured by the Gini coefficient, increased from 0.35 in 1997–98 to 0.43 in 2002–03, but it decreased slightly to 0.408

in 2005–06. The upper income quintile was the only income bracket that registered a significant welfare improvement between 1999 and 2003 (Ssewanyana et al. 2004). Recent statistics have shown that poverty has declined from 38 percent in 2002–03 to about 31 percent in 2005–06 (Table 3.1). The rate of decline in the poverty headcount and poverty gap were both greatest in the western region (38 percent and 40 percent, respectively) and smallest in the northern region (4 percent and 12 percent, respectively). The rate of poverty reduction in rural areas was much greater (20 percent for the headcount and 26 percent for the gap) than in urban areas. In the northern region poverty headcount in urban areas increased, probably as a result of the rebel activities that drove a large number of rural residents into urban areas.[1] Likewise income inequality decreased in all regions but remained unchanged in rural areas (Table 3.1). This is surprising given that poverty reduction has been declining much faster in urban areas. It is possible that income in the highest income quintile continued to grow at a much higher rate than that in the lowest income quintile. Such unequal income changes could still lead to greater income inequality even as more people are escaping from poverty.

The country's persistent poverty presents the government and its development partners with a significant challenge calling for well-targeted policies and strategies. The government seeks to reduce absolute poverty to below 10 percent by 2017 with a broad strategy called the Poverty Eradication Action Plan (PEAP). The major goals of PEAP are rapid economic growth and transformation, good governance and security, increased income for the poor, and improvement in their quality of life (MFPED 2001).

As articulated in PEAP, poverty reduction will be achieved by developing the agricultural sector, since the majority of the poor live in rural areas. The government has made concerted efforts to improve agriculture through its Plan for Modernization of Agriculture (PMA), which is one of PEAP's key programs. One of the major challenges facing agriculture is land degradation. Land pressure has reduced fallow periods and increased outflow of soil nutrients through crop harvests as well as through soil erosion and runoff. Soil erosion is on the increase for many farming systems. Smallholder farmers are unable to compensate for these losses by using manure, crop and other plant residues, or mineral fertilizers, resulting in negative soil nutrient balances.

Available estimates indicate that the rate of soil fertility depletion in Uganda is among the highest in SSA (Stoorvogel and Smaling 1990; Wortmann and Kaizzi 1998). A recent study of maize-producing households in eastern Uganda estimated that the average value of soil nutrient depletion in this region is equal to about one-fifth of average agricultural income (Nkonya et al. 2004). Soil fertility depletion thus represents a substantial loss of Uganda's natural capital, and it also reduces agricultural productivity and income. Soil erosion is another serious problem in the highlands (NEAP 1992; Magunda and Tenywa 1999; Nkonya et al. 2004). Together soil nutrient depletion and erosion pose a serious concern since they contribute to declining agricultural productivity (Vlek 1993; IBSRAM 1994; Sanchez et al. 1997; Bekunda 1999; Deininger and Okidi 2001; Pender et al. 2001b; Bai et al. 2008), which in turn contributes to food and nutrition insecurity. Soil nutrient depletion and erosion could also lead to deforestation and loss of biodiversity since farmers may be forced to abandon nutrient-starved soils and cultivate more marginal areas, such as hillsides and rainforests.

---

[1]However, rebel activities have decreased significantly following the signing in August 2006 of an agreement calling for the cessation of hostilities (International Crisis Group 2006, 1–19).

Table 3.1   Poverty headcount and poverty gap in Uganda, 2005/06

| Region | Residence | Change in poverty since 2002/03 | | | | | |
| | | Poverty estimates | | (Δ%)ᵃ | | Gini coefficient | |
		Poverty headcount	Poverty gap	Poverty headcount	Poverty gap	2005/06	Changes since 2002/03 (Δ%)ᵃ
	Rural	34.2	9.7	19.9	26.0	0.43	0.0
	Urban	13.7	3.5	4.9	10.3	0.36	10.6
Central		16.4	3.6	26.5	34.5	0.42	9.3
Eastern		35.9	9.1	22.0	35.5	0.35	3.0
Northern		60.7	20.7	3.7	11.5	0.33	5.4
Western		20.5	5.1	37.7	40.0	0.34	4.7
Central	Rural	20.9	4.7	24.3	31.9	—	—
	Urban	5.5	1.1	29.5	31.3	—	—
Eastern	Rural	37.5	9.5	22.4	36.2	—	—
	Urban	16.9	4.4	5.6	8.3	—	—
Northern	Rural	64.2	22.3	1.2	8.2	—	—
	Urban	39.7	11.5	−2.1	17.3	—	—
Western	Rural	21.4	5.4	37.6	39.3	—	—
	Urban	9.3	2.0	50.0	58.3	—	—
National		—	—	—	—	0.41	4.7

Source: UBOS (2006). However, the changes are computed from the UBOS data reported in UBOS (2006).

ᵃ$\Delta\% = \frac{2002/03 - 2005/06}{2002/03} \times 100$.

Efforts to Promote SLM in Uganda

The policies and strategies for poverty reduction in Uganda emphasize the need to protect the natural resources on which the poor depend heavily. Various legal instruments and policies support and encourage sustainable NRM. The constitution states that measures should be taken to protect and preserve the environment from abuse and degradation and to manage the environment for sustainable development. Accordingly the national parliament and local government councils have formulated a number of environmental protection regulations. (One of these, the Land Act, is discussed in the next section.) Uganda is one of the few countries that have incorporated the UNCCD National Action Plan into its PRSP. The country is also a signatory to the Ramsar Convention on Wetlands, the Convention for Biological Diversity, and a number of other natural resource and environmental conservation treaties and conventions.

The most recent strategy for SLM is the Strategic Investment Plan (SIP), which was developed as part of the TerrAfrica partnership to promote SLM in the region (Anonymous 2007b), building on and complementing ongoing SLM programs and projects.[2] The SIP identifies potentially suitable ap-

[2]TerrAfrica is a partnership that aims to address land degradation by scaling up harmonized support for effective and efficient country-driven SLM practices in the countries of SSA. TerrAfrica partners include African governments, NEPAD, regional and subregional organizations, the UNCCD Secretariat, the UNCCD Global Mechanism, the World Bank, the Global Environment Facility, the International Fund for Agricultural Development, the Food and Agricultural Organization of the United Nations, the United Nations Development Programme, the United Nations Environment Programme, and the African Development Bank, as well as multilateral organizations including the European Commission, bilateral donors, and civil, social, and scientific organizations including the Forum for Agricultural Research in Africa and centers of the Consultative Group on International Agricultural Research. For more information see www.terrafrica.org.

proaches for scaling up investments in SLM that have been successful in Uganda or in other countries with similar socioeconomic and biophysical environments. The SIP has identified the following areas of emphasis: promoting SLM on privately owned land, formulating and supporting SLM on rangelands and forest resources, stimulating diversification of income to reduce heavy reliance on natural resources, institutional support to enact and enforce sustainable NRM regulations, and effective NRM monitoring and evaluation (Anonymous 2007b). An interministerial SLM Technical Working Group has been formed to coordinate and implement SLM in Uganda (Republic of Uganda 2007). The working group consists of representatives of the key ministries, namely the Ministry of Agriculture, Animal Industry and Fisheries; the Ministry of Water and Environment; the Ministry of Energy and Mineral Development; and the Ministry of Lands, Housing and Urban Development (Anonymous 2007b). This committee will help to reduce the conflicting and uncoordinated NRM efforts that have undermined past attempts to promote SLM in the region (Anonymous 2007a).

Several projects and nongovernmental organizations (NGOs) also promote SLM in Uganda (Anonymous 2007b). The Lake Victoria Environmental Management project is one of the largest environmental undertakings, covering those eastern African countries that surround Lake Victoria. The project has been promoting SLM in order to reduce sedimentation in and pollution of Lake Victoria (Anonymous 2007b). A similar plan is promoting integrated soil nutrient management to attain sustainable productivity increases in Ethiopia, Kenya, and Uganda. The project, funded by the European Union, promotes SLM practices through field schools for farmers (Anonymous 2007b).

Donor funding for SLM in Uganda has been falling in the past few years. For example, donor-funded SLM expenditures fell from US$28 million in 2002–03 to US$8 million in 2005–06 (World Bank 2008). Government-funded SLM expenditures fell from US$8 million in 2002–03 to US$6 million in 2005–06. This downward trend suggests that the government must back its resolve to promote SLM with additional resources.

The Land Act of 1998

The Land Act of 1998 was passed with the broad objective of ensuring land tenure security and SLM. It recognizes four land tenure systems in Uganda: customary, freehold, leasehold, and *mailo*. Each is associated with its own land rights and obligations and with a specific period over which those rights can be exercised or enjoyed:

1. *Customary land tenure* is the most common land tenure system in Uganda and is regulated by customary rules. Under customary tenure, an individual, family, or traditional institution may occupy a specific area of land as prescribed by the customary laws. The landholder under customary tenure has the right to share and use the land for the good of the community. A landholder may apply for a certificate of ownership from the District Land Board. Once such a certificate is issued, the landholder may lease, mortgage, sell, sublet, give, or bequeath by will the land or part of it (Republic of Uganda 1998).
2. *Freehold land tenure* allows the landholder to own the land for an unlimited period of time. This system recognizes and protects the rights of lawful and bona fide (legal) occupants on the land as well as improvements on the land. The landholder may use the land for any lawful purpose; may sell, rent, or lease it or use it as collateral for a bank loan; may allow other people to use it; and may give or bequeath it by will (Republic of Uganda 1998).
3. *Leasehold land tenure* is a form of tenure created either by contract or by operation of law. Under this system

the landlord allows the tenant to use the land for a specific period. The lessee may change the lease ownership to freehold and may sell, sublet, mortgage, give, or bequeath by will the land during the period he or she is entitled to hold the land (Republic of Uganda 1998).

4. *Mailo* is a land tenure system under which the landholder owns the land forever in the same way as a freehold owner. After receiving land titles from the colonial government in the 1900s, the *mailo* owners divided their land into smaller parcels (*kibanja*) and rented them out to bona fide tenants. The landholder may lease, mortgage, pledge, sell, give away, or bequeath by will the land or part of it. The Land Act of 1998 prohibits a landholder from evicting a bona fide occupant. If the bona fide occupant has developed the land, the landowner is allowed to continue owning the land but not the development on the land. The rent and tribute that tenants pay to landowners entitle them to cultivate crops, plant trees, and reside on the *mailo* land. However, some restrictions are usually imposed by *mailo* owners, such as not allowing tenants to plant more than 0.4 ha of coffee or to grow cotton on *mailo* land. (The *mailo* landlords may have feared that if tenants planted coffee—a perennial commercial crop usually planted over a large area—they would get rich and seek to assume ownership of the land.) Tenants are also not allowed to cut and sell trees for profit (NEMA 2001).

The Ugandan land tenure system has both similarities to and significant differences from the systems in neighboring countries. As is the case in other SSA countries, customary land tenure is the most common form of tenure in Uganda. The freehold land tenure system in Uganda is not permitted in those countries in which land belongs to the

state (for example, Ethiopia, Rwanda, and Tanzania). In the East African region only Kenya and Uganda permit freehold land tenure (Migot-Adholla et al. 1991). *Mailo* tenure is only found in Uganda.

Biophysical Characteristics of Uganda and Their Relevance to SSA

There are several systems for classifying the AEZs and farming systems in Uganda, and the distinctions among these classifications are not always clear-cut.

The Ministry of Natural Resources (1994) divided Uganda into 11 AEZs and 20 ecological zones while Semana and Adipala (1993) identified 4 AEZs. Wortmann and Eledu (1999) divide Uganda into 33 AEZs that offer a detailed representation of the country's natural resource endowment and will therefore be used in this study. The AEZs as classified by Wortmann and Eledu fall into 14 major categories, shown in Figure 3.1. These categories are largely determined by the amount of rainfall, which drives the agricultural potential and farming systems within each category. Here we discuss these AEZs and assess their relevance to SSA's various biophysical features. Table 3.2 summarizes the agro-ecological characteristics of each zone and the SSA countries or regions with similar characteristics.

1. *Lake Victoria crescent.* This zone has a high level of rainfall (above 1,200 mm/year) distributed throughout the year in a bimodal pattern (bimodal high rainfall); it is characterized by the dominant banana-coffee farming system. The zone runs along the shores of Lake Victoria from the east in the Mbale district, through the central region to the Rakai district in southwestern Uganda. This zone is typical of most parts of central, eastern, and southern West Africa with rainfall above 1,200 mm/year and high agricultural potential (Figure 3.2).

Figure 3.1   Agroecological zones of Uganda

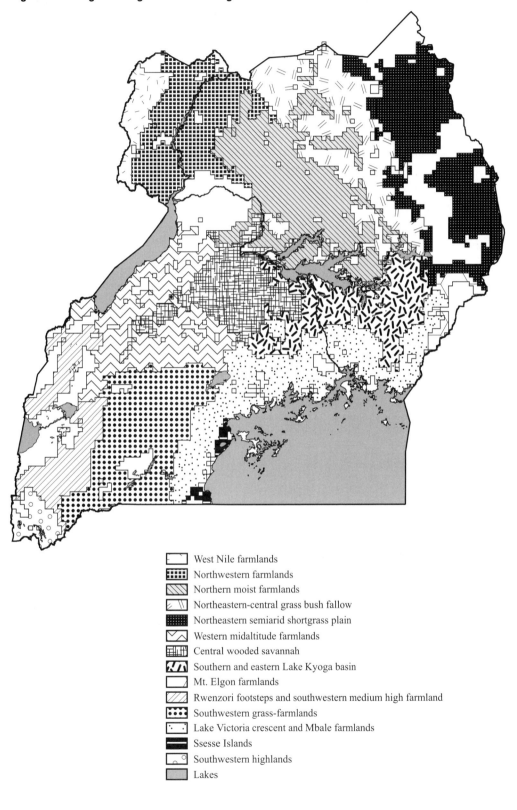

West Nile farmlands
Northwestern farmlands
Northern moist farmlands
Northeastern-central grass bush fallow
Northeastern semiarid shortgrass plain
Western midaltitude farmlands
Central wooded savannah
Southern and eastern Lake Kyoga basin
Mt. Elgon farmlands
Rwenzori footsteps and southwestern medium high farmland
Southwestern grass-farmlands
Lake Victoria crescent and Mbale farmlands
Ssesse Islands
Southwestern highlands
Lakes

Table 3.2   Summary of agroclimatic zones, SSA countries and regions with similar characteristics, and major forms of land degradation in Uganda

Agroclimatic zone	Biophysical characteristics and major farming system	SSA countries and regions with similar biophysical characteristics[a]	Major forms of land degradation in Uganda
LVCM	Bimodal high rainfall >1,200 mm/year; banana-coffee farming system	West-central (Democratic Republic of the Congo, Congo, etc.), and coastal region of western Africa	Soil erosion, soil nutrient depletion (especially potassium)
NW moist farmlands	Unimodal low to high rainfall (900–1,200 mm/year in lowlands to >1,200 mm/year in highlands); cereal and tuber crops and tobacco	Moist savannah (for example, Mozambique, central Nigeria, Southern Sudan, Tanzania, Zambia)	Deforestation due to tobacco curing, charcoal making, fuelwood harvesting; soil erosion and nutrient depletion
NM farmlands	Unimodal low to medium rainfall (700–1,200 mm/year); cereal and tuber crops, cotton, and legumes	Countries along the desert margin (e.g., Burkina Faso, Northern and central Nigeria, Namibia, central Sudan)	Leaching, overgrazing and deforestation due to charcoal making
Mt. Elgon farmlands	Unimodal high rainfall (>1,200 mm/year); cereals, banana, and coffee	Highlands of Cameroon, Ethiopia, Kenya, Malawi, Rwanda, and Tanzania (southern highlands)	Soil erosion and nutrient depletion
SW grass-farmlands	Bimodal low to medium rainfall (900–1,200 mm/year); livestock system	Savannah vegetation/climate: southern Africa, western and central Africa	Overgrazing, deforestation, and soil erosion
SWH	Bimodal high rainfall (>1,200 mm/year); banana, Irish potato, sorghum, and vegetables	Eastern and central African highlands	Soil erosion and soil nutrient depletion
Semiarid northeast shortgrass plains and northeast central grass bush fallow	Unimodal low rainfall (400–700 mm/year); pastoral livestock system	Semiarid and arid zones: Botswana, Burkina Faso, northern Kenya, Namibia, Niger, Somalia, Togo, and desert margins of western and northern Africa	Overgrazing and loss of vegetation

Note: LVCM—Lake Victoria crescent and Mbale; NM—northern moist; NW—northwestern; SW—southwestern; SWH—southwestern highlands.
[a]The list is not exhaustive. It gives only a few examples of countries or regions with similar agroclimatic characteristics. Like Uganda, countries have different agroecological zones. Any similarity does not imply that a particular description applies to the entire country or region.

2. *Northwestern (NW) moist farmlands.* This area is characterized by unimodal low to medium rainfall and covers the west Nile districts of Arua, Nebbi, and Yumbe. Common crops grown in the zone are coarse grains (such as sorghum, millet, and bulrush), maize, tubers, and tobacco. The region includes areas with high rainfall in the highlands (above 1,200 mm/year) and medium rainfall in the lowland plains (900–1,200 mm/year). This area typifies African countries with moderate agricultural potential in the medium and lowland plains and high agricultural potential in the highlands (for example, Mozambique, Nigeria, and Tanzania).

3. *Northern moist (NM) farmlands.* This zone is also characterized by unimodal low to medium rainfall (700–1,200 mm/year) and covers most of the northern districts. The NM zone represents areas with low agricultural potential with sandy soils (for example, countries along the desert margins, such as Burkina Faso, Namibia, and northern and central Nigeria). The common crops grown are coarse grains,

Figure 3.2   Intensity of precipitation in Africa

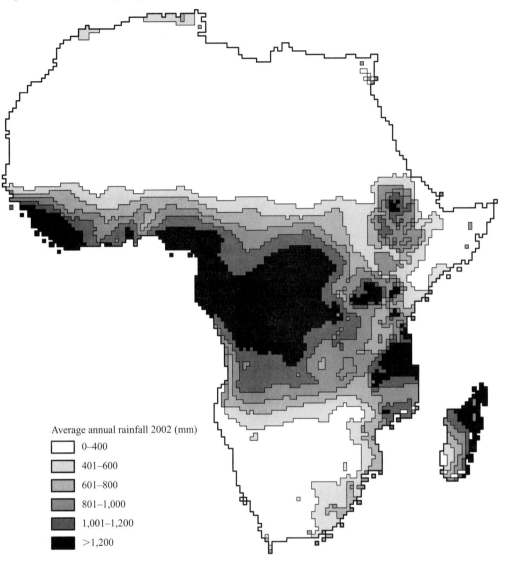

Average annual rainfall 2002 (mm)

	0–400
	401–600
	601–800
	801–1,000
	1,001–1,200
	>1,200

maize, tubers, cotton, and a variety of legumes.

4. *Mt. Elgon farmlands.* This zone is on the slopes of Mt. Elgon in the east and is characterized by unimodal high (above 1,200 mm/year) and well-distributed rainfall, high altitude and cooler temperatures, and relatively fertile volcanic soils. Countries with these agroecological features include Cameroon, Ethiopia, the Kenyan highlands, Malawi, and Rwanda. The only district covered by our survey that falls within this zone is Kapchorwa. The major crop in Kapchorwa is maize; farmers elsewhere in this zone also plant bananas and raise livestock.

5. *Southwestern (SW) grass-farmlands.* This zone receives medium to low rainfall (900–1,200 mm/year) in a bimodal distribution. The region is along the so-called cattle corridor, with mainly savannah vegetation suitable for livestock grazing. It is typical of countries in southern western and central Africa with savannah vegetation and climate.

The only district covered by our survey within this zone is Mbarara. Farmers in the district keep large herds of cattle and grow bananas, coarse grains, maize, and tubers.

6. *Southwestern highlands (SWH)*. This zone receives bimodal high rainfall (over 1,200 mm/year) and is characterized by high altitude, hence a cooler climate, and relatively fertile volcanic soils. Some areas in the lowlands receive medium rainfall ranging from 900 to 1,200 mm/year. Like the Mt. Elgon farmlands, the zone is typical of countries in which highlands predominate. The common crops in the SWH are bananas, Irish potatoes and other tubers, sorghum, maize, and vegetables.

7. *Semiarid northeast shortgrass plains and northeast central grass bush fallow*. These AEZs cover the Karamoja area in northeastern Uganda. The major economic activity in the area is pastoralism. This is the driest zone, and one with low agricultural potential. The area receives unimodal rainfall ranging from 400 to 700 mm/year (NWDR 2006), with poor distribution throughout the year. The Karamoja area typifies the arid and semiarid areas in SSA, with predominantly pastoral and transhumant livelihoods (for example, Botswana, Burkina Faso, northern Kenya, Namibia, Somalia, and Togo). We did not sample any district from this area.

In summary, Uganda provides a good case study owing to its diverse AEZs, which include most of the AEZs of SSA shown in Figure 3.2. However, Uganda is not typical of countries in the desert (for example, Mali, Mauritania, and Niger). Hence our results should be applied to such countries with caution.

CHAPTER 4

Methods of Data Collection and Analysis

n this chapter we discuss the methods and procedures used to collect and analyze primary data at the community, household, and plot levels. Since this report is intended for a wide audience—including policymakers, development practitioners, students, and researchers from different disciplines—we use nontechnical language to discuss the analytical methods.

Data Collection

The data used in this report were collected from four sources. The first source was the community, through group interviews during which community-level data—such as village wage rates, village (local council 1 [LC1], the lowest administrative unit in Uganda) area, and NRM regulations—were collected. The second source was the household survey, from which household-level data on endowments of all forms of capital and other household-level variables were collected. Households were randomly selected from communities sampled for the community-level survey. The third source was plot-level data, which were collected from each of the sampled households. The data collected were soil samples (used to conduct laboratory analyses of the physical and chemical properties of the soil), information on crop management practices, plot area, slope, and topsoil depth. The fourth source is secondary data from UBOS. We used the population census data to compute the community population density. Here we discuss how data were collected from the three primary sources.

Community-Level Data

The community survey drew a subsample of the communities included in the UBOS UNHS survey, which was conducted in 2002–03. A stratified two-stage sample was drawn for the UNHS. Using the 56 districts as strata, 972 enumeration areas (565 rural and 407 urban) were randomly selected at the first-stage sampling, from which a total of 9,711 households were randomly selected at the second-stage sampling.[1] The sampling was weighted in proportion to population size, using the population of each district. Data used in this report are derived from a smaller survey (hereafter referred to as the IFPRI-UBOS survey) including 123 communities, which were drawn from the 565 rural enumeration areas covered by the UNHS. This smaller survey drew a sample using the rural enumeration areas from eight districts as the sampling frame.

---

[1]Only 55 of the 56 districts were covered in the survey. One district (Pader) was not covered due to insecurity during the time of the survey. Some enumeration areas in Gulu and Kitgum were also not covered for the same reason. An enumeration area covers one or more LC1s. Enumeration areas are the smallest unit areas used for census purposes.

The districts selected for the IFPRI-UBOS survey were Arua, Iganga, Kabale, Kapchorwa, Lira, Masaka, Mbarara, and Soroti. Since the aim of the IFPRI-UBOS survey was to study poverty-NRM linkages, the criteria used to select the districts were level of poverty and endowment of natural resources at the district level (that is, districts were selected to represent variation along these dimensions). The poverty status of a district was determined using poverty incidence, which is the share of people living in households with real consumption per adult equivalent that falls below the poverty line of the region (UBOS 2003a). Data on the incidence of poverty were obtained from the UBOS. Table 4.1 summarizes the number of communities selected for the IFPRI-UBOS survey from each district and the poverty status and endowment of natural resources of the sample districts. Figure 4.1 shows the spatial distribution of the sampled communities.

For the community survey about 10–15 key informants were selected to provide information on institutions, natural resource governance and management, and labor issues on behalf of the entire community.

Among the village-level variables used in this study are access to markets and roads, and population density. Access to markets was classified according to the method of Wood et al. (1999), who defined it using the potential market integration index (PMI), a measure of the travel time from each location to the nearest five markets, weighted by the population size of those markets; a higher PMI value indicates better market access. The geographic coordinates of the survey communities were linked to geographic information on indicators of market access and population density. The areas classified as having relatively high market access include most of the Lake Victoria crescent region and areas close to main roads in the rest of the country (Figure 4.2).

Table 4.1   Selected districts, communities, and households

District	Number of communities selected	Number of households selected	Poverty incidence[a] (%)	Poverty status[b]	Natural resource endowment (agricultural potential)[c]	Mean altitude (masl)	Mean annual rainfall (mm)
Arua	16	112	65	High	Low potential (WNW farmlands)	1,047–1,261	>1,200
Iganga	16	112	43	Medium	High potential (LVCM farmlands)	1,174	>1,200
Kabale	16	112	34	Low	High potential (SWH)	1,420–2,123	>1,200
Kapchorwa	8	55	48	Medium	High potential (Mt. Elgon farmlands)	1,220–1,466	>1,200
Lira	17	112	65	High	Low potential (NM farmlands)	1,024	>1,200
Masaka	20	139	28	Low	High potential (LVCM farmlands)	1,235	>1,200
Mbarara	20	139	34	Low	Medium potential (SW grass-farmlands)	1,477	<1,000
Soroti	10	70	65	High	Low potential (NM farmlands)	1,075	1,000–1,200
Total	123	851	43				

Source: Data from UBOS (2003a, 2003b).

Note: LVCM—Lake Victoria crescent and Mbale; masl—meters above sea level; NM—northern moist; SW—southwestern. SWH—southwestern highlands; WNW—west Nile and northwestern.

[a]Poverty incidence measures the percentage of people living in households with real consumption per adult equivalent below the poverty line of the region. This indicator does not measure the depth of poverty, that is, how far below the poverty line are the poor (UBOS 2003a, 2003b).

[b]Using 2002/03 Uganda National Household Survey data, the rural poverty status of a district was ranked as follows: <40 = low; 40–50 = medium; <50 = high.

[c]Agricultural potential is an abstraction of many factors—including rainfall level and distribution, altitude, soil type and depth, topography, the presence of pests and diseases, and the presence of irrigation—that influence the absolute (as opposed to comparative) advantage of producing agricultural commodities in a particular place.

Figure 4.1   Spatial distribution of communities sampled

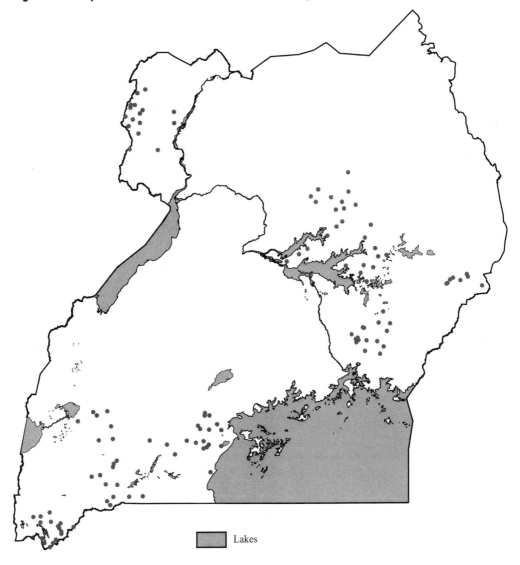

Lakes

To calculate the population density of the community, the area of the LC1 was measured using global positioning system (GPS) units and the population of the community was obtained from the census data.

Household- and Plot-Level Data

As noted previously, the households surveyed in this study were randomly sampled from communities selected for the IFPRI-UBOS survey (Table 4.1). The plot-level data were collected from all plots owned or operated by each household sampled. The IFPRI-UBOS survey interviewed the same households that were visited by the UNHS in 2002–03. Hence the IFPRI-UBOS survey collected only data that were not collected by the UNHS 2002–03 survey. Here we provide a detailed description of the data collected and the variables used in the econometric models.

Crop Productivity. Total value of crop production was measured by multiplying the quantity of crops produced per acre times the village-level price, which was

Figure 4.2   Classification of market access in Uganda

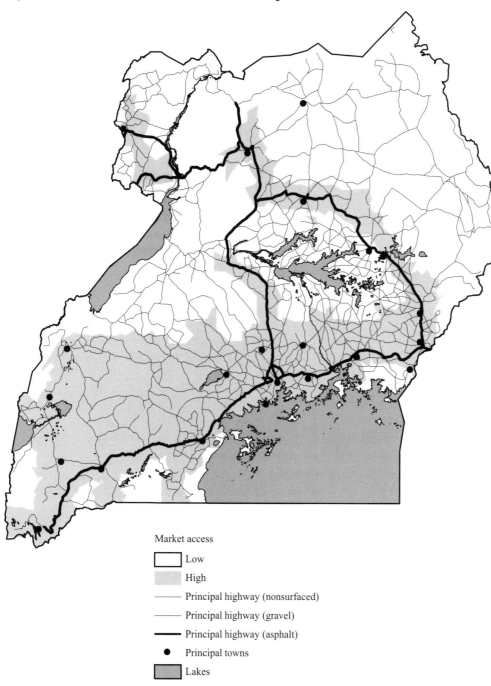

Market access

☐ Low

▨ High

—— Principal highway (nonsurfaced)

—— Principal highway (gravel)

—— Principal highway (asphalt)

● Principal towns

▨ Lakes

Source: Wood et al. (1999).

aggregated over the two planting seasons. Area cultivated was derived as the weighted average for both seasons. We use the value of crops produced as a measure of crop productivity instead of crop yield because most plots were planted with more than one crop, making the estimation of the area occupied by any one crop difficult to establish. This made estimation of crop yield difficult and at best inaccurate.

Household Endowments. As mentioned earlier, household endowments include physical, natural, human, and financial capital.[2] We discuss the measurement of only those few household endowments whose method of measurement may not be obvious to readers: the soil quality characteristics of the plot and education. The soil quality characteristics were measured by visiting the plot, measuring its slope using a clinometer, taking soil samples to a depth of 20 cm, analyzing the samples (as will be discussed further in the next section), and measuring the topsoil depth. The enumerators also measured the area of the plot using GPS units that automatically measure the area as the enumerator walks along the borders of the plot.

Household members pursue different activities that reveal a clear division of labor. For example, Gladwin and Thompson (1999) note that women in Africa produce much of the household food and are responsible for most of the land management activities. As observed earlier, the level of education of female and male members of the household is likely to have different impacts on land management. We therefore used eight variables that represent the level of education as shares of the female and male members of the household who have attained the following levels of education: no formal education, primary education, secondary education, and post-secondary education.

Soil Nutrient Flows and Balances. Soil samples obtained from depths of between 0 and 20 cm were collected from the plots. The biophysical characteristics of a total of 1,887 soil samples were analyzed in the laboratory, and these data were used to compute the soil nutrient flows and balances. The pH, organic matter, total N, extractable P, exchangeable K and calcium, and texture were measured using the analytical methods of Foster (1971).[3] Information on farm management practices, crop-livestock interactions, crop diversity, and other variables that affect nutrient flow was obtained from the household- and plot-level surveys.

These data were used to arrive at estimates of annual nutrient inflows and outflows for each plot. We restrict our analysis to the three major macronutrients, N, P, and K. The sources of inflows and outflows used in this study are according to Smaling, Stoorvogel, and Windmeijer (1993) and de Jager et al. (1998). The nutrient inflows are mineral fertilizers, organic inputs from outside the plot, atmospheric deposition, biological nitrogen fixation (BNF), and sedimentation. The major outflows are crop products and residues taken off the plot, leaching, soil erosion, and gaseous losses.[4]

Household- and Plot-Level Data Analysis

Descriptive Analysis

The severity of soil nutrient depletion was analyzed using descriptive statistical methods. Knowing the impact of soil nutrient depletion on crop yield is more important than merely quantifying the depletion, but there are no studies known to the authors that have measured agricultural productivity loss due to soil nutrient depletion in Uganda. We therefore use a simpler measure to estimate this impact, the economic nutrient depletion ratio (ENDR) (der Pol

---

[2]In the context of this report, natural capital comprises the quantity and quality of the land (the physical, biological, and chemical characteristics of the soil) and any land-improving investments. Physical capital includes assets that are not naturally occurring (for example, farm equipment, other durable assets, and livestock).

[3]For details on the soil nutrient analysis methods and results see Kaizzi (2002).

[4]For details on how the inflows and outflows were computed see Nkonya, Kaizzi, and Pender (2005).

1993). ENDR is the share of farm income derived from mining soil nutrients.[5] Soil nutrient mining is the practice of growing crops with insufficient replacement of the nutrients that are taken up by the crops. Mathematically,

$$ENDR = \frac{NDMV}{\pi} \times 100.$$

NDMV is nutrient deficit market value, the value of nutrients mined per hectare if such nutrients were to be replenished by applying fertilizer purchased from the cheapest sources. π is the profit from agricultural activities per hectare. The cost of production excludes family labor. *ENDR* measures the cost of replenishing nutrients depleted relative to farm income, and not the benefit. Holding other factors constant, decreasing fertilizer prices will both increase economic net returns to use of fertilizer and reduce ENDR.

Econometric Models

Our main objective is to analyze the relationships between different aspects of poverty and land management practices, crop productivity, household income, and measures of land degradation. We do this by using an empirical model based on the sustainable livelihoods framework (Carney 1998) and the literature on agricultural household models (Singh, Squire, and Strauss 1986; de Janvry, Fafchamps, and Sadoulet 1991). In our theoretical framework (presented in Chapter 2) we assume that rural households make choices about labor allocation, land management, input use, and savings and investment to maximize their discounted expected lifetime welfare, subject to the factors that determine their income opportunities, constraints, and risks, including their endowments of physical, human, natural, and financial capital; land tenure; agroecological potential; population pressure; commodity and factor prices; and access to markets, extension, and other services.

Under standard assumptions used in the dynamic programming literature (for example, Stokey and Lucas 1989), this life-cycle decision problem reduces to a series of decision problems in each year. In each of these the household decides what it is best to do in the current year, based on the endowments and information that it has at the beginning of the year and its expectations about how the decisions it makes will affect current consumption and the value of endowments that it will carry over to the next year.[6] These decision problems imply that current decisions about labor allocation, land management, input use, and investments will depend on the endowments of different types of capital that the household has at the beginning of the year, and on other factors influencing the household's income potentials and risks in the present and the future. The empirical models that we discuss in this report are based on such a dynamic household model, which was presented in Chapter 2.

Since there are considerable differences in how farmers manage land depending on the characteristics of specific plots, we analyze land management practices, crop productivity, and soil nutrient flows and balances at the plot level. Only household income is analyzed at the household level, since it is an aggregation of all sources of income, farm and nonfarm.

Determinants of Land Management Practices, Value of Crop Production per Acre, and per Capita Household Income. We assume that the value of crop production per acre (we also refer to it as crop pro-

---

[5]Farm income includes income from crop, livestock, and other agricultural activities. It excludes income from such sources as nonfarm activities and transfers.

[6]This is a narrative summary of the Bellman principle of dynamic programming (Stokey and Lucas 1989).

ductivity) by household h on plot p (Y_{hp}) is determined by the following:

labor use per acre on the plot (L_{hp}),

land management practices (LM_{hp}) on the plot (including slash and burn, fallow, crop rotation, short-term SWC practices, and use of purchased seed, organic matter, and fertilizer),[7]

the natural capital (size and quality) of the plot (NC_{hp}),

the tenure of the plot (T_{hp}),

the household's endowments of physical capital (PC_h), human capital (HC_h), and financial capital (FC_h),

the household's access to agricultural technical assistance (AS_h),

village- and higher-level factors influencing comparative advantage (agroecological potential, access to markets and roads, population density, community-level natural resource management regulations [RG_c], and wage level [X_v]), and

other random factors, such as weather in a given year and location (e_{vhp}^y) (equation 24).

Some of these factors may have only indirect impacts on crop production, by influencing use of labor and land management practices (for example, population density and the wage level). However, we include these in the full specification of the structural model, and then use hypothesis testing to eliminate such factors that have statistically insignificant impacts. We do not include the NRM regulations in the structural model since land management practices and labor intensity—which are affected directly by NRM regulations—are included. We include the NRM regulations in the reduced equations, which do not include land management practices and labor intensity.

The complete structural model of crop productivity including land management practices that affect crop productivity is as follows:

Value of crop production per acre:

$$Y_{hp} = f(L_{hp}, LM_{hp}, NC_{hp}, PC_h, T_{hp},$$
$$HC_h, FC_h, AS_h, X_v, e_{vhp}^y). \quad (24)$$

Labor use per acre:

$$L_{hp} = f(RG_c, NC_{hp}, PC_h, T_{hp},$$
$$HC_h, FC_h, AS_h, X_v, e_{vhp}^l). \quad (25)$$

Land management practices:

$$LM_{hp} = f(RG_c, NC_{hp}, PC_h, T_{hp},$$
$$HC_h, FC_h, AS_h, X_v, e_{vhp}^{lm}). \quad (26)$$

All variables are as defined previously, except RG_c, which represents natural resource management restrictions in the community. This variable has been included as a determinant of households' land management decisions to reflect the possible influence of community-level regulations on such decisions.[8] For example, restrictions on bush burning may affect households' decisions about whether to use slash and burn or whether to fallow their land. Equation (24) is the same as equation (5) in Chapter 2 (although expressed at the plot level). Equation (25) is the same as equation (18), and equation (26) is the same as equation (19), except that the explanatory variable RG_c has been included in both, as already noted.

Land management practices and labor use are potentially endogenous variables affecting crop productivity. FC_h, which in this report is measured as use of credit, and AS_h, which is measured as participation in the new demand-driven advisory services or the traditional extension service, are also

---

[7]Short-term SWC practices include trash lines, deep tillage, and zero tillage. Use of organic matter includes incorporation of organic residues from the same plot and biomass transfer of organic matter to one plot from another location (for example, manure from kraals, household residues, and other types of organic matter).

[8]This variable was added in response to a suggestion by one of the anonymous peer reviewers of the report.

potentially endogenous.[9] Hence, to assess the robustness of the estimates in the absence of the potentially endogenous variables, we also estimate the following reduced models for each set of the dependent variables, leaving out the potentially endogenous explanatory variables:

Value of crop production per acre:

$$Y_{hp} = f(RG_c, NC_{hp}, PC_h, T_{hp}, \\ HC_h, X_v, e_{vhp}^{yr}) \qquad (27)$$

Labor use per acre:

$$L_{hp} = f(RG_c, NC_{hp}, PC_h, T_{hp}, \\ HC_h, X_v, e_{vhp}^{l}) \qquad (28)$$

Land management practices:

$$LM_{hp} = f(RG_c, NC_{hp}, PC_h, \\ T_{hp}, HC_h, X_v, e_{vhp}^{lm}), \qquad (29)$$

where e_{vhp}^{yr}, e_{vhp}^{lm}, and e_{vhp}^{l} are unobserved random factors affecting the dependent variables in village v for household h at plot p.

To better understand the factors that affect income poverty reduction, we analyze the factors that affect total household income since crop production does not fully account for total household income. Additionally, we analyze the factors that affect land degradation, which is measured in terms of soil erosion and soil nutrient balances.

Per capita household income:

$$I_h = f(NC_h, PC_h, T_h, HC_h, \\ FC_h, AS_h, X_v, e_{vh}^{I}) \qquad (30)$$

Land degradation:

$$E_{hp} = f(RG_c, NC_{hp}, PC_h, T_{hp}, \\ HC_h, FC_h, AS_h, X_v, e_{hp}^{E}), \qquad (31)$$

where E_{hp} is a vector of indicators of land degradation, namely soil erosion on plot

p of household h and nutrient depletion represented by nutrient balances of macronutrients, namely N, P, and K from household h on plot p; I_h is income per capita of household h; e_{vhp}^{E} are unobserved random factors affecting land degradation in village v in household h on plot p; e_{vh}^{I} is an observed random factor affecting income of household h in village v; and other variables are as defined previously.

Equation (30) is the same as equation (23) in Chapter 2. Equation (31) can be derived by substituting equations (28) and (29) (for L_{hp} and LM_{hp}) into the expression for land degradation $[E(LM_{hp}, L_{hp}, NC_{hp}, X_v, u_e)]$ used in equation (14) in Chapter 2.

Table 4.2 reports the summary statistics of variables used in these models. The variables are listed under their main categories (for example, natural capital or physical capital).

It is likely that the error terms across equations (24)–(26) and (30) and (31) are not independently distributed; thus it would be desirable to estimate the models using a system of equations. Estimating them as single equations reduces the efficiency of estimation because correlation in error terms across equations cannot be accounted for and cross-equation restrictions cannot be imposed. However, estimation of a system of equations using such methods as three-stage least square (3SLS) is not possible because many of the dependent variables are qualitative response variables whose determinants cannot be consistently estimated using standard linear models (Maddala 1983). The inability to estimate a system of equations to account for cross-equation relationships does not cause the estimated coefficients to be inconsistent or biased (Davidson and MacKinnon 2004).

We estimated two systems of equations, the land management practices and land degradation equations, since the two

---

[9]Some components of NC_{hp} (nutrient stocks) are also potentially endogenous and thus are dropped from the reduced models, but we show NC_{hp} in these equations since it includes other components that are exogenous variables.

Table 4.2   Descriptive statistics for variables used in econometric analysis

Variable	Observations[a]	Mean	Standard deviation	Min	Max
Dependent variables					
Use slash and burn? (yes = 1, no = 0)	3,738	0.198	0.399	0	1
Practice fallow? (yes = 1, no = 0)	3,738	0.206	0.404	0	1
Practice crop rotation? (yes = 1, no = 0)	3,738	0.220	0.414	0	1
Use organic residues? (yes = 1, no = 0)	3,738	0.158	0.379	0	1
Practice short-term SWC? (yes = 1, no = 0)	3,738	0.127	0.333	0	1
Use inorganic fertilizer? (yes = 1, no = 0)	3,607	0.022	0.145	0	1
Use purchased seed? (yes = 1, no = 0)	3,607	0.392	0.488	0	1
Preharvest labor (hours/acre)	2,614	362.000	374.95	0.628	374.95
Value of crop production per acre (thousand Ush)	2,729[b]	166.85	287.42	0.0002[b]	1,983.081[b]
Per capita household income (thousand Ush)	851	759.18	1,765.63	−1.091	22,445.59
Independent variables					
Natural capital					
Average slope (%)	2,750	8.024	9.363	0	60
Topsoil depth (cm)	2,504	27.660	11.389	4	80
Land investment on plot dummies (yes = 1, no = 0)					
Practice agroforestry[c]	3,625	0.399	0.490	0	1
Have SWC structures[d]	3,625	0.209	0.407	0	1
Have other NRM investments[e]	3,625	0.053	0.223	0	1
Type of crop produced (cf. annual crop)					
Perennial crops	3,570	0.231	0.422	0	1
Pasture	3,570	0.031	0.172	0	1
Farm size (acres)	851	4.316	5.087	0.123	51.819
Physical capital					
TLU (no.)[f]	851	2.930	3.265	0	51,718.5
Value of buildings (thousand Ush)	851	777.508	190.572	0	30,000
Value of agricultural equipment (thousand Ush)	851	87.800	541.006	0	10,000
Human capital					
Share of education level of household female members (cf. no formal education)					
Primary	851	0.380	0.447	0	1
Secondary	851	0.092	0.258	0	1
Postsecondary	851	0.026	0.134	0	1
Share of education level of household male members (cf. no formal education)					
Primary	851	0.463	0.457	0	1
Secondary	851	0.148	0.315	0	1
Postsecondary	851	0.070	0.229	0	1
Primary activity of household head (cf. crop production)					
Nonfarm activity	851	0.306	0.461	0	1
Livestock	851	0.022	0.146	0	1
Sex of household head (male = 1, female = 0)	851	0.817	0.387	0	1
Household size	851	5.314	2.568	1	17
Share of farm area owned by female	851	0.134	0.326	0	1
Village-level factors					
Community NRM regulations	843	0.73	0.45	0	1
Distance from homestead to plot (km)	3,625	1.518	1.674	0	157.25
PMI	3,625	192.514	90.890	3.4838	415.073
Distance to all-weather road (km)	3,625	2.492	1.995	0	45.4167
Number of extension visits	851	0.960	3.803	0	48

(continued)

Table 4.2 Continued

Variable	Observations[a]	Mean	Standard deviation	Min	Max
Is there a NAADS program in the subcounty?					
(yes = 1, no = 0)	851	0.240	0.427	0	1
Number of programs and organizations with focus on					
agriculture and environment	851	1.873	1.694	0	7
Number of programs and organizations with focus on credit	851	1.245	1.368	0	6
Population density (persons/km^2)	851	9.679	3.025	1.264	402.333
Community wage rate (Ush)	851	1,279.683	1.881	475	10,000
Land tenure of plot					
Customary	3,625	0.450	0.498	0	1
Mailo	3,625	0.118	0.323	0	1
Freehold	3,625	0.419	0.494	0	1
Leasehold	3,625	0.020	0.109	0	1
Agroecological zones (cf. LVCM)					
WNW farmlands	851	0.133	0.340	0	1
NM farmlands	851	0.203	0.402	0	1
Mt. Elgon farmlands	851	0.041	0.198	0	1
SW grass-farmlands	851	0.137	0.343	0	1
SWH	851	0.241	0.428	0	1

Note: LVCM—Lake Victoria crescent and Mbale; NAADS—National Agricultural Advisory Services; NM—northern moist; NRM—natural resource management; PMI—potential market integration; SW—southwestern; SWC—soil and water conservation; SWH—southwestern highlands; TLU—tropical livestock units; Ush—Ugandan shillings.

[a]Number of observations for each variable varies due to missing observations.

[b]After removing outliers (crop productivity = 0 or crop productivity > Ush 2 million). About 819 plots reported yield = 0 due to unavailability of data during the survey, crop failure, or noncrop harvest (for example, fallow).

[c]Includes live barriers and planting trees in plot and on bunds.

[d]Includes stone bunds, fanya juu and fanya chini (bench terraces), drainage trenches, irrigation structures, and grass or other vegetative strips.

[e]Includes fish ponds, fences, paddocks, and pasture management.

[f]A standard animal with a live weight of 250 kg is called a TLU (Defoer et al. 2000). Average TLUs for common livestock in the Uganda area are as follows: cow = 0.9, oxen = 1.5, sheep or goat = 0.20, calf = 0.25.

groups each have equations whose dependent variables are similar: binary for the land management practices equations and continuous for the land degradation equations. We used the multivariate probit for the land management practices equation. The multivariate probit estimates maximum likelihood coefficients of M equations using the Geweke-Hajivassiliou-Keane smooth recursive simulator (Greene 2000). Simulated maximum likelihood estimators are consistent as the number of observations and replications increase.

Convergence becomes a problem as the number of equations in a multivariate probit estimation increases. To avoid this problem we excluded from the system the equation

for purchased seed, since the purchase of seeds is somewhat different from the other land management practices. While all other equations represent soil fertility management practices, the purchased seed equation represents soil fertility management indirectly. We achieved convergence after excluding the purchased seed equation, and we then estimated purchased seed as a single probit equation. We tested the independence of the error terms of the equation in the multivariate probit system of equations using the likelihood ratio test of the covariance of the error terms (ρ). We observed that the error term for the organic matter equation was not significantly associated with an error term of any other equation (at $p = .10$). Hence we used the results of the single-equation probit model for that practice in our discussion. For comparison purposes, we also reported the results from the multivariate probit model. Likewise we reported the results of the single-equation maximum likelihood coefficients for all other equations.

We estimated the land degradation system of equations using the seemingly unrelated regression (SUR). However, since we included explanatory variables that are potentially endogenous (participation in traditional extension services and in the new demand-driven extension services, and borrowing from credit institutions), we also estimated the system using the 3SLS method. We also estimated each equation as a single equation using instrumental variables (IV) to account for the endogeneity problem (that is, the two-stage least square method [2SLS]). We reported all these results to determine the robustness of the estimates. However, we test for the independence of the error term using the Breusch-Pagan test of independence of error terms. We also tested the exogeneity of the potentially endogenous variables using the C-statistic test (Baum, Schaffer, and Stillman 2002). When the C-statistic test does not reject exogeneity of the potentially endogenous variables, the preferred model is SUR.

In all regression models we corrected for sample weights, stratification, and plot clustering (possible nonindependence of error terms across plots within a household) at the household level.

Equation (24) includes endogenous right-side variables that could cause endogeneity bias. The endogenous choices are land management practices and preharvest labor input. Nutrient stocks could be endogenous since they are measured at the end of the current period (that is, the time of the survey). However, there are no suitable instruments to address this possible source of endogeneity bias. Thus we used estimated nutrient stocks at the beginning of the previous growing season, which according to the model in Chapter 2 are predetermined (that is exogenous) relative to the decisions of the current growing season (as are other household assets). The nutrient stocks at the end of the previous growing season were estimated by adding the nutrient outflows to and subtracting the nutrient inflows in the current growing season from the nutrient stocks at the end of the current season, that is,

Nutrient stocks at end of previous
growing season $NS_{t-1} = NS_t +$ nutrient
outflows$_t$ – nutrient inflows$_t$.

Even though we implemented this procedure, we dropped the estimated nutrient stocks from the reduced-form version of the crop production and household income models, to check the robustness of the results to their inclusion.

The participation variables, namely participation in agricultural extension or rural finance organizations, could also lead to endogeneity bias. To address this problem, we used IV estimation for all equations that contained some or all of these potentially endogenous variables.

IV coefficients are consistent, provided that a unique solution to the estimation problem exists and the IV are uncorrelated with the error term in the model (Davidson and MacKinnon 2004). However, in finite samples IV estimates are generally biased, and they can be more biased than ordinary least squares (OLS) estimates if the IV used are weak predictors of the endogenous explanatory variables (Bound, Jaeger, and Baker 1995; Davidson and MacKinnon 2004, 324–329). Furthermore, identification of the coefficients of a linear IV model is impossible unless restrictions are imposed on the model, such as excluding some of the IV from the regression. In linear IV estimation it is necessary to have at least as many restrictions as endogenous explanatory variables to be able to identify the model, and additional restrictions (overidentifying restrictions) can help to increase the efficiency of the model, provided that these exclusion restrictions are valid and that the excluded IV are significant predictors of the endogenous explanatory variables.

In our IV regressions we used several community-level variables as IV that are excluded from the regression model, including the degree of cropland degradation in a community (which is an indicator of land management practices in a community), the number of programs and organizations of different types present in a community (indicators of access to extension and credit), and ethnicity (a proxy for social factors that may influence participation in programs, livelihood, and land management decisions). We hypothesize that such variables are significant predictors of the endogenous variables (that is, they are "relevant"), but that they do not add additional explanatory power to the regression after controlling for the participation variables and other variables (that is, the over-identifying restrictions are valid). In estimating equation (24), we also exclude from the regression and use as IV those explanatory variables that were jointly statistically insignificant in the less-restricted version of the model. The explanatory variables that were dropped for being insignificant include the soil pH.

Other estimation and data issues considered included heteroskedasticity, multi-collinearity, and outliers. The distribution of each variable was examined and an appropriate monotonic transformation toward normality was determined using the ladder of power test, because this improves the model specification (that is, reduces problems of nonlinearity, outliers, and heteroskedasticity) (Mukherjee, White, and Wuyts 1998; Stata 2003). Most con-

tinuous variables were skewed; therefore we log-transformed all continuous variables to normalize their skewed distribution and to simplify interpretation of the regression results.[10] Despite these transformations, we still found heteroskedasticity in the regressions. We used the Huber-White robust standard errors in all cases to address heteroskedasticity.

In addition to the direct effects of the regressors, some variables may have interaction effects on value of crop production per acre and per capita income (for example, the effects of access to roads and services may vary across AEZs or by the asset level of the household). Such effects can be estimated by including interaction terms of such variables in the regression. However, a common problem with including interaction terms is that they can cause multicollinearity. We examined the interaction terms of some key variables and then tested for their validity (using Wald tests) and their impact on the multicollinearity (by investigating the variance inflation factors [VIFs]). The variables that we suspected to have significant interaction effects on value of crop production per acre were market access, soil quality indicators, and AEZ. The following interaction terms were significant according to the Wald test and did not cause a VIF larger than 10: SW grasslands × distance to all-weather road and SWH × distance to all-weather road. Hence we include these two interaction terms in the value of the crop production regression.

We also examined the interaction between poverty and policy-relevant variables in order to understand how such interactions affect crop productivity and per capita income. The interaction terms reflect how the relationships with policy-relevant variables

[10]To preserve observations with zero, the log-transformation was done as follows: $\ln(x + 1)$, where x is the variable being transformed (Battese 1997). Hence zero of the untransformed variable will correspond to zero of the transformed variable. However, the coefficients of the variables transformed are no longer elasticities, since their marginal effects are given by $d(\ln y)/d(\ln(1 + x))$.

differ according to asset level. For example the NAADS program could have different impacts across poverty groups. Well-off farmers may demand advisory services on high-value (and possibly risky) crops and technologies while poor farmers may demand advisory services on low-value (low-risk) crops and technologies. A positive interaction between NAADS and assets means that NAADS has a more positive association with crop productivity for households with more assets. Similarly a positive interaction of credit × value of assets in the crop productivity regression suggests that access to credit has a more positive association with crop productivity for farmers with more assets than for poorer farmers.

We used the total value of physical assets (houses, livestock, durable goods, and farm equipment) as an indicator of poverty level and interacted this variable with access to NAADS and traditional extension services, distance to nearest all-weather road, and access to credit as policy-relevant variables. We tested for multicollinearity and observed that, among the asset × policy interaction terms, the NAADS × asset and the credit × asset variables had VIF > 10; they were dropped.

Multicollinearity was also tested using pairwise correlations and VIF. Pairwise correlation showed very strong correlation among certain variables. For example, some of the ethnicity dummy variables showed a very strong correlation of over 0.7 (significant at $p = .001$) with certain AEZs. We

therefore dropped the ethnic group variable from the original specification. The over-identification tests (none of which were significant) verified that this and other exclusion restrictions in the IV models are valid. In the final specifications multicollinearity was not a major concern (maximum VIF = 7) (Mukherjee, White, and Wuyts 1998).

One of the weaknesses of our study is the use of cross-sectional data to assess the relationships between poverty, land management, and land degradation. As noted in Chapter 2, there are complex and multi-directional relationships among these variables over time. Given that we have only cross-sectional data, the ability to determine the direction of causality of observed relationships is limited, even though we have based our empirical specification on a theoretical dynamic model that specifies the temporal order of decisionmaking and have sought to control as much as possible for confounding factors affecting causal inference. For example, our ability to assess the effect of land degradation on crop productivity is weak. Hence we interpret our regression results only as showing empirical associations between dependent and independent variables, rather than as showing causal relationships. A similar approach to the interpretation of empirical results was taken by Minten and Barrett (2008) in a recently published paper on relationships between agricultural technology adoption, productivity, and poverty in Madagascar, and for similar reasons.

CHAPTER 5

Land Management and Severity of Land Degradation

To better understand the land management and soil fertility status of the AEZs analyzed in this study, in this chapter we first examine the soil characteristics using a set of critical values to determine the fertility level for each AEZ. We then use descriptive analysis to explore the severity of soil nutrient depletion for each AEZ and its economic implications. To better understand causes of soil nutrient depletion, we then investigate the determinant factors associated with land management decisions. The specific land management practices analyzed are fallow, crop rotation, land preparation methods, and use of animal manure, household trash, crop and plant residue, short-term SWC methods, and inorganic fertilizer. Use of animal manure, household trash, and crop and plant residues (hereafter referred to as organic matter or organic residues) included biomass transfer (animal manure or organic residues transferred from sources outside the plot) and incorporation of residues from crops grown on the same plot in the previous season. We also analyze the factors associated with use of purchased seeds and the intensity of preharvest labor. This analysis will help us to understand the linkages between land management and poverty. As discussed in Chapter 4, most of the factors expected to affect land management practices are different indicators of asset or access poverty. The chapter concludes with an econometric analysis of the factors associated with land degradation. We use soil nutrient balances and erosion as indicators of land degradation.

Soil Physical and Chemical Properties

The mean values of the soil properties of the sample plots are indicated in Table 5.1. According to Foster's (1971) criteria for classifying Ugandan soils, the mean values of different parameters in west Nile and northwestern (WNW) farmlands and NM farmlands indicate deficient conditions. Therefore crop yields on these soils are likely to be low. The low levels of organic matter for the soils in these two AEZs are partly attributable to the soils having a higher sand fraction as compared to those in other AEZs. Generally organic matter is not protected from decomposition in sandy soils. The mean soil organic matter content is moderate for the other zones, namely the Mt. Elgon farmlands, SW grass-farmlands, Lake Victoria crescent and Mbale (LVCM) farmlands, and the SWH. Soil organic matter and pH are among the factors determining the inherent fertility of Uganda soils and crop yields (Foster 1978, 1980a,b). The relatively low pH (acidity) of the soils in the SWH affects root growth and the availability of plant nutrients and, if severe, may also lead to problems of aluminum toxicity (Kochian, Hoekenga, and Piñeros 2004).

Table 5.1 Mean values of selected physical and chemical characteristics of soils from different agroecological zones

	WNW farmlands	NM farmlands	Mt. Elgon farmlands	SW grass-farmlands	LVCM farmlands	SWH	Critical value[a]
Number of samples	248	451	56	356	470	406	—
pH (water 1:2.5)	6.1	6.3	6.3	6.3	6.4	5.3	5.2
Organic matter (%)	2.29	2.30	4.66	3.92	3.15	5.20	3.0
Total nitrogen (%)	0.10	0.14	0.30	0.19	0.18	0.24	0.2
Exchangeable potassium (cmol/kg^{-1})	0.50	0.57	1.83	1.05	0.65	0.74	0.4
Total phosphorus (%)	0.06	0.07	0.16	0.08	0.09	0.13	—
Total potassium (%)	0.21	0.17	0.63	0.55	0.33	0.95	—
Sand, 0–20 cm (%)	76.2	69.9	43.2	58.6	61.6	48.9	—
Clay, 0–20 cm (%)	16.3	20.1	39.8	25.9	28.9	29.7	—
Silt, 0–20 cm (%)	7.6	10.1	17.0	15.5	9.6	21.4	—
Nitrogen stock 0–20 cm (kg/ha)	2,000	2,800	6,000	3,800	3,600	4,728	—
Phosphorus stock 0–20 cm (kg/ha)	1,200	1,400	3,200	1,600	1,800	2,673	—
Potassium stock 0–20 cm (kg/ha)	4,200	3,400	12,600	11,000	6,600	18,972	—

Note: LVCM—Lake Victoria crescent and Mbale; NM—northern moist; SW—southwestern; SWH—southwestern highlands; WNW—west Nile and northwestern.
[a]Below these values soil levels are low or deficient (Foster 1971).

Table 5.1 shows relatively higher nutrient stocks in the volcanic soils of the Mt. Elgon farmlands and SWH because geologically they are still young and less weathered compared to other soils in Uganda. The stocks are moderate for the SW grass-farmlands and LVCM farmlands and low for the WNW farmlands.

Plot-Level Soil Nutrient Inflows

Table 5.2 shows that the average annual total N inflow is 18.05 kg/ha across all zones, an amount that is well below the recommended N rates for most crops in most soils of Uganda. Inorganic fertilizer contributed only about 1 percent of the average N inflow and was mainly used in the Mt. Elgon farmlands, where it contributed 11 percent of N inflow, and in the WNW farmlands, where it contributed 5 percent of N inflows. Likewise inorganic fertilizers were the major sources of P and K only in the Mt. Elgon and WNW farmlands (Tables 5.3 and 5.4). Inorganic fertilizers

in the WNW farmlands are mostly used by tobacco growers, who receive them on credit from the British American Tobacco Company (Pender et al. 2004a). Fertilizer use in the Mt. Elgon farmlands is due to the proximity of that AEZ to Kenya, where the fertilizer market is well developed and the use of fertilizer is relatively common.

Symbiotic BNF from legumes is a major source of N inflow, on average contributing about a third of total N inflow. This is because legumes are important crops in all AEZs covered in this study. BNF thus has significant potential as a source of N, which is the most limiting soil nutrient for most smallholder farmers, few of whom use inorganic fertilizer. The advantage of BNF over other organic sources of N is that the N comes from the atmosphere, which is an almost inexhaustible source. Other organic sources such as biomass transfer from animal manure and plant residues may be quickly depleted, since biomass transfer redistributes N from the source to the plot (Palm, Myers, and Nandwa 1997).

Animal droppings and manure contributed about 35 percent of the average total

Table 5.2   Major sources of nitrogen inflows and channels of outflows at plot level

Nutrient flow	WNW farmlands	NM farmlands	Mt. Elgon farmlands	SW grass- farmlands	Lake Victoria crescent	SWH	All zones
Total inflows (kg/ha)	13.79	18.79	25.58	25.38	19.53	12.13	18.05
				Contribution to total inflow (%)			
Inorganic fertilizer	5.00	0.00	11.00	0.00	0.00	0.00	1.00
Plant organic matter	0.00	0.00	16.00	4.00	11.00	0.00	5.00
Animal manure and droppings	22.00	46.00	26.00	54.00	26.00	23.00	35.00
BNF	38.00	27.00	28.00	27.00	41.00	38.00	33.00
Atmospheric deposition	34.00	27.00	19.00	15.00	23.00	39.00	25.00
Total outflows (kg/ha)	55.00	75.89	116.75	132.56	114.38	137.00	104.20
				Contribution to total outflow (%)			
Crop harvest	33.00	21.00	38.00	54.00	56.00	17.00	37.00
Animal grazing	26.00	41.00	24.00	22.00	4.00	1.00	15.00
Leaching and denitrification	21.00	29.00	13.00	12.00	15.00	13.00	17.00
Soil erosion	20.00	8.00	25.00	11.00	24.00	69.00	31.00

Note: BNF—biological nitrogen fixation; NM—northern moist; SW—southwestern; SWH—southwestern highlands; WNW—west Nile and northwestern.

Table 5.3   Major sources of phosphorus inflows and channels of outflows at plot level

Nutrient flow sources and channels	WNW farmlands	NM farmlands	Mt. Elgon farmlands	SW grass- farmlands	Lake Victoria crescent	SWH	All zones
Total inflows (kg/ha)	1.30	1.74	4.09	4.00	3.37	1.51	2.46
				Contribution to total inflow (%)			
Inorganic fertilizer	10.00	0.00	25.0	0.00	0.00	0.00	3.00
Plant organic matter	0.00	0.00	28.00	12.00	37.00	1.00	17.00
Animal manure and droppings	30.00	52.00	28.00	73.00	42.00	47.00	50.0
Atmospheric deposition	60.00	48.00	19.00	16.00	22.00	52.00	31.00
Total outflows (kg/ha)	10.06	7.77	20.32	12.84	16.94	41.25	18.09
				Contribution to total outflow (%)			
Crop harvest	29.00	29.00	20.00	46.00	37.00	6.00	22.00
Animal grazing	17.00	42.00	19.00	24.00	3.00	0.00	9.00
Soil erosion	55.00	30.00	60.00	30.00	59.00	94.00	69.00

Note: NM—northern moist; SW—southwestern; SWH—southwestern highlands; WNW—west Nile and northwestern.

Table 5.4 Major sources of potassium inflows and channels of outflows at plot level

Nutrient flow sources and channels	WNW farmlands	NM farmlands	Mt. Elgon farmlands	SW grass-farmlands	Victoria crescent	SWH	All zones
Total inflows (kg/ha)	6.01	12.40	10.33	13.25	15.73	4.36	10.45
Contribution to total inflow (%)							
Inorganic fertilizer	2.00	0.00	11.00	0.00	0.00	0.00	1.00
Plant organic matter	0.00	0.00	15.00	15.00	66.00	4.00	27.00
Animal manure and droppings	46.00	73.00	44.00	66.00	16.00	25.00	44.00
Atmospheric deposition	52.00	27.00	30.00	19.00	18.00	72.00	29.00
Total outflows (kg/ha)	46.99	50.23	124.83	202.37	111.32	303.29	141.33
Contribution to total outflow (%)							
Crop harvest	29.00	24.00	42.00	69.00	62.00	6.00	34.00
Animal grazing	30.00	65.00	20.00	15.00	5.00	0.00	11.00
Leaching	0.00	0.00	0.00	0.00	0.00	0.00	0.00
Soil erosion	41.00	11.00	37.00	16.00	33.00	94.00	55.00

Note: NM—northern moist; SW—southwestern; SWH—southwestern highlands; and WNW—west Nile and northwestern.

annual inflow of N, 50 percent of that of P, and 44 percent of that of K across all zones (Tables 5.2–5.4). This finding demonstrates that animal waste is an important source of nutrients, especially where the animal population is large. For example, animal waste contributed an especially large share of total inflows for all three nutrients in the SW grass-farmlands, where the cattle population is largest among all the zones covered in this study. Plant residues and compost contributed only about 5 percent of the annual inflow of N, 17 percent of P, and 27 percent of K. Plant residues and compost contribute larger shares of nutrient inflows in zones where perennial crops are grown and where the agricultural potential is high. Atmospheric deposition, although not influenced by farmers' land management practices, contributes over a quarter of the estimated inflows of all three macronutrients.[1] It contributes the largest share of P and K inflow

in the NM farmlands and SWH, where the contribution of plant residues and compost and inorganic fertilizers is limited.

Table 5.5 compares the nutrient inflow and outflow of annual and perennial crops. The contribution of inorganic fertilizer to total nutrient inflow for annual crops is greater than that for perennial crops. As observed earlier, inorganic fertilizer is used mainly for maize production in the Mt. Elgon farmlands and for tobacco production in the WNW farmlands. The table also shows that farmers applied limited amounts of inorganic K fertilizers, probably because the supply of K from the soil was sufficient. However, the unbalanced application of only N and P fertilizers is likely to lead to K becoming limiting in the future. Contributions of animal waste, plant residues, and compost to N, P, and K inflows for perennial crops are greater than for annual crops because these organic sources are bulky and

---

[1]Atmospheric deposition of soil nutrients is caused by rainfall (wet deposition), which washes down dust rich in soil nutrients. Dry atmospheric deposition occurs when nutrient-rich dust settles on the ground (Bergametti et al. 1992).

Table 5.5   Soil nutrient flows for perennial and annual crops

Nutrient inflow/outflow	Perennial crops			Annual crops		
	Nitrogen	Phosphorus	Potassium	Nitrogen	Phosphorus	Potassium
Total nutrient inflow (kg ha^{-1} year^{-1})	24.19	4.87	15.58	14.96	1.42	6.95
			Share of total inflow (%)			
Inorganic fertilizer	0.2	0.4	0.0	2.0	4.4	1.3
Animal manure and deposit	46.8	59.0	28.5	20.2	38.8	43.4
Plant residues and compost	13.2	27.0	54.5	1.5	8.8	13.5
BNF	22.2	0.0	0.0	43.5	0.0	0.0
Atmospheric deposition	17.7	13.5	17.0	32.9	48.1	41.8
Total nutrient outflow (kg ha^{-1} year^{-1})	118.07	13.29	185.17	77.20	12.26	79.49
			Share of total outflow (%)			
Crop harvest	55.7	37.7	66.7	26.6	17.9	17.3
Animal grazing	4.8	4.4	3.0	13.4	8.4	12.0
Leaching	17.2	0.0	0.0	22.7	0.0	0.0
Denitrification	3.3	0.0	0.0	4.4	0.0	0.0
Soil erosion	19.0	58.0	30.2	32.9	73.7	70.7
Soil nutrient balance (kg ha^{-1} year^{-1})	−93.88	−8.42	−169.59	−62.24	−10.85	−72.54

Note: BNF—biological nitrogen fixation.

thus not likely to be applied to annual crops, which tend to be planted on more distant plots than perennial crops.

Regardless of the distance, farmers growing perennial crops also have the tradition of mulching and applying other plant residues, such as dead banana stems, leaves, and banana peelings. In the case of nitrogen fixation, annual crops receive a larger share of N inflow from BNF than perennial crops because of the annual grain legumes (for example, beans, cowpeas, and soybeans) that are often grown as pure stands in rotations or mixed with other annual crops. BNF in perennial crops occurs through intercropping legumes with perennial crops like bananas and coffee.

Plot-Level Soil Nutrient Outflows

Crop harvesting is the major outflow for N, contributing over one-third of total nutrient

outflows (Table 5.2). N and K losses through crop harvesting are especially high in the LVCM farmlands, SW grass-farmlands, and Mt. Elgon farmlands, where bananas and coffee are major crops and soil fertility is relatively good, resulting in high crop yields (Tables 5.2 and 5.4). In addition bananas have high K uptake—hence the high rate of K depletion in AEZs with banana farming systems. The share of total P lost through crop harvesting is the lowest for the three macronutrients. As expected, N, P, and K loss through soil erosion is greatest in the hilly areas with limited use of soil conservation technologies, namely the SWH. Soil erosion is not as serious in the Mt. Elgon zone since perennial crop farming in the zone is greater and the average slope of cultivated plots is less than in the SWH zone. Farmers in the Mt. Elgon zone also use more SWC practices than in the SWH.

Leaching and denitrification are the third most important channels of total N outflow. Loss of N through leaching is greater in the light, sandy soils and generally flat terrain of the NM and WNW farmlands. Sandy soils have low water-holding capacity, while the flat terrain leads to poor runoff, which in turn leads to percolation and subsequent leaching of nutrients. Nutrient loss through animal grazing is greater in the NM farmlands, Mt. Elgon farmlands, and SW grass-farmlands owing to the large livestock population in these areas.

Comparison of outflows of annual and perennial plots shows that the amounts of N and K outflow for perennial crops are greater than the equivalent amounts for annual crops (Table 5.5). Perennial crop harvesting contributes the greatest share of N and K outflow. The share of nutrients depleted through perennial crop harvesting is twice that for annual crops or even more. Many factors could contribute to this result, such as the high crop yields of perennial crops, which are usually planted on fertile soils. Perennial systems lose the greatest amount of K because bananas are an important perennial crop and one with high K uptake. Therefore replenishing K is important in banana farming systems. The share of nutrient outflow via soil erosion in perennial crop systems is lower than for annual crops because of good ground cover throughout the year and common use of SWC measures, such as mulching.

The contribution of leaching to nutrient outflow is greater for annual than perennial crops since annual crops are more likely than perennial crops to be planted on light soils.

Plot-Level Nutrient Balances

In most plots surveyed total nutrient outflow exceeds total nutrient inflow. These results underscore the severe depletion of soil nutrient stocks that results from the low-external-input agriculture practiced in Uganda. Only about 20 percent of plots had positive N or K balances, but about a quarter of the plots had positive P balances (Table 5.6). The LVCM zone has the second largest amount of N depletion after the SW grass-farmlands and the second largest rate of P depletion after the SWH. The amount of nutrient depleted per year is largely influenced by the level of fertility of the soils, which determines the amount of crop harvesting—the major channel of nutrient outflows. For example, the total amount of nutrients depleted in the AEZs with poor soils, the MN and WNW farmlands, is less than 100 kg/ha per year, while the average total nutrient depletion is about 179 kg/ha per year across all zones.

We use ENDR to determine the economic magnitude of the loss of soil nutrients. As discussed in Chapter 4, ENDR measures the share of farm income that would be required to replenish the lost nutrients using the cheapest available fertilizers (der Pol 1993). If farmers were to buy the cheapest source of nutrients to replenish the nutrients depleted, the average cost of fertilizer bought would be equivalent to one-fifth of the total household farm income across the eight districts studied.[2] Because of the low farm income in the NM farmlands, farmers in this AEZ would have to use more than a third of their farm income to replenish mined nutrients, compared to only about 11 percent for the Mt. Elgon farmers, who have greater income and use better soil fertility management practices. The nutrient requiring the largest cost to replenish is N, followed by K. These results show the heavy reliance of smallholder farmers on mining soil fertility. Using a fifth of farm income to avoid nutrient depletion would be very difficult for most farmers, who de-

---

[2]Household farm income includes only income from the farm enterprise; it excludes nonfarm income, gifts, and other forms of transfers. The average household income in 2002–03 was Ush 3.04 million, which is about US$1,788.

Table 5.6   Severity of soil nutrient depletion and its economic magnitude

Nutrient depletion and its economic value	WNW farmlands	NM farmlands	Mt. Elgon farmlands	SW grass-farmlands	LVCM	SWH	All zones
Nitrogen							
Nutrient balances (kg ha^{-1} year^{-1})	−35.55	−53.11	−70.01	−99.22	−82.19	−73.18	−70.60
Percent of plots with positive balances	21.16	19.17	22.58	14.73	14.75	28.40	20.14
Nitrogen stock (kg/ha)	1,944.2	2,897.0	6,017.3	3,842.0	3,700.5	4,746.1	3,695.0
Nitrogen balance as percent of total nitrogen stock	−1.83	−1.83	−1.16	−2.58	−2.22	−1.54	−1.91
Number of years to deplete nutrient stock[a]	55	55	86	39	45	65	52
NDMV (US$)/farm[b]	66.17	139.06	106.50	190.41	145.16	75.65	124.80
ENDR[c] (%)	12.0	23.0	6.0	13.0	11.0	6.0	11.0
Phosphorus							
Nutrient balances (kg/ha/year)	−6.29	−4.97	−8.01	−7.33	−9.29	−18.55	−9.98
Percent of plots with positive balances	25.19	26.11	33.45	26.94	19.32	32.16	26.41
Phosphorus stock (kg/ha)	1,160.2	1,412.1	3,127.8	1,655.2	1,828.7	2,759.8	1,916.5
Phosphorus balance as percent of total phosphorus stock	−0.54	−0.35	−0.26	−0.44	−0.51	−0.67	−0.52
Number of years to deplete nutrient stock	184	284	390	226	197	149	192
NDMV (US$)/farm	13.21	14.69	13.75	15.88	18.53	21.62	19.91
ENDR (%)	2.00	2.00	1.00	1.00	1.00	2.00	2.00
Potassium							
Nutrient balances (kg ha^{-1} year^{-1})	−31.97	−34.17	−81.25	−172.95	−78.75	−143.70	−94.85
Percent of plots with positive balances	23.11	30.53	14.42	15.50	14.10	30.70	22.99
Potassium stock (kg/ha)	4,207.5	3,407.2	11,992.6	10,888.4	6,560.1	18,579.9	9,618.9
Potassium balance as percent of total potassium stock	−0.76	−1.00	−0.68	−1.59	−1.20	−0.77	−0.99
Number of years to deplete nutrient stock	132	100	148	63	83	129	101
NDMV (US$)/farm	30.71	46.17	63.79	171.30	71.79	76.56	86.54
ENDR (%)	5.56	7.67	3.75	11.29	5.26	6.32	7.78
All nutrients (nitrogen, phosphorus, potassium)							
Nutrient balance (kg/ha)	−73.82	−99.48	−159.27	−279.50	−178.10	−235.53	−178.80
Nutrient balance as percent of stock	1.01	1.29	0.75	1.71	1.47	0.90	1.17
Percent of plots with positive balances	19.14	17.99	20.00	13.18	11.23	26.58	18.05
ENDR (%)	19.94	33.21	10.82	24.90	17.25	14.34	20.80

Note: ENDR—economic nutrient depletion ratio; LVCM—Lake Victoria crescent and Mbale; NDMV—nutrient deficit market value; NM—northern moist; SW—southwestern; SWH—southwestern highlands; WNW—west Nile and northwestern.

[a] Assuming constant rate of depletion; that depleted nutrients are replenished only from stocks from all three pools (soluble, labile, and inert) in the 0–20 cm of topsoil; that 100% of nutrients in the inert pool become available to plants over time; and that farmers do not change soil fertility management practices.

[b] NDMV is the value of nutrients mined per hectare if such nutrients were to be replenished by applying purchased fertilizer (der Pol 1993).

[c] ENDR is the share (%) of farm income derived from mining soil nutrients (der Pol 1993).

pend on agriculture as their primary source of income. This begs the question of what can be done to help farmers improve SLM practices. This question is the focus of this chapter.

Nutrient Balances in Relation to Stocks

The soil nutrient stocks consist of three pools: the soil solution, labile, and less labile (inert) pools.[3] Plants get their required nutrients from the soil solution pool, which is replenished from the labile pool, which in turn is replenished from the less labile pool. The three pools tend to be in equilibrium. Estimated soil nutrient depletion is high in AEZs with good soils, due to relatively high crop yields and high nutrient loss through erosion (Table 5.6).

The average amount of N depleted in all regions during the 2002 cropping seasons was about 1.9 percent of total N stock in the top 20 cm of the soil (the most critical zone for crops), which includes both the available and inert stocks (Table 5.6). The corresponding average rates of nutrient stock depletion for P and K are 0.5 percent of extractable P and 1.0 percent of exchangeable K in the top 20 cm of the soil.

Although high nutrient mining occurs in the AEZs with good soils, crop yields may not immediately decline because soils have large stocks of nutrients (Table 5.1) that replenish the deficit. The relatively lower negative nutrient balances observed in the WNW and NM farmlands are largely due to lower crop yields in these zones. The crop yields in these zones are likely to decline further as nutrient mining continues, because the soils are generally poor in plant nutrients (Table 5.1).

Assuming that the level of nutrient mining remains at the current level, farmers do not change their current management practices, nutrients lost from the system are

replenished from the soil stocks at a constant rate, and the inert nutrients eventually become available, the maximum numbers of years required for the nutrient stocks in the top 20 cm of soil to be depleted are presented in Table 5.6. The current N stocks will be depleted first, followed by K and then P. Crops require greater amounts of N, which is also more readily available, hence lost through more channels than the other two macronutrients. The LVCM farmlands and SW grass-farmlands show the smallest number of years to total depletion of nutrient stocks, emphasizing the unsustainable agricultural production practices in these regions. It should also be noted that although the number of years required to deplete the current P stocks is the highest, P might become a problem earlier than estimated because of its fixation into unavailable forms in the soil and its low potential for recycling through deep-rooted crops and trees. Trees are typically unable to capture P from below the rooting depth of crops (IAEA 1975).

Overall the average depletion rate for all nutrients combined is 1.2 percent of the stocks in the top 20 cm of soil per year. However, this does not mean the nutrient stocks would be depleted in less than a hundred years. First, the inert stocks are not readily available over the short term; hence their depletion rates are much slower. The amount depleted comes mainly from the soluble component of the nutrient stock. Second, as crops deplete nutrients, their yields decline exponentially, decreasing the rate of depletion since crop harvesting is the leading channel of nutrient outflow. Evidence of declining yields and soil fertility in Uganda since the early 1990s (Deininger and Okidi 2001; Pender et al. 2001b) supports the hypothesis that soil fertility declines are causing yield declines. Third, the regeneration of soils from parent material is not included as a nutrient inflow. Finally, we are not including nutrient stocks below

[3]Labile nutrients are unstable and constantly changing.

the top 20 cm of soil, which can be available to deeper-rooting crops and trees, or as a result of fallowing or deep tillage.

The roots of trees or tree crops such as coffee extend beyond the rooting depth of annual crops. The deep roots of trees can potentially intercept nutrients leaching down soil profiles and take up nutrients accumulated in the subsoil below the rooting depth of annual crops (Breman and Kessler 1995). The potential for trees to retrieve subsoil nutrients is generally greatest when they have deep-rooting systems and high demand for nutrients, water and/or nutrient stress occurs in the surface soil, and considerable reserves of plant-available nutrients or weatherable minerals occur in the subsoil.

Greater capture of subsoil resources by roots would be expected for water and mobile nutrients, such as nitrate, than for less mobile nutrients like P. Research on deep weathered soil in western Kenya showed that fast-growing trees with high N demand (*Calliandra calothyrsus, Sesbania sesban,* and *Eucalyptus grandis*) took up subsoil nitrate that accumulates beneath the rooting zone of annual crops (Hartemink et al. 1996; Mekonnen, Buresh, and Jama 1997; Jama et al. 1998). The retrieval of subsoil nitrate by trees and the subsequent transfer of the N to crops might be an important process in high- and medium-potential zones with deep soils and relatively high base status and anion sorption capacity (Mekonnen et al. 1999). Fallow grasses have a similar effect and help recycle leached nutrients, thus slowing the depletion of nutrient stocks.

The next two sections discuss the land management practices and the determinant factors associated with them. The discussion will help us better understand the factors contributing to soil nutrient depletion and erosion and the policy options to address the problem.

Land Management Practices

Table 5.2 shows that about 16 percent of plots received organic matter. Only around 20 percent were fallowed or were subject to crop rotation. Earlier soil research in Uganda developed input recommendations and soil conservation practices for sustainable production, including a six-year rotation in which land is rested half the time (Foster 1976), application of 22 tons/ha of manure (dry matter) from kraals (livestock enclosures) spread over three years, and use of inorganic fertilizers. The low percentage of farmers who applied organic matter shows that this recommendation is not followed by the majority of farmers, owing to the high labor intensity of biomass transfer and the lack of available organic matter.

Use of inorganic fertilizer is even lower, as only about 2 percent of the plots sampled received fertilizer, at an average rate of 48 kg/acre. Inorganic fertilizer is used mainly by large-scale plantation farmers, who account for 95 percent of fertilizer consumption in Uganda (NARO and FAO 1999). The remaining 5 percent is accounted for by small-scale farmers, mainly maize producers in Kapchorwa and tobacco farmers in the west Nile region. The majority of smallholder fertilizer users in the rest of the country use fertilizer on small plots planted with vegetables or other high-value crops. Adoption of SWC measures is also low, as short-term SWC practices (including trash lines, deep tillage, zero tillage, and cultivation along contour lines) were in place on only about 13 percent of plots.

The results show the low level of use of organic land management practices and the even lower rate of use of inorganic fertilizer. The low rate of adoption of improved soil fertility management technologies contributes to the severe soil nutrient depletion discussed in this chapter.

Factors Associated with Land Management Practices

The land management practices analyzed in this section are the most common land management practices reported by farmers, including slash and burn, fallow, crop rotation, short-term SWC practices (such as trash lines, deep tillage, and zero tillage), crop rotation, fertilizer application, and use of organic matter.

NRM regulations in the community generally do not have a statistically significant association with organic land management practices, but they do have a negative association with application of fertilizer (Table 5.7). Most of the NRM regulations require farmers to use organic land management practices (for example, calling for the planting of trees or prohibiting slash and burn or cultivating on steep slopes) (Nkonya, Pender, and Kato 2008) to prevent or remedy land degradation. Our results suggest that such NRM regulations are less accepted in communities where the potential for inorganic fertilizer use is greater.

Household ownership of physical assets has mixed associations with land management practices. As expected, larger farms are more likely to fallow since they have enough land to continue crop production while resting part of their land. Farmers with larger farms are less likely to use short-term SWC measures such as trash lines, deep tillage, and zero tillage but more likely to practice crop rotation, apply organic manure, or incorporate crop residues. These results give mixed evidence concerning Boserup's (1965) theory of agricultural intensification and the findings of Tiffen, Mortimore, and Gichuki (1994) on the impacts of population pressure on intensity of land use and the propensity to invest in SWC measures. The results are contrary to a long-term study in the Kabale district, which found that fallowing increased with population pressure (Lindblade, Tumuhairwe, and Carswell 1996).

Controlling for farm size, wages, and other factors, population density has no association with fallowing. Population density is positively associated with the probability of using short-term SWC, but it is also positively associated with the use of slash and burn. These results also give mixed

evidence regarding the Boserupian theory of intensification.

Higher wages are positively associated with the use of slash and burn, suggesting that farmers rely on this practice as a labor-saving strategy. However, a higher wage rate is, surprisingly, associated with a greater probability of using SWC measures and applying organic matter; both of these practices are likely to be labor intensive.

Greater ownership of livestock is associated with greater probability of using inorganic fertilizer but with a decreased likelihood of using crop rotation and fallowing. This is perhaps because crop rotation and fallowing are less necessary for soil fertility management if farmers own more livestock, because of the soil fertility benefits of manure. It is also possible that farmers with more livestock use the fallowed plots to graze their animals, which in turn increases the incentive to fallow. The positive association of livestock ownership with fertilizer use suggests that livestock ownership enables farmers to finance the purchase of such inputs, possibly by selling small livestock or livestock products (such as milk) to buy fertilizer. Households that own more farm equipment are, surprisingly, less likely to apply fertilizer.

The human capital of the household has mixed associations with land management practices. Primary, secondary, and postsecondary education of males is associated with a higher probability of applying fertilizer. This could be due to the greater financial ability of households with better-educated males to purchase fertilizer and their greater awareness of the importance of fertilizer in crop production. Postsecondary education of men and women is associated with a lower probability of using short-term SWC. This is probably due to the higher labor opportunity cost of better-educated farmers, which makes it harder for them to adopt labor-intensive practices. Education of males and females has no significant association with organic land management practices, suggesting the need to promote

Table 5.7 Factors associated with land management practices and purchase of seeds (multivariate and single probit models)

Variable	Slash and burn MV	Slash and burn Single	Fallow MV	Fallow Single	Crop rotation MV	Crop rotation Single	SWC MV	SWC Single	Fertilizer MV	Fertilizer Single	Organic matter MV	Organic matter Single
Natural capital												
ln(average slope, %)	−0.004	−0.003	0.008	0.009	0.015	0.024	0.191***	0.200***	−0.032	−0.037	−0.011	−0.063
ln(soil depth, cm)	0.003	0.003	0.109	0.115	0.251***	0.250***	−0.235***	−0.235***	0.500***	0.504**	0.004	−0.099
ln(% sand)	0.001	0	−0.001	−0.001	0.000	0	0.007	0.006	0.002	0.001	0.001	0.004
Practice agroforestry	−0.078	−0.081	0.115*	0.114*	0.038	0.042	0.101	0.089	−0.155	−0.167	0.015	−0.169
SWC structures	−0.053	−0.061	0.103	0.109	0.013	0.018	0.055	0.018	−0.105	−0.107	0.196**	0.201
Perennial crops (cf. annual crops)	−0.275***	−0.271***	−0.355***	−0.355***	−0.171**	−0.169**	−0.111	−0.116	−0.109	−0.104	0.184***	0.243**
Have other NRM investments	0.083	0.074	0.028	0.034	0.180	0.188	0.010	−0.021	−0.138	−0.145	0.265*	0.342
ln(plot area, acres)	0.067	0.072*	−0.031	−0.032	−0.064*	−0.064*	0.026	0.038	0.102	0.104	0.044	−0.291***
ln(farm area, acres)	−0.048	−0.051	0.148***	0.147***	0.097*	0.098*	−0.101*	−0.115*	−0.092	−0.098	−0.061	0.312***
Physical capital												
ln(TLU)	−0.022	−0.013	−0.115***	−0.113***	−0.099*	−0.089	0.053	0.071	0.166*	0.177*	−0.046	0.073
ln(value of farm equipment, Ush)	0.022	0.022	0.001	0.002	0.008	0.008	0.017	0.006	−0.086*	−0.089*	0.028	−0.024
Human capital												
Proportion of female household members with: (cf. no formal education)												
Primary education	−0.058	−0.055	−0.061	−0.065	−0.078	−0.077	−0.062	−0.055	0.007	0.014	0.111	0.054
Secondary education	−0.033	−0.037	−0.011	−0.006	−0.005	0.016	0.058	0.042	0.326	0.327	−0.02	−0.243
Postsecondary education	−0.360	−0.337	0.018	0.013	0.270	0.279	−0.912***	−0.832**	0.921	0.938	0.085	0.098
Proportion of male household members with: (cf. no formal education)												
Primary education	0.089	0.087	−0.081	−0.083	−0.092	−0.083	−0.040	−0.044	0.710***	0.718***	0.104	0.057
Secondary education	−0.179	−0.18	−0.105	−0.104	0.055	0.064	−0.149	−0.125	0.683***	0.699***	−0.089	0.031
Postsecondary education	−0.113	−0.108	0.007	0.008	0.122	0.124	−0.880***	−0.787***	1.077***	1.095**	0.148	0.229
Male household head	0.034	0.038	−0.252	−0.249	0.024	0.015	0.075	0.105	0.350	0.339	0.274*	0.252
ln(household size)	−0.204**	−0.205**	0.013	0.011	0.021	0.013	−0.070	−0.059	0.067	0.071	−0.073	−0.179
Primary activity of household head (cf. crop production)												
Nonfarm activity	−0.086	−0.097	0.265***	0.269***	−0.042*	−0.031	0.064	0.06	0.029	0.039	−0.280***	−0.176
Livestock	−0.039	−0.04	−0.336	−0.307	0.032	0.033	0.125	0.19	−3.195***	—	−0.158	0.363
Proportion of land area owned by women	0.126	0.128	−0.089	−0.081	0.093	0.09	0.275	0.267	−0.096	−0.127	0.444***	−0.147
Land tenure (cf. leasehold and freehold)												
Customary	0.230	0.223	−0.111	−0.103	−0.263**	−0.276**	−0.197	−0.238*	−0.162	−0.158	0.125	0.288
Mailo	−0.164	−0.166	−0.165	−0.16	−0.119	−0.12	−0.317*	−0.354**	0.466	0.5	0.309**	0.005

Rural services

ln(distance to residence + 1, km)	0.138**	0.074	0.071	-0.125	-0.131	0.202***	0.176**	-0.410**	-0.413**	0.009	-0.122
PMI	0.000	0.000	0	0.000	0	0.001**	0.002**	0.000	0	0	0
ln(distance to all-weather road + 1, km)	0.173***	0.023	0.02	-0.015	-0.016	0.132*	0.140**	0.085	0.092	-0.113**	-0.193**
ln(contact hours with extension agent + 1)	0.05	-0.033	-0.033	-0.023	-0.024	0.040	0.035	0.154*	0.150*	0.046	-0.137
Participates in NAADS	0.129	-0.063	-0.064	-0.185**	-0.04	-0.071	0.171	-0.498**	-0.507**	0.004	0.159
Has access to credit	0.069	-0.014	-0.015	-0.031	-0.181**	0.166	-0.102	-0.056	-0.044	0.107	0.028
Village-level factors											
Community NRM regulations	0.025	0.099	0.096	0.029	0.021	0.082	0.079	-0.391***	-0.397***	-0.132*	0.183
ln(population density, persons/km^2)	0.048**	-0.037	-0.039	-0.014	-0.018	0.118***	0.120***	-0.013	-0.013	0.007	0.044
ln(village wage rate, Ush/day)	0.204***	0.009	0.01	0.132	0.153**	0.176*	0.195*	0.239	0.227	0.160**	0.032
Agroecological zone (cf. LVCM)											
NW moist farmlands	0.176	0.564***	0.544***	-0.067	-0.035	0.249	0.289	1.814***	1.822***	0.093	-0.204
Northern moist farmlands	-0.513***	0.826***	0.818***	0.353*	0.395**	-0.495**	-0.453**	-0.016	0.047	-0.374**	-0.275
Mt. Elgon farmlands	-0.416	-0.082	-0.081	0.061	0.074	0.937***	0.958***	1.995***	2.003***	0.878***	-0.15
SW grass-farmlands	-0.546	0.150	0.157	-0.234	-0.22	-0.453**	-0.482**	-3.337***	—	0.338**	0.729***
SWH	-0.572***	0.809***	0.821***	0.744***	0.758***	-2.536***	-2.626***	0.241	0.232	-0.148	0.454
Constant	-2.121***	-1.482*	-1.529*	-2.651***	-2.826***	-2.811***	-2.969***	-6.768***	-6.688***	-2.518***	0.931
Observations	2,827	2,827	2,827	2,827	2,827	2,827	2,827	2,827	2,827	2,827	2,827
Positive observations (%)	20.15	20.85			22.30	13.22		2.23		15.78	

Covariance of error terms (σ_{ij})

	Coefficient (σ)	χ^2		Coefficient (σ)	Probability > χ^2
Slash and burn versus fallow (σ_{21})	0.093	0.039	Fallow versus SWC σ_{42}	0.191	0.000
Slash and burn versus crop rotation (σ_{31})	0.194	0.000	Fallow versus fertilizer σ_{52}	0.016	0.867
Slash and burn versus SWC (σ_{41})	0.390	0.000	Crop rotation versus SWC σ_{43}	0.357	0.000
Slash and burn versus fertilizer (σ_{51})	0.096	0.183	Crop rotation versus fertilizer σ_{53}	0.076	0.399
Fallow versus crop rotation (σ_{32})	0.211	0.000	SWC versus fertilizer σ_{54}	0.051	0.507

Notes: *, **, *** indicate that the coefficient is statistically significant at the 10, 5, or 1 percent level, respectively. Likelihood ratio test of $\sigma_{21} = \sigma_{31} = \sigma_{32} = \sigma_{41} = \sigma_{42} = \sigma_{43} = \sigma_{51} = \sigma_{52} = \sigma_{53} = \sigma_{54} = 0$, prob. $> \chi^2 = 0.000$. LVCM—Lake Victoria crescent and Mbale; MV—multivariate probit; NAADS—National Agricultural Advisory Services; NM—northern moist; NRM—natural resource management; NW—northwestern; PMI—potential market integration; SW—southwestern; SWC—soil and water conservation; SWH—southwestern highlands; TLU—tropical livestock units; Ush—Ugandan shillings.

agricultural education in schools. Larger households have a lower probability of practicing slash and burn, perhaps because of the ability of larger families to use more labor-intensive land preparation practices. However, household size does not have a statistically significant association with other land management practices.

Controlling for education and other household capital endowments, male-headed households are more likely to use organic matter than female-headed households. This is not surprising, as male-headed households are likely to be better endowed to use labor-intensive practices. The multivariate probit results show that the proportion of farms owned by women is positively associated with the probability of using organic matter, but the results were not significant in the single-equation probit, which is the model of choice. Other aspects of human capital have statistically insignificant associations with land management practices.

The livelihood strategy of the household, measured by the primary source of income of the household head, has limited association with most land management practices. Nonfarm activity as a primary source of income is associated with a higher probability of fallowing relative to households for which crop production is the primary activity. This suggests that nonfarm activities enable less-intensive crop production by providing households with alternative sources of income and increasing the opportunity cost of family labor. However, nonfarm activities are associated with a lower probability of using crop rotation. Having livestock production as the major source of income is associated with a lower probability of using fertilizer. This might be expected as a result of these farmers having a large supply of organic manure, which can replace fertilizers. However, contradicting this explanation is our finding that livestock as a source of income did not have a significant association with the use of organic matter. Instead our findings suggest that farmers who depend on livestock have

less incentive to invest in crop production, whether this involves using inorganic or organic fertilizers.

Natural capital has significant associations with several land management practices. Farmers are more likely to practice short-term SWC technologies on steeper slopes. This is probably because the need for and benefits of SWC practices are greater on steeper slopes. Crop rotation and fertilizer application are more likely to be used on deeper topsoils. This suggests that farmers take advantage of deeper and more fertile soils to practice better management to maximize returns, since the response to better land management practices on more fertile soils is likely to be higher (Kaizzi 2002, 64–69). However, farmers are less likely to use SWC practices on deeper soils. It is possible that farmers see no need to practice SWC on plots with deep soils.

Prior investments on the plot have limited associations with current land management practices. Fallowing is more common on plots where agroforestry (noncrop) trees have been planted. This could be part of an improved fallow. The limited influence of prior investment on current land management practices is contrary to the results of Nkonya et al. (2004), who observed that prior land investments do influence current land management practices.

Slash and burn, fallowing, and crop rotation are less likely on plots where perennials dominate than where annual crops dominate. Clearly these are practices associated with the production of annual crops. Application of organic matter is more likely on perennial crops than on annual crops. This is to be expected, since farmers who plant coffee and bananas usually apply manure, household trash, and other organic matter on their plots.

Access to markets, as measured by the PMI, and access to all-weather roads have limited associations with most land management practices. However, better access to markets is associated with a higher probability of adopting SWC practices, while slash and burn practices are more likely to be implemented farther from an all-weather road. These results are consistent with the findings of Tiffen, Mortimore, and Gichuki (1994) that better market access can promote expanded use of SLM practices by increasing the return to labor and other inputs invested in the effort. However, access to all-weather roads is associated with a lower probability of adopting organic matter. This could be a reflection of the better opportunities enjoyed by farmers who live closer to all-weather roads, the limited availability of organic matter, or the higher demand closer to roads for crop residues as fuelwood or fodder for zero-grazed animals. Generally the impacts of market and road access on land management practices in Uganda are mixed (Nkonya et al. 2004; Pender et al. 2004b). Surprisingly, access to roads is not significantly associated with use of fertilizer. Fertilizer use may simply be too far from profitable for most farmers for marginal improvements in road access to make much difference. Other factors that affect the profitability and adoption of fertilizer may need to be addressed before roads can have a significant impact on the adoption of fertilizer.

Access to agricultural technical assistance services (measured by the number of contact hours of the household with agricultural extension agents and participation in the new extension-advisory program, NAADS) has statistically insignificant associations with most of the land management practices considered. The number of visits of traditional extension agents is positively associated with the probability of using fertilizer, but participation in NAADS is negatively associated with the probability of using fertilizer and crop rotation and positively associated with the probability of using slash and burn. This could be due to the focus of NAADS on building profitable enterprises rather than on land management, and it may contribute to increased land degradation where NAADS is operating. Results of the land degradation regressions,

reported in the next section, support this concern.

Access to rural financial services has statistically insignificant associations with all land management practices, except a significant negative association with crop rotation (in the single-equation probit model). The lack of significant association of credit with land management practices may arise because credit is used to facilitate nonfarm activities, rather than to increase soil fertility and crop production. Consistent with this, we find that participation in rural finance organizations is associated with higher per capita income (the findings are discussed in Chapter 6). These findings suggest that credit constraints are not a major impediment to the adoption of improved land management practices, and that access to credit may promote less-intensive land management practices by facilitating more remunerative nonfarm activities. This result is similar to findings reported by Nkonya et al. (2004) and Pender et al. (2004b).

There are significant differences in some land management practices across different land tenure types. Crop rotation and short-term SWC practices are less likely to be practiced on plots under customary tenure than plots under freehold or leasehold. Use of SWC practices is less common on *mailo* than freehold and leasehold plots. However, use of organic matter is more likely on plots under *mailo* tenure than those under freehold and leasehold tenure. This could be due to the traditional practice among farmers in the Lake Victoria crescent region, where *mailo* tenure is common, of growing perennial crops and applying organic manure.

Other factors significantly associated with land management practices include the size of the plot, the distance of the plot from the household residence, and the AEZ and farming system. We do not emphasize the impacts of such factors in this report, as they are static factors not directly related to the issues of poverty and access to markets and services, which are the main focus.

Use of Purchased Seeds and Labor Intensity

Use of purchased seeds and labor intensity are associated with many of the same factors as land management practices. Larger farms are less likely to use purchased seeds and more likely to use less labor per acre (Table 5.8). These results are consistent with the Boserupian theory of intensification and the findings of Nkonya et al. (2004) and Pender et al. (2004b). They are also consistent with the finding, reported in Chapter 6, that larger farms obtain a lower value of crop production per acre. It is also possible that farmers who purchase seeds consumed seeds from previous harvests owing to food insecurity. Hence seed purchases could be an indication of food insecurity rather than of the use of improved seeds. For example, farmers are more likely to plant purchased seeds on plots with sandy soils. This could be due to the lower yields on sandy soils, which lead to consumption of seeds from previous seasons. Consistent with this finding, farmers with other NRM investments (for example, fish farming, paddock construction, pasture management, and fences) and households with a greater proportion of women with secondary education are less likely to plant purchased seeds.

Consistent with Boserupian theory, labor intensity on larger farms is lower than that on smaller farms. This result is consistent with the lower crop productivity on larger farms (reported in Chapter 6). Controlling for farm size, however, we find a negative association of population density and labor intensity. This could be due to the effects of high population density on the intensity of agricultural labor, which are not fully captured by the variables included in the model. For example, the dummy for nonfarm activity does not capture the intensity of nonfarm activities, which is likely to be higher in areas with high population density.

Primary and secondary education of women members of a household have opposite associations with labor intensity. Com-

pared to households with women members having no formal education, households with a larger proportion of women with primary education use more preharvest labor and those with a greater proportion of women members with postsecondary education use less preharvest labor.

Land Degradation

In this section we analyze the factors associated with soil erosion and soil nutrient depletion, which are the most important forms of land degradation in Uganda. Predicted soil erosion is not significantly associated with the size of the farm or the household's physical assets (Table 5.9). Consistent with expectation, the enactment of NRM regulations is associated with higher K balances. These regulations encourage farmers to adopt improved land management practices in their communities. Compliance is higher for those regulations that are enacted by the local community (Nkonya, Pender, and Kato 2008), suggesting the need to strengthen local institutions to enable the enactment of NRM regulations. Female primary education is associated with more soil erosion and lower N and P balances, although the reasons for this finding are not clear. It may be related to the association, discussed earlier, of primary education with labor-intensive crop production, which may cause erosion and subsequent N and P depletion. Likewise male postsecondary education is associated with lower N and P balances. This is consistent with the results on land management, where we observed that male postsecondary education reduces the probability of using short-term SWC practices.

Livestock ownership is, surprisingly, associated with more rapid depletion of N. This is likely due to the feeding of crop residues to livestock after harvest, a common practice in areas with large cattle populations. The resulting nutrient outflows through crop harvests and grazing outweigh the positive impact of organic matter on nutrient inflows.

Table 5.8   Factors associated with intensity of preharvest labor and probability of buying seeds (ordinary least squares)

Variable	Labor full	Labor reduced	Labor instrumental variables	Seed full	Seed reduced
Natural capital					
ln(slope, %)	0.005	0.016	0.017	–0.036	–0.033
ln(soil depth, cm)	–0.034	–0.021	0.032	–0.054	–0.052
ln(% sand)	–0.003	–0.003	–0.001	0.006**	0.006**
Investments on plot					
Practice agroforestry	–0.059	–0.053	–0.048	–0.038	–0.035
Have SWC structures	0.067	0.084	0.115	0.033	0.044
Perennial crops	–0.053	–0.051	–0.051	0.056	0.06
Have other NRM investments	–0.059	–0.026	–0.056	–0.252*	–0.244*
ln(plot area, acres)	—	—	0.086**	0.082**	—
ln(farm area, acres)	–0.301***	–0.301***	–0.260***	–0.175***	–0.170***
Physical capital					
ln(TLU)	0.017	0.033	0.05	–0.049	–0.04
ln(value of farm equipment, thousand Ush)	0.011	0.012	0.002	–0.023	–0.022
Human capital					
Proportion of female household members with: (cf. no formal education)					
Primary education	0.231***	0.226***	0.211**	–0.04	–0.036
Secondary education	0.049	0.053	0.108	–0.255**	–0.234**
Postsecondary education	–0.449*	–0.472*	–0.531*	0.106	0.128
Proportion of male household members with: (cf. no formal education)					
Primary education	0.073	0.072	0.047	0.089	0.09
Secondary education	–0.034	–0.058	–0.064	–0.04	–0.042
Postsecondary education	–0.092	–0.142	–0.214	0.075	0.078
Male household head	–0.064	–0.097	–0.028	0.055	0.052
ln(household size)	0.151	0.151	0.117	0.022	0.031
Primary activity of household head (cf. crop production)					
Nonfarm activity	–0.147*	–0.15*	–0.159*	–0.09	–0.098
Livestock	–0.103	–0.074	–0.027	0.082	0.095
Proportion of land area owned by women	–0.025	–0.06	0.016	–0.146	–0.159
Land tenure (cf. leasehold and freehold)					
Customary	0.316***	0.277**	0.257**	0.098	0.081
Mailo	0.302*	0.286*	0.356**	0.018	0.009
Access to rural services					
ln(distance to residence + 1, km)	0.032	0.039	0.074	–0.141**	–0.138**
PMI	0.000	0.000	0.000	0	0
ln(distance to all-weather road + 1, km)	–0.017	–0.02	0.00	0.052	0.057
ln(contact hours with extension agent +1)	0.010	—	0.059	0.028	—
Participates in NAADS	–0.019	—	–0.400	0.101	—
Has access to credit	–0.181	—	0.113	–0.076	—
Village-level factors					
Community NRM regulations	–0.080	–0.096	–0.105	—	—
ln(population density, persons/km²)	–0.080**	–0.082	–0.071**	0.004	0
ln(village wage rate, Ush/day)	0.028	0.039	0.016	–0.017	–0.012
Agroecological zone (cf. LVCM)					
NW moist farmlands	–0.255	–0.231	–0.286	–0.604***	–0.565***
NM farmlands	–0.085	–0.069	–0.154	–1.179***	–1.170***

(continued)

Table 5.8   Continued

Variable	Labor full	Labor reduced	Labor instrumental variables	Seed full	Seed reduced
Agroecological zone (cf. LVCM)					
Mt. Elgon farmlands	0.045	−0.061	−0.14	−0.619***	−0.643***
SW grass-farmlands	0.367**	0.290*	0.181	−0.450***	−0.475***
SWH	0.388**	0.301	0.188	−0.168	−0.188
Constant	5.507***	5.389***	5.270***	0.413	0.341
C-statistic (exogeneity/orthogonality) (p-value)	—	—	0.295	—	—
Relevance tests of excluded variables (p-values)					
Contact hours with extension agent	—	—	0.000	—	—
NAADS	—	—	0.000	—	—
Access to credit	—	—	0.000	—	—
Hansen J-test of overidentification restrictions (p-value)	—	—	0.119	—	—

Notes: *, **, *** indicate that the coefficient is statistically significant at the 10, 5, or 1 percent level, respectively. Standard errors are not reported but are available from the authors on request. LVCM—Lake Victoria crescent and Mbale; NAADS—National Agricultural Advisory Services; NM—northern moist; NRM—natural resource management; NW—northwestern; PMI—potential market integration; SW—southwestern; SWC—soil and water conservation; SWH—southwestern highlands; TLU—tropical livestock units; Ush—Ugandan shillings.

Table 5.9   Factors associated with soil nutrient depletion and soil erosion

Variable	Nitrogen balance			Phosphorus balance		
	SUR	3SLS	2SLS	SUR	3SLS	2SLS
Natural capital						
ln(slope, %)	−24.269***	−22.365***	−21.460***	−5.498***	−5.079***	−4.486***
ln(soil depth, cm)	2.859	5.84	4.573	−0.841	0.244	−0.196
ln(% sand)	0.450*	0.471*	0.101	0.125**	0.103**	0.033
Investments on plots						
Practice agroforestry	9.009	10.822	8.704*	2.109*	2.115	2.295**
Have SWC structures	8.37	7.708	12.964*	2.52	2.799	3.355**
Perennial crops (cf. annual crops)	−12.666*	−13.053*	−14.604**	−0.52	0.337	−0.67
Have other NRM investments	−6.274	−1.668	−4.919	−4.05	−5.006*	−4.000
ln(plot area, acres)	6.301*	6.750*	11.069***	−0.004	0.018	1.544**
ln(farm size, acres)	−1.602	−1.612	−10.965***	0.102	0.305	−2.163***
Physical capital						
ln(TLU)	−15.242***	−13.676***	−10.733***	−0.666	0.015	−0.102
ln(value of farm equipment, thousand Ush)	−2.072	−1.739	−1.248	0.004	0.109	0.14
Human capital						
Proportion of female household members with: (cf. no formal education)						
Primary education	−17.092**	−16.176**	−15.789***	−3.297**	−3.555**	−3.272***
Secondary education	−1.962	−4.857	−11.948	4.194*	2.979	2.077
Postsecondary education	−10.603	−5.374	−13.228	−6.968	−5.783	−5.94
Proportion of male household members with: (cf. no formal education)						
Primary education	4.956	5.923	2.404	−0.893	−0.735	−1.231
Secondary education	−3.8	−12.872	−1.438	−1.846	−1.979	0.046
Postsecondary education	−30.633**	−36.340**	−28.213	−7.190**	−6.030*	−6.291**

Table 5.9   Continued

Variable	Nitrogen balance			Phosphorus balance		
	SUR	3SLS	2SLS	SUR	3SLS	2SLS
Male household head	5.169	3.166	11.174	0.552	0.461	1.817
ln(household size)	11.875	12.666	13.623**	3.790**	3.790**	3.841***
Primary activity of household head (cf. crop production)						
Nonfarm activity	–3.158	–1.8	4.425	1.132	2.350*	2.812**
Livestock	–0.196	5.706	–17.32	8.819**	12.569***	5.639
Proportion of land area owned by women	5.886	2.743	10.449	0.425	0.274	1.904
Land tenure (cf. leasehold and freehold)						
Customary	14.472	11.825	5.527	–0.01	–0.33	–0.385
Mailo	8.95	8.755	–1.661	2.337	1.284	0.631
Access to rural services						
ln(distance to residence + 1, km)	2.066	0.679	9.513**	1.343	1.155	2.311***
PMI	0.042	0.047	0.073**	–0.01	–0.009	0
ln(distance to all-weather road + 1, km)	–7.963*	–8.993**	–5.822	–3.806***	–4.040***	–2.915***
ln(contact hours with extension agent +1)	9.405**	1.591	3.37	1.388	–1.911	0.072
Participates in NAADS	–5.166	–5.362	0.575	–1.691	–0.8	0.355
Has access to credit	2.068	14.561	1.496	0.443	0.062	0.452
Village-level factors						
Community NRM regulations	5.281	5.334	10.769**	0.947	0.191	1.709
ln(population density, persons/km^2)	–0.437	–0.739	–4.587*	–0.56	–0.539	–1.013*
ln(village wage rate, Ush/day)	9.962	9.293	6.831	0.239	0.139	0.548
Agroecological zone (cf. LVCM)						
NW moist farmlands	38.598**	38.380**	38.571***	–1.006	–1.558	0.998
NM farmlands	18.633	15.047	19.620*	1.351	0.982	3.044
Mt. Elgon farmlands	42.821*	28.63	26.01	6.545	4.903	3.924
SW grass-farmlands	2.556	–8.734	–4.891	5.653**	4.273	4.658**
SWH	18.665	6.449	25.561*	–13.044***	–15.831***	–5.799**
Constant	–179.349***	–182.358**	–132.505**	–9.407	–10.008	–10.729
C-statistic (exogeneity/orthogonality)						
(*p*-value)	—	—	0.215	—	—	0.586
Relevance tests of excluded variables (*p*-values)						
Contact hours with extension agent	—	—	0.000	—	—	0.000
NAADS	—	—	0.000	—	—	0.000
Access to credit	—	—	0.000	—	—	0.000
Hansen *J*-test of overidentification restrictions (*p*-value)	—	—	0.951	—	—	0.763
Number of observations	2,236	2,099	2,835	2,236	2,099	2,835
R^2	0.090	0.093	0.069	0.174	0.185	0.101

	Potassium balance			Soil erosion		
	SUR	3SLS	2SLS	SUR	3SLS	2SLS
Natural capital						
ln(slope, %)	–34.065***	–32.255***	–28.625***	8.617***	8.194***	8.463***
ln(soil depth, cm)	4.105	11.879	8.627	1.178	0.884	0.972
Sand	1.173***	1.693***	0.482	–0.070***	–0.064**	–0.067**
Investments on plot						
Practice agroforestry	21.352*	27.960**	20.390**	–2.226***	–2.528***	–2.247***

(continued)

Table 5.9 Continued

Variable	Nitrogen balance			Phosphorus balance		
	SUR	**3SLS**	**2SLS**	**SUR**	**3SLS**	**2SLS**
Have SWC structures	21.621	30.526*	19.364*	–1.696*	–1.814*	–1.628**
Perennial crops (cf. annual crops)	–37.471***	–37.078***	–42.552***	0.212	0.626	0.559
Have other NRM investments	8.972	14.29	5.515	–0.311	–0.815	–0.194
ln(plot area, acres)	1.899	1.523	12.111*	–0.131	–0.055	–0.113
ln(farm size, acres)	0.6	3.595	–15.422**	0.61	0.558	0.51
Physical capital						
ln(TLU)	–7.146	–5.146	–5.567	–0.682	–1.222**	–0.693*
ln(value of farm equipment, thousand Ush)	–1.041	–2.843	–1.372	–0.128	–0.177	–0.095
Human capital						
Proportion of female household members with: (cf. no formal education)						
Primary education	8.511	3.321	–1.031	1.770**	1.878**	1.964**
Secondary education	11.641	15.51	–6.402	1.158	1.416	1.257
Postsecondary education	–11.412	–29.368	–17.955	3.39	1.082	2.724
Proportion of male household members with: (cf. no formal education)						
Primary education	10.974	11.719	1.631	0.383	–0.087	0.352
Secondary education	–32.726*	–50.858**	–17.49	–3.094***	–3.086**	–3.009***
Postsecondary education	–10.982	–56.682*	–15.898	–0.994	–1.652	–0.663
Male household head	15.469	10.565	20.54	0.379	0.257	–0.033
ln(household size)	36.876***	39.483**	42.340***	–1.534*	–1.47	–1.347
Primary activity of household head (cf. crop production)						
Nonfarm activity	4.849	7.054	14.354	–1.616**	–1.826**	–1.627**
Livestock	77.142**	73.817*	50.486	–1.424	–3.792	–1.501
Proportion of land area owned by women	23.794	21.131	21.484	0.443	0.702	0.287
Land tenure (cf. leasehold and freehold)						
Customary	29.544	22.213	15.989	0.051	0.953	0.129
Mailo	3.659	1.113	–7.92	–0.629	–0.591	–0.465
Access to rural services						
ln(distance to residence + 1, km)	1.21	2.962	14.299**	0.329	0.442	0.303
PMI	–0.054	–0.037	–0.021	0.004	0.003	0.003
ln(distance to all-weather road + 1, km)	–27.701***	–30.644***	–24.246***	2.326***	2.331***	2.413***
ln(contact hours with extension agent +1)	7.398	–1.241	3.685	0.423	3.795***	0.465
Participates in NAADS	–19.832*	–36.023**	–10.643	1.765**	1.654*	0.377
Has access to credit	–9.426	113.752**	–7.771	0.137	0.926	1.660**
Village-level factors						
Community NRM regulations	22.552*	19.804	25.343***	–0.317	0.157	–0.392
ln(population density, persons/km^2)	–0.355	–1.489	–5.119	–0.015	0.187	0.097
ln(wage rate, Ush/day)	22.711*	30.736**	22.416***	0.381	0.092	0.281
Agroecological zone (cf. LVCM)						
NW moist farmlands	20.193	27.984	31.982	1.374	0.731	1.329
NWM farmlands	26.336	19.482	36.707**	–0.239	–1.077	–0.297
Mt. Elgon farmlands	52.017	–13.629	27.009	–7.378***	–6.873**	–7.420***
SW grass-farmlands	–74.478***	–117.961***	–67.349***	–5.257***	–5.079***	–5.488***
SWH	–67.728**	–101.658***	–17.655	9.378***	10.745***	9.873***
Constant	–363.357***	–486.984***	–318.643***	–6.763	–4.796	–5.652
C-statistic (exogeneity/orthogonality)						
(p-value)	—	—	0.637	—	—	0.061*

Table 5.9   Continued

Variable	Nitrogen balance			Phosphorus balance		
	SUR	3SLS	2SLS	SUR	3SLS	2SLS
Relevance tests of excluded variables (*p*-values)						
Contact hours with extension agent	—	—	0.000	—	—	0.000
NAADS	—	—	0.000	—	—	0.000
Access to credit	—	—	0.000	—	—	0.000
Hansen *J*-test of overidentification restrictions (*p*-value)	—	—	0.493	—	—	0.593
Number of observations	2,236	2,099	2,835	2,236	2,099	2,099
R^2	0.157	0.126	0.102	0.406	0.391	0.403

Notes: *, **, *** indicate that the coefficient is statistically significant at the 10, 5, or 1 percent level, respectively. Breusch–Pagan test of independence of equations in the SUR: *p*-value = .000.*** Standard errors are not reported but are available from the authors on request. LVCM—Lake Victoria crescent and Mbale; NAADS—National Agricultural Advisory Services; NM—northern moist; NRM—natural resource management; NW—northwestern; PMI—potential market integration; 2SLS—two-stage least square method; 3SLS—three-stage least square method; SUR—seemingly unrelated regression; SW—southwestern; SWC—soil and water conservation; SWH—southwestern highlands; TLU—tropical livestock units; Ush—Ugandan shillings.

Covariance matrix of error terms:

	Nitrogen balance	Phosphorus balance	Potassium balance	Soil erosion
Nitrogen balance	1.00	—	—	—
Phosphorus balance	0.56	1.00	—	—
Potassium balance	0.58	0.448	1.00	—
Soil erosion	–0.207	–0.371	–0.245	1.00

Larger households have significantly lower (at $p = .10$) soil erosion, probably because the availability of more family labor enables households to adopt labor-intensive soil conservation practices. This finding supports the optimistic "more people, less erosion" hypothesis (Tiffen, Mortimore, and Gichuki 1994) at the household level, and it is consistent with the better P and K balances of larger households.

Not surprisingly, soil erosion is greater on steeper slopes, is lower on sandy soils, and is reduced by investments in agroforestry and SWC structures. Sandy soils have higher N, P, and K balances, probably due to the low yields on such soils. Sandy soils also reduce erosion, as noted earlier, which is a major channel of outflows. Agroforestry investment is associated with higher K and P balances, probably due to its effect in reducing soil erosion.

Plots with perennial crops have significantly lower N and K balances than those with annual crops. As noted earlier, bananas have high K uptake, and farmers in Uganda do not apply K fertilizer to banana plots. This explains the negative balances for plots with banana crops. The more negative N balance is probably due to the cropping intensity on plots with perennial crops. Farmers often plant annual crops, such as yams or beans, on plots with perennial crops.

Participation in NAADS is associated with higher soil erosion and lower K balances. These results are consistent with the negative association between NAADS participation and use of crop rotation and inorganic fertilizer and the positive association with the use of slash and burn (Table 5.7). They demonstrate a potential negative effect of the new prodigality- and market-oriented enterprises that NAADS is promoting without emphasizing the need to address concerns about SLM. By contrast, contact with traditional extension service providers is associated with higher N balances, consistent with the positive association between traditional extension and the use of inorganic fertilizer.

Access to roads is associated with significantly less soil erosion. Consistent with this, access to roads is associated with higher N, P, and K balances, suggesting that farmers closer to roads manage their land more sustainably than those in the remote areas.

Erosion is lower for households dependent on nonfarm activities as their primary source of income than for households dependent on crop income, probably because such households use the land less intensively (for example, we observed that farmers with nonfarm activities are more likely to fallow and are less likely to use slash and burn than those dependent on crop production). Households dependent on livestock production have higher P and K balances than those dependent on crop production. This could be due to limited production of crops that deplete these nutrients and to lower soil erosion, which is the major outflow channel for these nutrients (Table 5.5).

Erosion differs across AEZs, being the worst in the steeply sloping, high rainfall SWH and least in the NM, LVCM, and WNW zones.

CHAPTER 6

Factors Associated with Crop Productivity and Household Income

U sing a number of poverty indicators, this chapter analyzes the linkages between asset and access poverty and crop productivity and per capita income. We analyze the determinants of crop productivity and per capita household income using the econometric model specified in Chapter 4.

We divide the discussion below into seven major groups of factors expected to affect crop productivity and household income: land management practices and intensity of labor (for the crop productivity model only), natural capital, physical capital, human capital, access to rural services, land tenure, and village-level factors.[1]

Land Management Practices and Intensity of Labor

Regression models for the factors associated with the value of crop production per acre are shown in Table 6.1. The regression models used include OLS; quantile regressions for the lower, median, and upper quartiles; and IV. The Hansen *J*-test in the IV model supports the validity of the IV and identifying assumptions used, and the relevance test indicates that the IV are highly relevant. However, the exogeneity test (*C*-test) fails to reject statistical exogeneity of these inputs and practices, so OLS is the preferred model, as it is more efficient than the IV model.

As expected, the value of inorganic fertilizer applied is associated with higher crop productivity in the OLS model, but the impact is statistically insignificant in all quantile regression models and the IV model. The minor impact of inorganic fertilizer on productivity is consistent with the findings of Pender et al. (2004b) and explains the limited adoption of inorganic fertilizer use in Uganda.

Intensity of preharvest labor is positively associated with crop productivity in all regression models, while the coefficient of crop residue incorporation is statistically significant in OLS and median regressions but insignificant (at $p = .10$) in the IV and other quantile models (Table 6.1). The positive association of labor intensity with crop productivity is consistent with the findings of Nkonya et al. (2004) and Pender et al. (2004b). The positive association found for incorporation of crop residues contrasts with the results of Nkonya et al. (2004) and Pender et al. (2004b), who found insignificant impacts of organic fertilizer on crop productivity, perhaps because of differences in the sample frames or in the way organic fertilizer was mea-

---

[1]See Chapter 2 for detailed discussion of these groups of factors. (Chapter 2 discusses land management practices as endogenous variables.)

Table 6.1   Factors associated with value of crops produced per acre

Variable	Ordinary least squares	Lower quartile	Median	Upper quartile	Instrumental variables
Land management practices					
ln(value of fertilizer + 1, Ush)	0.052**	0.051	0.024	0.037	0.039
ln(value of purchased seed, Ush)	–0.012	–0.014	0.016	0.007	0.01
ln(value of organic fertilizer, Ush)	–0.015	–0.034	–0.013	0.016	0.003
Incorporate crop residues	0.266**	0.333	0.350**	0.108	0.19
ln(preharvest labor)	0.207***	0.207***	0.196***	0.210***	0.182***
Natural capital					
Topsoil depth (cm)	0.037	0.419***	0.221***	0.043	0.142
Average slope (%)	–0.026	0.071	0.059	0.025	0.037
ln(nitrogen stock, kg/ha)	0.002	0.039	0.06	0.042	–0.053
ln(phosphorus stock, kg/ha)	0.153***	0.201***	0.052	0.073*	0.124*
ln(potassium stock, kg/ha)	0.062	0.014	–0.01	0.049	0.083
Practice agroforestry	0.320***	0.299**	0.402***	0.387***	0.399***
Have SWC structures	0.452***	0.262	0.532***	0.465***	0.478***
Perennial crops (cf. annual crops)	0.214**	0.025	0.076	0.155*	0.141
Have other NRM investments	0.106	0.071	–0.145	0.084	–0.09
ln(plot area, acres)	0.255***	0.364***	0.353***	0.251***	0.307***
ln(farm size, acres)	–0.907***	–1.025***	–0.962***	–0.883***	–0.965***
Physical capital					
TLU	0.027	0.069	0.084	0.082	0.066
ln(value of farm equipment, Ush)	–0.048**	–0.029	–0.021	–0.019	–0.027
Human capital					
Proportion of female household members with: (cf. no formal education)					
Primary education	0.019	0.038	0.037	0.056	–0.025
Secondary education	–0.284	–0.053	–0.043	–0.215	–0.078
Postsecondary education	0.27	0.568	0.629*	0.29	0.496
Proportion of male household members with: (cf. no formal education)					
Primary education	0.09	–0.1	–0.189	0.002	–0.031
Secondary education	0.472***	0.546**	0.305*	0.194	0.387**
Postsecondary education	0.529**	0.501**	0.028	–0.107	0.261
Male household head (cf. female)	0.033	0.452**	0.18	–0.193	0.189
ln(household size)	0.141	0.15	0.194	0.254*	0.258*
Primary activity of household head (cf. crop production)					
Nonfarm activity	0.022	0.066	0.068	0.429***	0.077
Livestock	–0.34	–0.17	–0.204	–0.611*	–0.454
Proportion of farm size owned by female household members	–0.074	0.380*	–0.095	0.089	0.126
Land tenure (cf. leasehold and freehold)					
Customary	0.253*	0.31	0.470***	0.559***	0.346**
Mailo	0.009	0.107	0.256	–0.063	0.203
Village-level factors					
ln(population density, persons/km^2)	–0.076*	–0.037	–0.001	0.012	–0.055
ln(community level wage rate, Ush/day)	–0.243***	–0.335***	–0.222	–0.325***	–0.213*
Access to rural services					
ln(distance to residence +1, km)	–0.224***	–0.353***	–0.270***	–0.123	–0.221**
ln(distance to all-weather road +1, km)	–0.12	–0.006	–0.046	–0.046	–0.134
PMI	0	0	–0.001	–0.001*	–0.001
ln(number of contact hours with traditional extension agent +1)	–0.093	–0.116	–0.173	–0.024	–0.003

Table 6.1   Continued

Variable	Ordinary least squares	Lower quartile	Median	Upper quartile	Instrumental variables
Participates in NAADS	0.270***	0.266**	0.176*	0.201*	0.177*
Has access to credit	0.177	0.134	0.323**	0.501***	0.191
Agroecological zone (cf. LVCM)					
NW moist farmlands	−1.166***	−1.097***	−1.047***	−1.444***	−1.058***
NM farmlands	−0.870***	−0.815***	−0.604***	−0.945***	−0.576**
Mt. Elgon farmlands	−0.34	−0.451	−0.356	−0.237	−0.149
SW grass-farmlands	0.422*	0.596	0.760**	0.274	0.799**
SWH	−0.724***	−1.205***	−0.538*	−0.730**	−0.730**
Interaction terms (agroecological zone × distance to all-weather road)					
Southwestern grasslands × distance to all-weather road	−0.049	−0.236	−0.013	−0.027	−0.135
SWH × distance to all-weather road	−0.143	0.016	−0.019	−0.270*	0.006
Value of asset × extension	0.002***	0.002*	0.003***	0.002*	0.001
Value of assets × distance to all-weather road	0.003**	0.003**	0.002	0	0.003**
Constant	10.366***	7.935***	9.848***	11.830***	9.668***
Hausman test (*p*-value)	—	—	—	0.000	—
Hansen *J*-test of overidentification restrictions (*p*-value)	—	—	—	0.230	—
C-statistic (exogeneity/orthogonality) (*p*-value)	—	—	—	0.140	—
Relevance tests of excluded variables (*p*-value)					
Value of purchased seed	—	—	—	0.000	—
Value of inorganic fertilizer	—	—	—	0.000	—
Value of organic fertilizer	—	—	—	0.000	—
Crop residue	—	—	—	0.095	—
Nitrogen stock	—	—	—	0.038	—
Phosphorus stock	—	—	—	0.010	—
Potassium stock	—	—	—	0.000	—
Contact hours with extension agent	—	—	—	0.000	—
NAADS	—	—	—	0.000	—
Access to credit	—	—	—	0.000	—

Notes: *, **, *** indicate that the coefficient is statistically significant at the 10, 5, or 1 percent level, respectively. Interaction terms for other agroecological zones that are not reported jointly failed the Wald test at $p = .10$. For brevity the reduced crop productivity regression results are not reported but are available from the authors on request. See equivalent results without the asset × policy interaction terms in Table A.1; the results are similar with only a few exceptions. LVCM—Lake Victoria crescent and Mbale; NAADS—National Agricultural Advisory Services; NM—northern moist; NRM—natural resource management; NW—northwestern; PMI—potential market integration; SW—southwestern; SWC—soil and water conservation; SWH—southwestern highlands; TLU—tropical livestock units; Ush—Ugandan shillings.

sured in these studies. However, the non-significant association of the value of organic fertilizer with crop production is consistent with the findings of Nkonya et al. (2004) and Pender et al. (2004b).

Natural Capital

Not surprisingly, natural capital also has significant associations with crop produc-

tivity and household income. Controlling for use of inputs and land management practices, land quality, and other factors, larger farms have a lower per-acre value of crops produced for all productivity quartiles, supporting the inverse farm size–land productivity relationship observed in many empirical studies in developing countries (for example, Chayanov 1966; Sen 1975; Berry and Cline 1979; Carter 1984; Bhalla

1988; Barrett 1996; Heltberg 1998; Lamb 2003; Nkonya et al. 2004; Pender et al. 2004b). We find this inverse relationship even when controlling for use of labor, other inputs, land management practices, plot size, and observable indicators of land quality, suggesting not only that smaller farmers tend to farm more intensively (as we have already seen) but also that they are more productive in their use of inputs.[2]

These results suggest that market imperfections (such as limitations in the markets for some factors of production and for outputs) limit the productivity of larger farms (Carter 1984; Feder 1985; Barrett 1996; Heltberg 1998). Unobserved differences in the quality of land operated by larger versus smaller farms may also account for part of this finding (Bhalla 1988; Lamb 2003), although we have controlled for many indicators of land quality at the plot level, unlike many of the previous studies. By contrast, plot area is positively associated with crop productivity per acre, suggesting that land fragmentation reduces the ability to achieve economies of scale.

Despite having lower land productivity, larger farms have higher per capita household income for all the income quartile and OLS regressions (Table 6.2), suggesting that they have higher labor productivity (Pender 2001). Hence larger farms appear able to compensate for lower land productivity with higher labor productivity, leading to higher incomes.

The P stock in the topsoil has a positive association with crop productivity in the OLS, lower-quartile, and upper-quartile regressions. Similarly P stock is positively associated with per capita household income in the OLS regression. These results suggest that P is a key limiting nutrient in Uganda. A 1 percent increase in the P stock is associated with a 0.15 percent increase in the value of crop productivity in the OLS regression and with a 0.20 percent increase among farmers in the lower productivity quartile.

We can use these results to estimate the productivity loss due to P depletion. Loss of productivity is a common measure of the cost of land degradation (Bojö 1996). Taking the average crop productivity (166,850 Ugandan shillings [Ush]/acre) and stock of P (767 kg/ acre) as benchmarks, a 1 percent decrease in the stock of P, equivalent to 7.7 kg/acre, is associated with a predicted decrease of crop productivity equivalent to only Ush 334/ acre or approximately Ush 43/kg of soil P lost among farmers in the lower quartile.[3] This demonstrates the large difference between the price of commercial P fertilizer (averaging about 930 Ush/kg for diammonium phosphate in 2005, equivalent to about 4,600 Ush per kilogram of elemental P) and the value of soil P. The value of loss of productivity due to a 1-kg loss of soil P is equivalent to less than 0.9 percent of the price of the cheapest commercial P (43/ 4,600).[4] The results show the low value that farmers impute to soil P and explain the low adoption rate of fertilizer in Uganda. This is a common problem in SSA, where adoption rates of fertilizer are low and soil nutrient depletion is high.

Most soils in Uganda and elsewhere in tropical Africa are deficient in P (Mokwunye, Chien, and Rhodes 1986). Worse still, replenishment of P using organic matter is not effective since organic inputs have

---

[2]Nkonya et al. (2004) noted a similar finding from their analysis of data from a different sample in Uganda.

[3]The stock of P per hectare is 1,917 kg/ha (Table 5.5), which is equivalent to 767 kg/acre.

[4]The P stock measured in this study includes the soil solution, labile, and less labile (inert) pools. Dissolved P is readily available to plants; the labile and inert pools are not readily available, but they replenish the soluble stock over time. Since we include the stocks that are not readily available to plants, it is likely that we have underestimated the benefits of increased available P in the soil. Further research is required to estimate more accurately the impact of land degradation on crop productivity and the value that farmers impute to depleted nutrients.

Table 6.2   Factors associated with per capita household income

Variable	Ordinary least squares	Instrumental variables	Quantile regression Lower quartile	Median	Upper quartile
Natural capital					
ln(slope %)	–0.001	–0.001	0.01	–0.004	–0.02
ln(topsoil depth, cm)	0.005	0.006	0.004	0.006	0
ln(nitrogen stock, kg/ha)	0.076	0.089	0.278*	0.184	0.199
ln(phosphorus stock, kg/ha)	0.260***	0.245**	0.107	0.172	0.173
ln(potassium stock, kg/ha)	–0.093	–0.11	–0.09	–0.137	–0.182
Practice agroforestry	0.201*	0.203*	0.176**	0.155	0.361**
Have SWC structures	0.476***	0.504***	0.567***	0.498***	0.556**
Perennial crops (cf. annual crops)	0.419***	0.402***	0.2	0.216	0.465**
Have other NRM investments	1.017**	1.205***	0.731	1.07	0.939
ln(farm area, acres)	0.382***	0.413***	0.388***	0.405***	0.325***
Physical capital					
TLU	0.228***	0.223***	0.288***	0.229***	0.262***
ln(value of farm equipment)	0.01	0.014	–0.011	0.001	0.006
Human capital					
Proportion of female household members with: (cf. no formal education)					
Primary education	0.034	0.088	–0.075	0.001	–0.006
Secondary education	–0.242	–0.222	0.028	–0.076	–0.213
Postsecondary education	0.369	0.221	0.592	0.469	0.848
Proportion of female household members with: (cf. no formal education)					
Primary education	0.159	0.099	0.094	0.08	–0.04
Secondary education	0.383**	0.318*	0.204	0.23	0.296
Postsecondary education	0.344	0.17	0.464	0.201	–0.148
Male household head (cf. female)	0.228	0.203	0.426	–0.081	0.204
ln(household size)	–0.219	–0.321**	–0.267*	–0.188	–0.015
Primary activity of household head (cf. crop production)					
Nonfarm activity	0.221**	0.18	0.151	0.294*	0.07
Livestock	–0.521	–0.759**	–0.509	0.109	–0.517
Proportion of farm area owned by female household members	0.104	0.191	0.155	–0.148	0.121
Land tenure (cf. leasehold and freehold)					
Mailo	–0.11	–0.057	–0.083	–0.064	0.049
Customary	0.187	0.163	0.117	0.201	0.235
Access to rural services					
ln(distance to residence, km)	0.161*	0.154*	0.241*	0.158	0.224
PMI	0.000	0.000	0.000	0.001	0.000
ln(distance to all-weather road, km)	–0.321***	–0.344***	–0.358**	–0.308**	–0.294
Participates in NAADS	0.005	1.387**	0.219	0.134	–0.201
ln(contacts with traditional extension agent +1)	0.046	–0.128	0.092	0.045	0.046
Has access to credit	0.455***	0.822*	0.403***	0.326***	0.546***
Village-level factors					
ln(population density, persons/km^2)	0.01	0.019	–0.001	–0.024	–0.02
ln(community wage rate, Ush/day)	0.088	0.066	–0.138	0.042	–0.016
Agroecological zone (cf. LVCM)					
NW moist farmlands	–0.356	–0.512	–0.602**	–0.353	–0.677
NM farmlands	0.254	0.102	–0.481*	–0.048	0.421
Mt. Elgon farmlands	–0.133	–0.287	–0.543*	-0.151	–0.39
SW grass-farmlands	0.644***	0.439	0.353*	0.656**	0.503
SWH	0.216	0.01	0.036	0.162	0.299

(continued)

Table 6.2 Continued

Variable	Ordinary least squares	Instrumental variables	Quantile regression		
			Lower quartile	Median	Upper quartile
Interaction terms					
Asset × extension	0.000	0.000	–0.001	–0.001	0.000
Asset × distance to all-weather road	0.003***	0.003***	0.004**	0.004**	0.003
Constant	2.716**	3.271***	3.452**	3.564**	4.686**
Hansen J-test of overidentification restrictions (p-value)	—	0.249	—	—	—
C-statistic (exogeneity/orthogonality) (p-value)	—	0.325	—	—	—
Relevance tests of excluded variables (p-value)					
Nitrogen stock	—	0.038	—	—	—
Phosphorus stock	—	0.010	—	—	—
Potassium stock	—	0.000	—	—	—
Contact hours with extension agent	—	0.000	—	—	—
NAADS	—	0.000	—	—	—
Access to credit	—	0.000	—	—	—
Number of observations	—	759	—	—	—

Notes: *, **, *** indicate that the coefficient is statistically significant at the 10, 5, or 1 percent level, respectively. LVCM—Lake Victoria crescent and Mbale; NAADS—National Agricultural Advisory Services; NM—northern moist; NRM—natural resource management; NW—northwestern; PMI—potential market integration; SW—southwestern; SWC—soil and water conservation; SWH—southwestern highlands; TLU—tropical livestock units; Ush—Ugandan shillings.

low P content (Palm 1995; Nziguheba et al. 1998). P deficiency is common in SSA, where application of inorganic P fertilizer is limited. Hence fertilizer recommendations targeting P application may be particularly useful for these zones. P stock also has a significant impact on per capita income.

As expected, topsoil depth has statistically significant associations with crop productivity for the median- and lower-quartile regressions. However, for farmers in the upper quartile, the association of topsoil depth with crop productivity is not significant (at $p = .10$). Even though we controlled for the major crop management practices and land investments, we may not have captured the intensity and impacts of these variables. For example, farmers in the upper quartile are more likely to use improved varieties or higher-intensity application of inorganic fertilizer. The inorganic fertilizer and seed variables used do not fully capture the intensity and impacts of these

inputs since they are based on the value rather than the intensity of use of the inputs. Topsoil depth does not have a statistically significant association with the household per capita income across quartiles.

Even though agroforestry trees and SWC structures may potentially compete with crops for space, light, and moisture, we find that these investments are significantly associated with higher crop productivity across all quartiles. However, the association of SWC structures with agricultural productivity in the lower quartile is not significant (at $p = .10$). The magnitude of the impact of agroforestry interventions on the crop productivity of the lower-quartile households is also the smallest. Agroforestry is associated with a 30 percent increase in the predicted productivity for farmers in the lower productivity quartile regression and with a 40 percent increase in productivity for farmers in the median and upper quartiles. The lower returns for farmers in the lower productivity quartile could be due to the low intensity of land investment by the poor households.

SWC structures are associated with a 53 percent increase in the predicted crop productivity for farmers in the median quartile and with a 47 percent increase for farmers in the upper quartile. These investments can help increase crop productivity by reducing soil erosion, fixing N if leguminous trees and shrubs are planted, recycling leached nutrients, and improving moisture conservation and soil physical characteristics. Hence investments in land improvement appear to offer significant potential for reducing poverty in Uganda. For example, SWC structures and other land investments are associated with significantly higher per capita incomes, probably due to their positive impact on crop productivity. It is possible that reverse causality contributes to this positive relationship (that is, people with higher incomes are better able to invest), although we have controlled for many factors that determine households' capacity to invest.

Investments in perennial crop production are also associated with a higher value of crops produced per acre and per capita household income in the OLS and upper-quartile regressions. The values of crop production per acre and income per capita are significantly higher on plots and for households for which perennial crop production dominates than for those for which annual crop production dominates (Tables 6.1 and 6.2). For the farmers in the upper productivity quartile, perennial crop production is associated with a 16 percent increase in the predicted value of crop production per acre compared to annual crop production in the same productivity quartile. These results are consistent with the findings of Collier (2002) and Nkonya et al. (2004).

Other NRM investments—including fish pond development, paddock and pasture development, and construction of kraals and other livestock structures—are also positively associated with higher per capita household income. The association is significant in the OLS regression but insignificant in the quantile regressions. Investments like those in fish farming contribute directly to household income, while other NRM investments, like improvement of pastures and construction of paddocks, are likely to increase livestock productivity.

Physical Capital

Livestock ownership is associated with higher per capita income for all quartiles but not higher crop productivity. The insignificant association of livestock assets with crop productivity is probably due to the limited use of animal manure and animal power in crop production. The positive association between livestock and per capita income is due to revenue from the sale or home consumption of livestock and their products.

Ownership of farm equipment has a significant negative association with crop productivity in the OLS regression but an insignificant association in the quantile regressions, controlling for land management practices and input use. The main impacts of mechanization may be to enable farmers to farm on a larger area, rather than increasing their productivity on a given area (for example, farmers who use ox-plows for land preparation may not have enough labor for timely weeding [Lubwama 2000]). We find statistically insignificant associations of farm equipment with household income per capita, but this is controlling for farm size (Table 6.2). Since equipment may enable households to farm a larger area—a hypothesis supported by the correlation between farm area and the value of farm equipment, which is 0.214 (significant at $p = .01$)—this effect of farm equipment may be implicitly reflected in the association of farm size with household income.

Human Capital

Male secondary and postsecondary education, as expected, is also associated with significantly higher crop productivity in the OLS and lower-quartile regressions (Table 6.1) and with household income per capita in the OLS regression (Table 6.2). This is consistent with other studies of income determinants in Uganda (Appleton 2001b; Deininger and Okidi 2001; Nkonya et al. 2004) and numerous other developing countries. Surprisingly, we find that female education has no statistically significant associations with crop productivity, and only postsecondary female education has a significant (at $p = .10$) positive association with household income in the median regression. The generally weak association of female education with crop productivity could be due to the limited role of women in household decisionmaking (Udry 1996). These weak effects are also probably due to the small share of females with secondary or higher education in our sample (only 9 percent with secondary and less than 3 percent with higher education), and they do not necessarily mean that female education has no impact on income. Indeed, the estimated coefficients of postsecondary education in the household income regressions are positive and quite large (0.63 in the median regression), indicating that the association between this level of education and income may be large, even if the ability to measure this association precisely is limited by a small sample of educated women.

Male-headed households were associated with higher crop productivity in the lower-quartile regression. This is probably due to the higher resource endowments (for example, income) of male-headed house-

holds, which enhance crop productivity.[5] However, the gender of the household head did not have a significant association with productivity in the median and upper productivity quartiles.

The gender of the household head does not have a significant association with per capita income. This is contrary to some other studies, which have shown that female-headed households have lower incomes than male-headed households (for example, Nerina and Roy 1998; IFAD 1999), but it is consistent with the findings of Pender et al. (2004b), who also found insignificant differences between the incomes of female- versus male-headed households.[6] Gender of the household head also did not have significant associations with land management and land degradation, as shown earlier.

Family size is associated positively with crop productivity in the upper quartile and IV regressions (weakly significant at $p = .10$), suggesting, consistent with Boserup, that population pressure (at the household level) leads to agricultural intensification and higher land productivity. However, family size has a nonsignificant association with crop productivity in the lower and median productivity quartiles. Family size has a negative association with income per capita (significant at $p = .10$ only in the median regression), suggesting that such Boserupian responses do not improve the household's welfare but only help to mitigate the effects of larger family size on income per capita.

Nonfarm activity as the primary income source of the household head has a positive

---

[5]Even though we controlled for the major resource endowments (for example, natural, human, and physical capital) and access to agricultural services, there are still some crop productivity–enhancing factors that we did not capture. For example, men could have higher income and better access to market information since they travel more frequently than women.

[6]Pender et al. (2004b) did find lower crop production by female-headed households, but not significant differences in income by gender of household head. Nkonya et al. (2004) found that female-headed households have higher incomes in their study region of Uganda. Differences in the regions studied may be responsible for the variation in findings in these reports.

but insignificant association with crop productivity for the OLS and the lower quartile and median regressions but a significant association (at $p = .01$) for the upper quartile regression. Crop productivity is 43 percent higher for households in the upper productivity quartile with nonfarm activities. Similarly nonfarm activities are positively associated with household income per capita for the OLS and median regressions. For the OLS and median regressions the predicted per capita income is respectively 22 percent and 29 percent higher for households dependent on nonfarm activity rather than crop production as the primary income source.[7]

The positive association of nonfarm activities with household income per capita is as expected, although different from the findings of Nkonya et al. (2004), who did not find a statistically significant association of nonfarm activities with household income. The finding that nonfarm activities did not have a significant association with crop productivity in the OLS and lower and median quartile regressions—despite having a negative association with soil erosion and a positive impact on the propensity to fallow, both of which are likely to have favorable impact on soil productivity—could be due to the offsetting effect of less management effort being devoted to crop production by these households.

We do not find statistically significant differences between per capita incomes of households dependent on livestock versus crop production. This result contrasts with the findings of Nkonya et al. (2004), who found that households dependent on livestock income earned higher incomes.

Access to Rural Services

As expected, distance to an all-weather road has a negative and significant association with per capita household income for the OLS regression and for the lower and median quartile regressions (Table 6.2). Similarly distance to an all-weather road is negatively associated with crop productivity for the OLS and all quartile regressions, but the association is not significant (at $p = .10$) (Table 6.1). However, the roads × value of asset interaction has a positive association (significant at $p = .05$) with crop productivity and per capita household income for the OLS regression and the lower quartile regressions (Tables 6.1 and 6.2). The association is also significant for the median regression for the per capita income. The results suggest higher per capita income and crop productivity for wealthier farmers in remote areas than for those closer to roads. These results are similar to those of Nkonya et al. (2004), who observed a puzzling negative association between access to an all-weather road and household income. They are contrary to the results of Pender et al. (2004b), who found that better road access is associated with higher incomes in the central region of Uganda (but an insignificant association in other regions), and Fan, Zhang, and Rao (2004), who found that road investment (especially in rural feeder roads) contributes to greater income growth and reduced poverty in Uganda.

The type of equipment owned could contribute to this result. Hence we examined the association between distance to roads and the value of different types of assets. Distance to roads was negatively associated

---

[7]Note that the dummies are not in log form, hence the percent change follows the computation of semielasticity (percent change per [nonpercent] unit change). Specifically the dummy variables (x) are related to the dependent variable (y) as follows: $\ln(y) = b_1 x$. Taking the antilog of both sides, $y = e^{b_1 x} \rightarrow y(x=1) = e^{b_1 x}$, $y(x=0) = e^0 = 1$. Hence percent change in y as x changes from 0 to 1 is $[y(x=1) - y(x=0)] \times 100/[y(x=0)]$, that is, $[y(x=1) - 1] \times 100 = [e^{b_1} - 1] - 1] \times 100$. If the value of b_1 is small (<0.05), a simpler approximation method could be used. Taking the differentials of y with respect to x, $\Delta\ln(y)\, b_1\Delta x$. Multiplying both sides by 100, $100\Delta\ln(y)\, b_1 100\Delta x$, or percent $\Delta\ln(y)\, (100b_1)_{\Delta x}$, implying that, to get the percent change in value of crops produced per acre as one starts using, say, SWC structures, we simply multiply the b_1 coefficient by 100 (Wooldridge 2003, 685–688).

(significant at $p = .01$) with the value of farm equipment (for example, ox-plows, tractors, or ox-carts) and with the value of durable goods (most of which are nonproductive assets like home appliances), suggesting that farmers closer to roads are better positioned to have higher crop productivity and per capita income. The results are puzzling, and further research is required to better understand the impacts of the road × asset interaction on crop productivity and income. It is possible that multicollinearity of the variables road, asset, and road × asset interaction may still affect their results (even though the maximum VIF was less than 10) and could contribute to these puzzling results. So we estimated the crop productivity and per capita household income regressions without the policy × asset interaction terms; the results show that access to roads did not have a significant association with crop productivity but was positively associated with household income (Tables A.1 and A.2).

Agricultural technical assistance programs appear to have favorable impacts on the value of crop production. Participation in the NAADS program is associated with a significantly higher value of crop production per acre (Table 6.1). Based on the OLS and lower quartile regression results in Table 6.1, the value of crop production per acre in 2002–03 is predicted to be 27 percent higher for households that participated in NAADS than those who did not. Participation in NAADS has a higher positive association with crop productivity for farmers in the lower quartile (27 percent) than for those in the median and upper quartiles. This suggests that, controlling for all explanatory variables, households who tend to have lower productivity respond better to NAADS than those who tend to have higher productivity. These results are consistent

with the findings of Nkonya et al. (2004) concerning the positive impacts of access to agricultural extension and training on the value of crop production, and with those of Fan, Zhang, and Rao (2004) concerning the positive agricultural productivity impacts of expenditures on agricultural research, and extension expenditures more generally, in Uganda.

The positive association of NAADS with the value of crop production per acre probably has less to do with improving farming practices than with promoting production of higher-value crops, since we found insignificant associations of the presence of NAADS with most land management practices and labor intensity, and negative associations with some soil fertility management practices and land degradation (Tables 5.7–5.9). Hence NAADS may be causing a trade-off between improving returns to agriculture in the near term and its influence on the longer-term productivity and sustainability of crop production. We do not find robust, statistically significant associations of NAADS or other extension programs with income per capita, however.

It is possible that these positive associations are due in part to program placement or participant self-selection bias; that is, these programs may be operating in areas where productivity was already higher prior to the advent of the NAADS program, or program participants may be those who were more productive even before participating in the program. We have sought to address this concern by including in the regressions numerous explanatory factors influencing productivity potential, but it is still possible that some excluded factors that are associated with technical assistance program placement or participation are partly responsible for these positive associations.[8] To address

---

[8]Participants in regional seminars held to disseminate the findings of this study also expressed concern regarding potential NAADS program bias. However, the site selection criteria for NAADS programs were based on compliance with local government development programs, which are not supposed to be influenced by income levels, and are supposed to reflect variety with respect to the nature of the local agricultural economy and AEZs.

the endogeneity of program participation and possible selection bias, we estimated the model using IV regressions. We found that the positive association of NAADS with the value of crop production was still weakly significant (at $p = .10$) in the IV model, although the magnitude of the coefficient for NAADS in the IV model is somewhat smaller (0.18) than that of the coefficient in the OLS model (0.27). The exogeneity test fails to reject exogeneity of NAADS, hence OLS is the preferred model because it is more efficient (and less prone to bias caused by weak instruments [Bound, Jaeger, and Baker 1995]).

We also estimated the model using the presence of NAADS in a subcounty rather than household-level participation as the explanatory variable, and we found similar positive associations of the presence of NAADS with productivity.[9] This finding reduces our concern that household-level self-selection bias is responsible for the positive association of productivity with NAADS participation. However, there still could be bias caused by the initial placement of NAADS in more productive subcounties.

We investigated the possibility of bias in the selection of NAADS subcounties using data from the 1999–2000 UNHS and survey data from this study. Tables 6.3 and 6.4 show the differences in mean value of crop production per acre and per capita income in 1999–2000 between NAADS and non-NAADS subcounties in the districts where our study was conducted.[10] These tables show that there was no bias toward selecting subcounties where productivity or income was already higher. In only one district (Kabale) was there a statistically significant difference in pre-NAADS productivity between NAADS and non-NAADS subcounties, and in that case pre-NAADS productivity was higher in the non-NAADS subcounties. In all other cases, average pre-NAADS productivity was quite similar in the NAADS versus non-NAADS subcounties, and for all six subcounties the average difference in pre-NAADS productivity was less than 2 percent (slightly lower in the NAADS subcounties). In no district was there a statistically significant difference in pre-NAADS income per capita between NAADS and non-NAADS subcounties, and the average differences are quantitatively small (less than 0.5 percent difference in all six districts).

These results strengthen our confidence that NAADS is indeed having significant positive impacts on crop productivity. It is still theoretically possible that some other factors besides the introduction of NAADS or the factors that we control for in our regressions have changed since 1999–2000 in NAADS and non-NAADS subcounties, and that these are responsible for the higher current productivity in the NAADS subcounties and among NAADS participants. But it is difficult to imagine what those factors are, given that we have controlled for so many factors affecting productivity, or why such factors would have affected NAADS versus non-NAADS subcounties differentially, in favor of NAADS subcounties. These results therefore support the emphasis in the PMA on increasing the availability of agricultural technical assistance in Uganda through expansion of NAADS, at least in terms of increasing the value of crop production. Nevertheless, the negative impacts of NAADS on land management and land degradation are of concern.

A current IFPRI-led study on NAADS —which uses panel data collected from NAADS and non-NAADS farmers—will help to better understand the impacts of

---

[9]Results of these regressions using the presence of NAADS in a subcounty, rather than household-level participation, were included in an earlier version of this report and are available on request.

[10]NAADS had not yet begun to operate in the other two districts covered by this study (Masaka and Kapchorwa) in the year covered by the IFPRI-UBOS survey (2002–03).

Table 6.3   Pre-NAADS value of crop production per acre in NAADS versus non-NAADS subcounties of sample districts

District	First year in NAADS	Mean value of crop production per acre, 1999/2000 (thousand USh/acre) (no. of observations)				Statistical significance (*p*-level)
		Non-NAADS subcounties		NAADS subcounties		
		Mean	Standard error	Mean	Standard error	
Arua	2001/02	246.2 (234)	18.1	253.5 (65)	20.7	0.8417
Kabale	2001/02	470.5 (137)	60.7	303.3 (146)	23.3	0.0105**
Soroti	2001/02	124.8 (143)	26.4	126.4 (65)	12.9	0.9405
Iganga	2002/03	272.8 (303)	11.3	318.0 (65)	47.4	0.1598
Lira	2002/03	99.3 (229)	6.5	78.5 (61)	10.5	0.1420
Mbarara	2002/03	298.4 (247)	12.9	342.2 (31)	50.5	0.2912
All six districts		246.7 (1,293)	9.5	242.6 (433)	12.6	0.8059

Source: Data from 1999/2000 Uganda National Household Survey.
Note: ** indicates that the difference in means is statistically significant at the 5 percent level.

Table 6.4   Pre-NAADS income per capita in NAADS versus non-NAADS subcounties of sample districts

District	First year in NAADS	Mean income per capita, 1999/2000 (thousand USh) (no. observations)				Statistical significance (*p*-level)
		Non-NAADS subcounties		NAADS subcounties		
		Mean	Standard error	Mean	Standard error	
Arua	2001/02	238.5 (233)	12.5	213.5 (65)	23.3	0.3524
Kabale	2001/02	258.0 (137)	14.5	264.8 (146)	17.4	0.7686
Soroti	2001/02	205.8 (143)	39.6	226.5 (65)	26.6	0.7002
Iganga	2002/03	232.9 (303)	16.2	254.8 (65)	20.9	0.4654
Lira	2002/03	143.5 (229)	8.4	131.7 (61)	28.3	0.5972
Mbarara	2002/03	328.8 (247)	17.7	320.7 (31)	32.6	0.8835
All six districts		236.1 (1,292)	6.7	235.1 (433)	9.9	0.9436

Source: Data from 1999/2000 Uganda National Household Survey.

NAADS, which has covered all 80 districts. The results will help to design the new government rural development programs— Prosperity for All, the Rural Development Strategy, and the National Development Plan—all of which give high priority to agricultural advisory services.

The coefficient of the number of contacts with the traditional extension program did not have statistically significant asso- ciations with the value of crops produced per acre and per capita household income. Since we also included the interaction of extension contacts with asset level, this result suggests that traditional extension has little impact on the productivity or income of very poor households.[11] These results are consistent with the insignificant impacts of traditional extension found by Pender et al. (2004b). One of the possible reasons for

---

[11]More precisely, the coefficient of the traditional extension variable in the crop productivity and income regressions represents the predicted impact of traditional extension for households with zero assets.

this observation is the limited resources and weak institutional approaches and strategies of the local governments for running the traditional extension services (MAAIF/ MFPED 2000; NAADS Secretariat 2000). However, the asset × traditional extension interaction has a positive and significant association (at $p = .01$ for the OLS and median regressions and at $p = .10$ for the lower- and upper-quartile regressions) with crop productivity, although the magnitude of the coefficients in all regressions is small and comparable across all four regressions (coefficient = 0.003 in all regressions). A 1 percent increase in the value of the asset × extension interaction is associated with a 0.2 percent increase in crop productivity. This means crop productivity is predicted to increase by Ush 334 when the value of assets increases by Ush 12,590 and the farmer receives an hour-long extension visit.[12] These results suggest that traditional extension yields greater impacts on crop productivity for wealthier households, although the predicted impact is still relatively small even for wealthier households. As a result, the associations of traditional extension with income are statistically insignificant, even for wealthier households in our sample.

Participation in rural finance organizations is associated with significantly higher per capita incomes in the OLS and in all quantile regression models (Table 6.2), and with significantly higher crop productivity only in the median- and upper-quartile regressions (Table 6.1). As in assessing the impacts of NAADS, we have used IV estimation to address potential self-selection bias in the use of credit, but the results are robust to this concern. The favorable association of credit on income, while having no significant association with crop productivity for the lower-quartile households, is likely due to the use of credit to develop nonagricultural enterprises with greater returns than agricultural enterprises. The re-

sults suggest that increasing access to credit may not increase agricultural productivity for the poorest households as envisaged in the PMA and other government strategies, although it may contribute to improved income and reduced poverty for all farmers and to increased agricultural productivity for wealthier farm households.

These results support the current government efforts to promote savings and credit cooperative societies in every subcounty as part of the strategy to reduce poverty (MAAIF 2005; GOU 2007). However, the government's strategy of providing credit at a subsidized interest rate (MAAIF 2005; GOU 2007) is not likely to be sustainable in the long run and may undermine the private microfinance institutions (MFIs) that have been growing in Uganda (Okurut, Schoombee, and van der Berg 2005).

Land Tenure

Compared to freehold and leasehold tenures, customary land tenure has a statistically significant positive association with crop productivity in the OLS regression and the median- and upper-quartile regressions. The results suggest that the assumed tenure security for freehold and leasehold tenure does not have the desired favorable impact on crop productivity. Farmers holding land under freehold and leasehold may not be as dedicated to farming as those holding land under customary tenure, as they may be holding land for speculative purposes or they may have other noncrop enterprises with greater returns, so that they do not invest much effort in crop production.

Consistent with the reports of Nkonya et al. (2004) and Pender et al. (2004b), land tenure does not have a significant association with household per capita income in any regression. These results suggest that lack of land titles and other differences in land tenure are not major constraints to

---

[12]The average crop productivity is approximately Ush 167,000 (Table 4.2) and the average value of assets is approximately Ush 1,259,000.

productivity or income in Uganda. Similar limited impacts of land titles in areas of secure customary tenure have been reported elsewhere in Africa (for example, Place and Hazell 1993; Platteau 1996).

The proportion of farm area owned by female members of the household is positively associated with higher crop productivity in the lower-quartile regression. This supports the view that increasing poor women's access and ownership of land will increase agricultural productivity, since they contribute a larger share of agricultural production in Africa (Udry 1996; Quisumbing, Estudillo, and Otsuka 2004; Sender and Johnston 2004). However, the share of farms owned by women was not significantly associated with crop productivity (in the median- and upper-quartile regressions) or with per capita income (for all regressions).

Village-Level Factors

Higher village wage rates are associated with significantly lower crop productivity in the OLS regression and in the lower- and upper-quartile regressions. This suggests that in areas with higher wages, crop productivity may be competing for farmers' management inputs or other inputs not controlled for in this model. Controlling for farm size and other variables, population density has no significant association with crop productivity and per capita household income.

Not surprisingly, different AEZs are associated with differences in both crop productivity and income, as expected. These results are fairly consistent with the findings of Nkonya et al. (2004) and Pender et al. (2004b) (although the classification of zones in this study is somewhat different).

CHAPTER 7

Summary and Discussion of the Results and Their Relevance to Sub-Saharan Africa

T his chapter summarizes and discusses the major results from the Ugandan case study and compares them with past studies, especially those in SSA. The chapter also discusses the limits of this study and the gaps that need to be addressed in future studies. We first discuss the severity of land degradation in Uganda and then focus on the association of the major socioeconomic factors with land management, land degradation, crop productivity, and household income, since these factors will need to be considered in the design of policies to address poverty and land degradation.

While discussing the applicability of our results to other countries in the world, we specifically focus on SSA. The linkages between poverty and land management are likely to be context specific, and therefore they would need to be extrapolated to other regions and countries with care, ensuring that these had characteristics comparable to those of the study country.

Severity of Land Degradation

Land degradation, in the form of soil erosion and soil nutrient depletion, is a serious problem in Uganda. Our study shows that farmers in the eight districts studied (representing six major agroecological and farming system zones) deplete an average of 179 kg/ha of N, P, and K per year, which is about 1.2 percent of the nutrient stock stored in the topsoil (0–20 cm depth). The value of replacing the depleted nutrients, using the minimum price of inorganic fertilizer, is equivalent to about one-fifth of the household income obtained from agricultural production. This emphasizes the heavy reliance of smallholder farmers on soil nutrient mining for their livelihoods and the high costs of addressing the problem.

The findings of this study also underscore the significance of soil nutrient depletion, which contributes to declining agricultural production in the near term as well as over the longer term. For example, we find that a 1 percent decrease in the P stock in the topsoil is associated with a predicted 0.15 percent reduction in crop productivity. The loss of productivity is the relevant value, which the farmer is likely to impute to soil nutrient depletion. However, this value is far less than the minimum cost of replenishing the depleted nutrients using purchased fertilizer. These results further demonstrate why farmers deplete soil nutrients in Uganda and in many other parts of SSA. The very low returns to additional soil nutrients compared to their costs imply that even very large subsidies for fertilizer, as have been advocated by many observers, are unlikely to have a major impact on fertilizer use and soil fertility depletion in situations similar to those in Uganda. This finding is consistent with those of several other studies on the low returns to fertilizer use in Uganda (Woelcke 2003; Nkonya et al. 2004; Pender et al. 2004b). Addressing this problem will require identifying more-profitable SLM practices, as well as technical assistance to help farmers use available technologies more productively.

Relationships between Household Capital Endowments and Land Management, Land Degradation, Crop Productivity, and Income

Table 7.1 summarizes the econometric results reported in Chapters 5 and 6. For brevity the table reports only the qualitative relationships between the explanatory variables and the outcomes. Similarly only the OLS results of the crop productivity and per capita household income regressions are reported.

Our study supports the inverse farm size–crop productivity relationship reported by other studies (for example, Chayanov 1966; Sen 1975; Berry and Cline 1979; Carter 1984; Bhalla 1988; Barrett 1996; Heltberg 1998). We also observed that farm size is positively associated with per capita household income. The inverse relationship between farm size and crop productivity is probably due primarily to the inefficient financial and labor markets that limit efficient resource allocation (Lamb 2003). For example, we find that labor intensity is inversely related to farm size. Similar results were reported by Clay, Reardon, and Kangasniemi (1998) in Rwanda and Jagger and Pender (2006) in Uganda. Farm size is also associated with higher propensity to fallow but has no significant association with the use of inorganic fertilizer. This is contrary to the results of Benin (2006), who found a positive association of farm size and chemical fertilizer in the high-rainfall region of Ethiopia. Our results on the relationship between farm size and land management and crop productivity are consistent with a large body of literature, and they can be extrapolated to other SSA countries where credit and labor markets are not efficient.

As expected, prior investments in land improvement (namely SWC structures and agroforestry) are associated with higher per capita household income and crop productivity. They are also associated with better land management (for example, agroforestry is positively associated with propensity to fallow, and SWC structures are positively associated with propensity to apply organic matter). Consequently plots with agroforestry and SWC structures have lower soil erosion. Investments in land improvement may be win-win options for both improving incomes and reducing land degradation.

These results are consistent with findings from success stories in many other parts of Africa showing that SWC measures, agroforestry interventions, and other land management practices can have immediate positive impacts on productivity and income while contributing to reduced land degradation (for example, Tiffen, Mortimore, and Gichuki 1994; Scoones et al. 1996, 1–20; Adams and Mortimore 1997; Haggblade and Tembo 2003; Kaboré and Reij 2004; Holden, Shiferaw, and Pender 2005; Benin 2006; Pender and Gebremedhin 2006). These results confirm that investments in land improvement can help reduce poverty as well as land degradation. The results are relevant to other countries, but it is important to recognize that the impacts of such measures are highly context dependent and are often limited by various constraints (Place et al. 2005; Pender and Mertz 2006; Pender, Place, and Ehui 2006). As will be discussed shortly, it is especially important to know the profitability of these land investments in order to establish their competitiveness and potential to help reduce poverty in particular contexts.

Physical assets generally have limited associations with land management but are associated with higher income. Consistent with Freeman and Coe (2002), Mekuria and Waddington (2002), Benin (2006), and Jagger and Pender (2006), we find that livestock ownership is associated with greater propensity to use inorganic fertilizer. However, livestock ownership is associated with lower N balances, supporting studies that have shown that livestock ownership is associated with an increase in land-degrading practices (for example, Clay, Reardon, and Kangasniemi 1998 in Rwanda). Our mixed results on the association of livestock ownership with land management confirm the context specificity of the findings, as observed in previous studies. Such results should therefore be verified in other contexts.

We do not find a significant association of the gender of the household head with land management. Some other studies have found a significant relationship. For example, Place et al. (2002) found in western Kenya that female-headed households were less likely to use chemical fertilizer but more likely to use compost. Consistent with Jollife (1997), our results suggest that the level of education of members of the household has different impacts on household-level decisions. Compared to the female household members with no formal education, those with primary education are more likely to operate farms on which there is depletion of soil nutrients and greater soil erosion. This suggests that female primary education leads to more severe degradation of land, probably because of the higher opportunity cost of educated females, which limits adoption of labor-intensive practices (Scherr and Hazell 1994). However, female postsecondary education is associated with higher crop productivity on the plots of farmers in the median quartile. Contrary to this finding, education of male members of the household is positively associated with a greater likelihood of using fertilizer, lower soil erosion, and higher crop productivity and income. The relationship of male education to income supports past studies that observed a positive impact of education on household income (for example, Appleton 2001a; Deininger and Okidi 2001; Nkonya et al. 2004). Regarding the positive associa-

tion of male education with land management, these results are likely to be context specific and should be extrapolated to other countries with care. The positive association of female primary education with soil erosion and nutrient depletion is likewise context specific.

Consistent with studies showing no significant difference between the productivity of plots owned by female and male members of the household (for example, Quisumbing, Estudillo, and Otsuka 2004), the share of farm area owned by women does not have a significant association with crop productivity in the OLS model. However, women's share of farm area is positively associated with crop productivity in the lower quartile. This is consistent with other studies that have shown that reallocating landownership from male to female—after controlling for all other factors—could increase crop productivity (Mock 1976; Udry 1996) and that have demonstrated better livelihoods when women's access to land is improved (Alderman et al. 1995; Kunze, Waibel, and Runge-Metzger 1998). However, given that agricultural investments in women's plots are less than those in men's plots and that women are more likely to inherit plots of lower quality (Quisumbing, Estudillo, and Otsuka 2004), studies have shown lower crop productivity for women's plots (for example, Kevane and Wydick 2001). Overall our results suggesting a nonsignificant relationship between productivity and the gender of the owner of the plot, and those showing higher productivity for women-owned plots in the lower quartile, are supported by other studies and are therefore applicable to other SSA countries.

Nonfarm activities are positively associated with use of fallow and lower soil erosion in our study region. Nonfarm activities are also associated with higher household income and crop productivity in the upper productivity quartile. The positive associations of nonfarm activities with per capita

Table 7.1 Qualitative summary of results

Variable	Slash and burn	Fallow	Crop rotation	SWC	Inorganic fertilizer	Organic fertilizer	Value of seed	Preharvest labor	Crop productivity	Per capita income	Erosion	Nitrogen balance	Phosphorus balance	Potassium balance
Land management practices														
Use purchased seed? (yes = 1, no = 0)														
Use inorganic fertilizer? (yes = 1, no = 0)									++					
Use organic fertilizer? (yes = 1, no = 0)														
ln(preharvest labor + 1)									+++					
Crop residue incorporated									++					
Natural capital														
ln(plot slope, %)			+++	+++							+++	–––	–––	–––
ln(topsoil depth, cm)				–	+++									
ln(nitrogen stock, kg/ha)														
ln(phosphorus stock, kg/ha)									+++	+++				
ln(potassium stock, kg/ha)														
Percentage of sand		+	–								–––	+	++	+++
Practice agroforestry			–	–			++		+++	+	–––		+	+
Have SWC structures						++			+++	+++	–			
Perennial crops		–––		–		+++	–		++	+++		–		–––
Have other NRM investments						+	++	+		++		+		
ln(plot area, acres)		–––	+		+		––		+++					
ln(farm area, acres)	–––	+++			–				–––	+++				
Physical capital														
ln(TLU)		–––	–							+++		–––		
ln(value of farm equipment +1, thousand Ush)														
Human capital														
Share of female household members with: (cf. no formal education)														
Primary education								+			++		––	
Secondary education							–						+	
Postsecondary education				–––				–						

Share of male household members with:

(cf. no formal education)

Primary education

Secondary education

Postsecondary education

Sex of household head

Household size

Share of farm owned by women

Primary activity of household head (cf. crop production)

Nonfarm activity

Livestock

Access to rural services

ln(distance from plot to residence +1, km)

PMI

ln(distance to all-weather road +1, km)

ln(number of contact hours with extension agent +1)

Participates in NAADS

Has access to credit

Land tenure of plot (cf. freehold and leasehold)

Customary

Mailo

Village-level factors

Community NRM regulations

ln(population density, persons/km²)

ln(village wage rate, Ush/day)

Agroecological zone (cf. LVCM)

NW moist farmlands

NM farmlands

Mt. Elgon zone

SW grass-farmlands

SWH

Notes: +++ (− − −), ++ (− −), and + (−) indicate positive (negative) association between dependent and independent variables, which is statistically significant at the 1, 5, or 10 percent level, respectively, in the preferred specification. LVCM—Lake Victoria crescent and Mbale; NAADS—National Agricultural Advisory Services; NM—northern moist; NRM—natural resource management; NW—northwestern; PMI—potential market integration; SW—southwestern; SWC—soil and water conservation; SWH—southwestern highlands; TLU—tropical livestock units; Ush—Ugandan shillings.

income and crop productivity demonstrate their potential to contribute to reduction of both poverty and land degradation. However, nonfarm activities are also associated with lower intensity of labor, suggesting that farmers with nonfarm activities will be less likely to adopt labor-intensive strategies, as observed by Clay, Reardon, and Kangasniemi (1998) in Rwanda and Hagos and Holden (2006) in Ethiopia. It is likely that farmers with nonfarm activities use other practices to increase crop productivity since nonfarm activities are associated with higher crop productivity.[1] The mixed associations of nonfarm activities with land management are, as expected, ambiguous —a finding that must be considered when these results are applied in other SSA countries. However, the positive association of nonfarm activities with poverty reduction is less ambiguous and has been observed by many other studies in SSA countries (for example, Barrett, Reardon, and Webb 2001; Lanjouw 2007). It is therefore likely to be applicable to other countries.

Land Tenure

Contrary to studies that have found that formalized land tenure through land titling is associated with investment in land and higher agricultural productivity (for example, Feder et al. 1988; Alston, Libecap, and Schneider 1996; De Soto 2000; Deininger and Chamorro 2006), we found that customary land tenure was associated with higher agricultural productivity. Similarly there was no significant association between land tenure and most of the land management practices in our study, or between land tenure and land degradation. The assumption that customary land tenure is insecure and causes farmers to use land-degrading practices is thus not supported by our research. Many other studies have reported similar results in SSA, that is, that farmers holding

land under customary tenure employ land management practices comparable to or better than those of framers who hold land under freehold or leasehold tenure with formal titles (for example, Shipton 1988; Atwood 1990; Migot-Adholla et al. 1991; Place and Hazell 1993; Toulmin and Quan 2000; Hunt 2003). Hence these results appear to be quite applicable to other SSA countries, where secure customary land tenure on croplands is common. The situation concerning customary tenure of common rangelands and other common lands may be quite different; we have not addressed this important issue in this study.

Access to Rural Services

Consistent with Binswanger and McIntire (1987), Tiffen, Mortimore, and Gichuki (1994), Boyd and Slaymaker (2000), and Pender, Place, and Ehui (2006), our results show that farmers with greater market access adopt better land management practices than those in remote areas. However, greater market access may lead to land degradation if farmers face seriously imperfect capital and factor markets and produce low-value products that do not afford them the incentive to increase the productivity of their land (Barbier, Joanne, and Burgess 1997; Boyd and Slaymaker 2000). Market access may also increase the incentive to degrade land, especially common lands (Benin and Pender 2006). Hence the impacts of market access on land management and land degradation are likely to be quite context dependent, as found by Pender, Place, and Ehui (2006). Negative impacts of market access can also occur in institutional environments that do not give farmers incentives to invest in SLM.

Consistent with the findings of Fan and Rao (2003) and Fan and Chan-Kang (2004), access to roads is also positively associated with household income. The association of

---

[1]However, the association is only significant on the plots of farmers in the upper quartile.

access to roads with per capita household income is more significant among farmers in the lower and median quartiles. These results are consistent with the conventional wisdom that access to roads reduces transaction costs and increases economic opportunities. Hence the results are likely to be applicable in other SSA countries.

Access to the new demand-driven advisory services is positively associated with the value of agricultural production, as expected, but is negatively associated with the use of fertilizer and crop rotation and positively associated with the use of slash and burn, soil erosion, and nutrient depletion. These results reflect NAADS's emphasis on creation of profitable enterprises and its limited emphasis on SLM; hence they may not be relevant to other countries where extension services promote improved land management. However, NAADS is being seen by many in the development community as a model for agricultural extension reform in Africa. These results could therefore be very relevant to other SSA countries that are implementing or planning to implement similar demand-driven advisory services with a primary emphasis on commercialization of agriculture but limited emphasis on soil fertility. Our results suggest that demand-driven advisory services may lead to negative trade-offs for land degradation while being effective in promoting higher-value production. In the case of NAADS, farmers apparently demand high-value enterprises and not improved SLM technologies. Nkonya et al. (2008) observed similar results in Nigeria, where beneficiaries of a project that promoted postproduction advisory services were more likely to demand postharvest technologies—in conformity with the orientation of the project—than soil fertility technologies.

The associations between access to credit and input use, soil nutrient depletion, and soil erosion are not significant. However, access to credit is associated with higher crop productivity on the plots of farmers in the median and upper quartiles

and with higher per capita household income. The nonsignificant association of credit with the use of external inputs like inorganic fertilizer and seeds is contrary to the expectations of agricultural credit services, which are provided to increase farmers' ability to purchase and use external inputs (Barbier and Burgess 1996; Angelsen and Kaimowitz 1999). The results suggest that the borrowed money is used to finance other activities that are more profitable than agriculture—hence contributing to higher income. The nonsignificant association of credit with land management and degradation is context specific and may not be applicable to other countries, but it questions the effectiveness of providing financial credit as a means of reducing land degradation.

Gaps and Future Studies

This study has limitations in its ability to assess linkages between poverty and land degradation. Because the study is based only on a cross-sectional survey, the ability to assess the dynamic linkages between poverty and land degradation—including the effects of land degradation on agricultural productivity and poverty over time—is limited. Some tentative inferences have been drawn by assessing the associations of soil nutrient stocks with current agricultural productivity and income, and combining this data with information on the estimated impacts of poverty on soil nutrient depletion. Nevertheless, drawing robust conclusions about these dynamic impacts requires longitudinal data (ideally panel data) on both poverty and land degradation, as well as on intervening factors such as land management decisions. The present study has laid the foundation for future longitudinal studies of the relationship between poverty and land degradation in Uganda.

This study is also limited in its focus on associations of poverty (broadly defined) with household-level land management decisions and plot-level estimates of land degradation. We do not assess the associations of poverty with community-level land management institutions or with management of common pool resources, although we do investigate the relationship between community-level institutions (that is, local land management bylaws) and household-level land management decisions. In a separate paper (Nkonya, Pender, and Kato 2008) we investigated the determinants of awareness of, enactment of, and compliance with such bylaws. We also do not attempt to address linkages between poverty and broader aspects of environmental degradation, such as depletion of biodiversity, water and air pollution, or contributions to greenhouse gas emission. Addressing such issues was beyond the scope of what we could achieve within the time frame and budget available for the study, but these would all be valuable topics for future research in Uganda and elsewhere in SSA.

In addition our study did not assess the profitability of most major land management practices, except the use of inorganic fertilizer, which was found to be unprofitable, as in other studies in Uganda. Assessment of the profitability of land management practices will help to better understand their cost effectiveness and potential for adoption. Unfortunately past studies have also looked at the factors that affect adoption of land management practices without assessing their profitability (for example, Feder, Just, and Zilberman 1985; Mercer 2004). Our study also did not analyze the risks of land management practices—a factor that is important in adoption decisions. Future studies need to address these gaps.

CHAPTER 8

Conclusions and Policy Implications

In this chapter we summarize the empirical results and draw conclusions and potential policy implications. Since we used cross-sectional data to analyze the dynamic relationships between poverty and land management, our ability to establish firm causal relationships between the outcomes and their determinants is limited. This in turn restricts our ability to draw definitive policy implications and make recommendations. Rather our results establish associations between the outcomes and the factors investigated that suggest tentative policy implications for formulating poverty reduction and SLM policies and strategies (for example, see Minten and Barrett 2008) in SSA, and Uganda in particular. Further research is needed to more clearly test the key causal relationships suggested by these results. As discussed in the previous chapter, our results can provide a baseline for future research to more firmly establish causality in the relationships between poverty, land management, and land degradation.

Soil Fertility Management

The severe soil nutrient depletion and soil erosion in Uganda highlight the challenges that the country faces as it accelerates the implementation of the PMA and other agriculture and rural development strategies. In addition to contributing to food insecurity, land degradation may contribute to deforestation and loss of biodiversity, since farmers may be forced to abandon nutrient-depleted soils and cultivate more fragile areas, such as hillsides and rainforests.

To forestall the potential medium- and long-term impacts of land degradation, policymakers in Uganda and other countries in SSA need to design strategies to reduce soil nutrient depletion, soil erosion, deforestation, bush burning, water pollution, and other forms of land degradation. Such strategies could include, but are not limited to, reducing the cost of inorganic fertilizer—for example, by promoting the development of markets for fertilizer, so that economies of scale can be realized in transporting fertilizer (Omamo 2002; Bumb, Debrah, and Maene 2006)—and developing and promoting alternative low-external-input soil fertility technologies that are cost effective and relevant to local farming systems. The organic soil fertility technologies are especially crucial in areas with low fertility, where fertilizer is less profitable (Kaizzi 2002; Kaizzi et al. 2007) and where farmers are less likely to apply fertilizer.

Given the low returns to inorganic fertilizer application found in this and other studies in Uganda (Woelcke 2003; Nkonya et al. 2004; Pender et al. 2004b), a potential alternative for addressing soil nutrient depletion in Uganda and elsewhere in SSA is a combination of organic and inorganic fertilizers. Inorganic fertilizer could be used judiciously to replenish nutrients (for example, P) that are limited in the organic inputs. The organic inputs could be used to improve the N status, soil biophysical characteristics, organic matter status, and buffering capacity of the soil in general.

For example, we observed that BNF was one of the most important sources of N, hence it offers a potential means of addressing the depletion of N where it is profitable and feasible to do so. This can be achieved by increasing the acreage under legumes, through planting legumes for grain and fodder, in improved fallows, and as green manure or cover crops. For example, the high value of herbaceous legumes in N cycling is illustrated by Giller, McDonagh, and Cadish (1994) and Kaizzi (2002), who reported that Velvet bean (*Mucuna pruriens*) accumulated 68–220 kg N per hectare in eastern Uganda, 50 percent of which was derived from the atmosphere through BNF. This is equivalent to applying two to five bags of urea. By using *Mucuna* or another herbaceous legume for one season, either as a relay crop or an improved fallow, the negative N balances reported in this study could be reduced considerably.

Unfortunately many of the efforts by SSA countries to address soil nutrient depletion have not emphasized the important role of organic soil fertility practices (Anonymous 2007a). A number of countries have instead spent a considerable share of their agricultural budgets to subsidize fertilizer. For example, Zambia used about 37 percent of its agricultural budget in 2005 to subsidize fertilizer (Jayne and Boughton 2006). Support and promotion of organic soil fertility practices in Zambia—as elsewhere in SSA—are mainly through international organizations, NGOs, and donor-funded projects (Kwesiga et al. 2005). There is a need to support and promote such practices in SSA, especially in low-potential areas, where the impacts of inorganic fertilizer by itself tend to be lower (Benin 2006; Pender and Gebremedhin 2006).

Poverty–Land Management Linkages

The results of this study provide suggestive evidence of linkages between poverty and land management practices. We find that natural capital in the form of some prior land investments is associated with better current land management practices, higher crop productivity and income, lower soil erosion, and, in the case of agroforestry, better soil nutrient balances. These findings suggest that SWC investments can lead to win-win-win outcomes, since they are associated with higher income and crop productivity and conserve natural resources.

These results also suggest that some farmers facing investment poverty may be in a poverty–land degradation trap that limits their ability to make capital- or labor-intensive land investments. Some of the land investments are appropriate for resource-poor farmers, but they have received weak support from SSA governments and donors. For example, certain agroforestry practices —such as planting indigenous trees and shrubs—are appropriate for investment-poor farmers. Therefore they need to be promoted more aggressively by government and nongovernment poverty reduction and sustainable NRM programs, where they are profitable. Unfortunately donor support for sustainable NRM in Uganda and other SSA countries has fallen in the past decade (Anonymous 2007a). Both SSA governments and donors must commit more resources to supporting low-cost sustainable NRM practices.

Consistent with other studies (for example, Collier 2002), we observe that farmers with perennial crops realize higher crop productivity and higher income. However, our results show that perennial crops (especially bananas) are associated with depletion of K in Uganda. Perennial crop production in this case involves trade-offs among the objectives of increasing productivity, reducing poverty, and ensuring sustainable use of natural resources. Promoting measures to restore soil nutrients in the production of perennial crops (especially bananas) should be a high priority for agricultural technical assistance programs.

Not surprisingly, the quality of land also influences land management practices and outcomes. For example, topsoil depth is associated with higher crop productivity on the plots of farmers in the lower and median productivity quartiles and with greater likelihood to apply fertilizer and to practice crop rotation. These results suggest that farmers are not likely to apply fertilizer or use crop rotation on shallow soils. Kaizzi (2002) observed that fertilizer was not profitable in low-agricultural-potential areas or on poor soils. This emphasizes the need to promote organic soil fertility management practices in such areas.

The inverse farm size–crop productivity relationship that we observe in this study (and many others) suggests that improving small farmers' access to land—for example, by improving the functioning of land markets or through land reforms—is essential to improving agricultural productivity and addressing rural poverty in SSA. Despite the importance of farm size for productivity and household income, we find no significant differences in soil erosion or soil nutrient depletion related to farm size. Thus it appears that improving small farmers' access to land will increase aggregate agricultural production and their incomes and reduce income inequality in Uganda, with no apparent trade-off in terms of land degradation.

Livestock ownership has mixed relationships with land management practices and outcomes. It is associated with lower probability to fallow and lower N balances but with higher per capita income. These results suggest that livestock-poor farmers are more likely to remain in poverty. However, in the long run, farmers with a large number of livestock may experience more rapid depletion of soil nutrients, hence reduction of land quality, unless steps are taken to remedy their land-degrading practices.

The results highlight the importance of the livestock sector in poverty reduction efforts in SSA, where the contribution of livestock to national GDPs is low due to poor management and the low genetic potential of the local breeds. For example, livestock contributes only 35 percent of the agricultural GDP in SSA (Sumberg 2002) and a much smaller share of the total GDP. The sector has a much greater potential to contribute to GDP and to poverty reduction and improved land management, owing to its potential to recycle soil nutrients and to provide animal power for transporting bulky organic residues and agricultural products. To achieve this potential, greater attention to livestock producers, and their priorities and constraints, in agricultural research and development programs is needed.

Human capital has mixed associations with land management practices, crop productivity, and land degradation, although it has a clear positive association with income. Female education has a weaker positive association with land management practices and sustainability than male education. This may be due to a greater tendency of educated females to focus on other livelihood activities besides agriculture. These results suggest that simply investing in education will not solve the problem of land degradation in Uganda and elsewhere in SSA, even though education is critical to the long-term success of poverty reduction efforts. These findings support current efforts by Uganda and other SSA countries to introduce agricultural and NRM education into school curricula in order to prepare students to become better farmers, who can manage natural resources sustainably (Riedmiller 2002).

Consistent with the findings of Boserup (1965) and Tiffen, Mortimore, and Gichuki (1994), our results show that household size is positively associated with P and K balances and negatively associated with soil erosion, highlighting the importance of family labor in achieving SLM. Nevertheless, increased household size is not associated with higher incomes, while smaller farm size is associated with lower incomes. Hence such Boserupian intensification responses appear not to be sufficient to prevent poverty from increasing as population grows and farm sizes decline, consistent with Malthusian predictions. Increasing small farmers' access to land and other assets, and reducing household fertility rates, should therefore be key components of poverty reduction strategies.

The share of farm area owned by female members of the household is positively associated with crop productivity for households in the lower productivity quartile. This result confirms the key role that women play in agricultural production in SSA and suggests the need to increase their access to and ownership of land.

Households pursuing nonfarm activities are better able to fallow their land, have less soil erosion, and earn higher per capita income. Crop productivity and nonfarm activities for farmers in the upper quartile are also positively associated. However, households with nonfarm activities have a lower propensity to use labor-intensive organic matter and invest less preharvest labor. These results suggest that promoting nonfarm activities can yield win-win benefits by increasing household incomes while reducing land degradation pressure, by enabling households to fallow and by reducing households' exposure to agricultural price and production risks. However, the results also suggest that there may be tradeoffs between increasing opportunities for nonfarm activities and agricultural production due to rising labor opportunity costs.

Such relationships must be anticipated in developing rural development strategies, and sufficient attention paid to developing and promoting agricultural technologies (such as mechanization) that increase labor productivity and are more likely to be useful to and adopted by farmers who face rising labor opportunity costs. Potential impacts of such changes on land management and land degradation must also be closely monitored and addressed through promotion of appropriate (given increasing labor costs) land management approaches. Conservation farming systems that yield higher labor productivity could be one promising option

in such contexts (Haggblade and Tembo 2003). Other interventions are likely to be needed to enable poor farmers and women to access profitable off-farm opportunities, given that barriers to entry are common in this sector (Gladwin 1991; Reardon 1997; Barrett, Reardon, and Webb 2001). Promotion of nonfarm vocational education, rural electrification programs, road development, and rural MFIs can help increase opportunities for poor people to participate in nonfarm activities.

We have used a number of poverty measures to show the linkage of poverty to a number of indicators of SLM. In many cases we found strong associations between poverty indicators and unsustainable land management practices. These results suggest that efforts to reduce poverty can also help to reduce land degradation. However, some results showed that farmers who are wealthier in some dimensions may degrade their land more than poor farmers. For example, farmers growing perennial crops were found to deplete soil nutrients more rapidly than those growing annual crops. Similarly farmers with a greater number of tropical livestock units (TLU) were less likely to fallow and had lower N balances. These results suggest that the impact of poverty on land degradation depends on the specific type of poverty and specific form of land degradation considered, as well as on the particular biophysical and socioeconomic context.

Hence there is a need to design policies and strategies that take into account the complex relationship between poverty and land management, and that allow for variation in approaches depending on the local context. The increased emphasis on decentralized approaches to policymaking, provision of public services, and NRM regulations are promising developments in this regard. Nevertheless more evidence is needed on the actual implementation of such policies in Africa and their impacts on NRM and poverty (Ribot 2002).

Access to Rural Services

Access to financial capital, in the form of household participation in programs and organizations providing financial services, is associated with higher per capita income for all quartiles and with higher crop productivity in the median and upper quartiles, suggesting the importance of MFIs in poverty reduction efforts in SSA. However, the fact that access to credit is not significantly associated with the purchase of fertilizer, seeds, or other inputs suggests that Ugandan households borrow mainly to finance non-agricultural activities that appear to offer greater returns than agriculture. The results suggest a limited direct impact of access to credit on the purchase of agricultural inputs. The challenge posed by MFIs lies in their high interest rates and the short terms of the loans they offer. Both constraints make it harder for smallholder farmers to borrow from MFIs. This highlights a need to promote development of rural MFIs with a specific focus on agriculture. For example, Sasakawa Global 2000 offers in-kind agricultural input loans that successfully attract borrowers, who use the credit to finance agricultural production.

Our results show less soil erosion, lower likelihood to use the destructive slash and burn practice, and more favorable soil nutrient balances on plots closer to roads. We also observe that farmers closer to large markets are more likely to use SWC practices and that those closer to roads earn higher per capita income. These findings are consistent with the favorable impacts of market and road access found in some other studies in East Africa (for example, Tiffen, Mortimore, and Gichuki 1994; Banana and Gombya-Sembajjwa 2000; Pender et al. 2001b; Fan, Zhang, and Rao 2004), although findings of such favorable impacts are not universal (for example, Mertens and Lambin 1997; Angelsen and Kaimowitz 1999; Nkonya et al. 2004). We also observe that farmers are less likely to apply organic matter on plots closer to roads. These results support the efforts of SSA countries

and their development partners to build rural roads as investments that can reduce poverty as well as potentially help to reduce land degradation. However, they also underscore potential trade-offs that can result from the improvement of roads, hence the need to rely on other strategies to enhance the positive impacts and to minimize the potential negative impacts of improved access to roads and markets.

Participation in the demand-driven advisory services program (NAADS) has a positive association with the value of crop production, as expected. This is consistent with the findings of Nkonya et al. (2004) and suggests that remote areas with poor access to technical assistance (Jagger and Pender 2006) are likely to continue to face low productivity and poverty. This finding suggests the need to offer incentives for technical assistance programs to operate in remote areas. However, we also observed that participation in NAADS is associated with a lower probability of using fertilizer or crop rotation and with increased soil erosion and nutrient depletion. Given that NAADS provides demand-driven advisory services, this suggests that farmers choose enterprises and practices that lead to higher near-term productivity, with land degradation as a consequence.

Apparently either the demand for SLM approaches among poor farmers is low or poor farmers' awareness of and capacity to demand such approaches is low, as argued by Qamar (2005, 25–56). There is a need to better understand the extent to which lack of farmers' awareness and capacity to demand such technologies is the reason for this result, and to build the capacity to demand SLM practices where this is a key constraint. Qamar suggested that one way to build such capacity would be to supply SLM practices during the initial stages of demand-driven advisory services. For these efforts to be successful in stimulating further demand for such practices, it is essential to identify and promote practices that are profitable within a relatively short period of time and that are consistent with farmers' available resources. Otherwise farmers' demand for such practices is likely to continue to be limited.

The results also suggest the urgent need for demand-driven advisory services like NAADS to devote greater attention to combining promotion of improved soil fertility management practices with promotion of high-value enterprises in order to address the potential soil fertility depletion resulting from higher productivity and promotion of more profitable farming enterprises. As farmers adopt higher-value enterprises, the returns to investing in improved land management are likely to increase, so there is likely to be complementarity in these emphases.

Land Tenure

Many SSA countries have set policies and institutions to ensure the security of customary tenure through land titling (Toulmin and Quan 2000). However, this research, as well as many other studies, shows a nonsignificant association of freehold tenure or land titling with improved land management and incomes. We observed that farmers holding land under customary tenure obtained greater crop productivity, but that income per capita was not statistically different across land tenure systems. These findings call into question the assumption of the Ugandan Land Act of 1998, and similar efforts in other SSA countries, that conversion of customary land to leasehold or freehold tenure would lead to improvements in SLM practices, crop productivity, and household income. Nevertheless there remains a need to facilitate access to credit in customary tenure areas, since owners of land under customary tenure are unable to pledge their land as collateral with formal credit services, and this research has shown that such services could help reduce poverty. Alternative forms of collateral, such as the group collateral used by many MFIs, may be helpful in this regard.

Summary

Our findings suggest that some modernization strategies can achieve win-win-win outcomes, simultaneously increasing productivity, reducing poverty, and reducing land degradation. Examples of such strategies include promoting investments in SWC and agroforestry. Certain strategies appear able to contribute to some positive outcomes without significant trade-offs for others, such as road development, nonfarm activities, and rural finance.

Other strategies are likely to involve trade-offs among different objectives. For example, participation in the demand-driven extension approach (NAADS) is likely to lead to increased adoption of higher-value commodities with potential income benefits, but it may also contribute to increased land degradation. Investing in livestock appears to improve household income but is also associated with more rapid soil nutrient depletion and a decreased tendency to fallow. Expansion of perennial (especially banana) production is likely to cause more soil nutrient depletion and also promote higher income and productivity, unless greater efforts to restore soil nutrients are made. Female education may contribute to improved health, nutrition, or other development indicators not analyzed in this research, but it also appears to contribute to some indicators of land degradation. The presence of such trade-offs is not an argument to avoid these strategies; rather it suggests the need to recognize and find ways to ameliorate such negative impacts where they may occur. For example, teaching the principles of sustainable agriculture and NRM in educational curricula—as well as in the traditional extension services and the demand-driven advisory services that are currently being promoted in SSA—is one important way of addressing such trade-offs.

Overall our results provide support for the hypothesis that promotion of poverty reduction and agricultural modernization through technical assistance programs and investments in infrastructure and education can improve agricultural productivity and help reduce poverty. However, they also show that some of these investments do not necessarily reduce land degradation, and they may contribute to worsening land degradation in the near term. Thus investing in poverty reduction and agricultural modernization by themselves may not be sufficient to address the problem of land degradation in Uganda and other countries in SSA; these strategies must be complemented by greater efforts to address this problem.

APPENDIX

Results for Crop Productivity and per Capita Household Income without the Asset × Policy Interaction Terms

Table A.1   Factors associated with agricultural productivity without the asset × policy interaction terms

	Ordinary least squares	Reduced ordinary least squares	Instrumental variables
Land management practices			
ln(value of seed purchased + 1, Ush)	−0.012	—	0.01
ln(value of inorganic fertilizer purchased + 1, Ush)	0.046	—	0.033
ln(value of organic fertilizer applied + 1, Ush)	−0.014	—	0.003
ln(preharvest labor used on plot + 1)	0.211***	—	0.188***
Were crop residues incorporated into plot? (yes = 1, no = 0)	0.275**	—	0.196
Natural capital			
ln(soil depth, cm)	0.034	0.050	0.123
ln(slope, %)	−0.024	0.009	0.033
ln(nitrogen stock, kg ha⁻¹ year⁻¹)	−0.01	—	−0.072
ln(phosphorus stock, kg ha⁻¹ year⁻¹)	0.143**	—	0.115*
ln(potassium stock, kg ha⁻¹ year⁻¹)	0.084	—	0.093
Practice agroforestry	0.296***	0.312***	0.376***
Have SWC structures	0.474***	0.495***	0.481***
Perennial crops (cf. annual crops)	0.233**	0.246**	0.161
Have other NRM investments	0.067	0.124	−0.138
ln(plot area, acres)	0.253***	0.077	0.312***
ln(farm size, acres)	−0.902***	−0.901***	−0.957***
Physical capital			
ln(TLU)	0.023	−0.004	0.059
ln(value of farm equipment, Ush/household)	−0.034	−0.017	−0.013
Human capital			
Proportion of female family members with: (cf. no education)			
Primary education	0.041	0.030	0.001
Secondary education	−0.165	−0.091	0.019
Postsecondary education	0.207	0.144	0.406

Table A.1   Continued

	Ordinary least squares	Reduced ordinary least squares	Instrumental variables
Proportion of male household members with: (cf. no formal education)			
Primary education	0.103	0.025	−0.011
Secondary education	0.486***	0.429***	0.391**
Postsecondary education	0.472	0.327	0.215
Sex of household head (cf. female)	0.126	0.144	0.260
ln(household size)	0.155	0.289*	0.276*
Primary activity of household head (cf. crop production)			
Nonfarm activity	0	−0.041	0.046
Livestock	−0.355	−0.473	−0.454
Proportion of land area owned by women	0.002	0.064	0.167
Land tenure system (cf. freehold and leasehold)			
Customary	0.204*	0.182	0.314*
Mailo	−0.007	0.053	0.225
Access to rural services			
ln(number of contact hours with extension agent + 1)	0.104	0.111	0.101
Participates in NAADS	0.245**	0.157	0.172
Has access to credit	0.176	0.195	0.200
Village-level factors			
ln(population density, persons/km^2)	−0.085	−0.095*	−0.064
ln(wage rate in community, Ush/day)	−0.248**	−0.264**	−0.204*
ln(distance to residence + 1, km)	−0.220**	−0.234***	−0.222**
ln(distance to all-weather road + 1, km)	0.04	0.037	0.053
PMI	0	−0.000	−0.001
Agroecological zone (cf. LVCM)			
NW moist farmlands	−1.193***	−1.178***	−1.024***
NM farmlands	−0.882***	−0.830***	−0.570*
Mt. Elgon farmlands	−0.343	−0.242	−0.058
SW grass-farmlands	0.382	0.497	0.818**
SWH	−0.734*	−0.794**	−0.684**
Interaction terms (agroecological zone × distance to all-weather road)			
SW grasslands × ln(distance to all-weather road + 1, km)	−0.086	−0.167	−0.173
SWH × ln(distance to all-weather road + 1, km)	−0.185	−0.143	−0.017
Constant	10.244***	12.784***	9.593***
Number of observations	2,189	2,441	2,002
R^2	0.297	0.278	0.299
Hansen *J*-test of overidentification restrictions (*p*-value)	—	—	0.116
C-statistic (exogeneity/orthogonality) (*p*-value)	—	—	0.1389

Relevance tests of excluded variables (*p*-values)	
Value of purchased seed	0.000
Value of inorganic fertilizer	0.000
Value of organic fertilizer	0.000
Crop residue	0.095
Nitrogen stock	0.000
Phosphorus stock	0.000
Potassium stock	0.000
Contact hours with extension agent	0.000
NAADS	0.000
Access to credit	0.000

Notes: *, **, *** indicate that the coefficient is statistically significant at the 10, 5, or 1 percent level, respectively. Interaction terms for other agroecological zones that are not reported jointly failed the Wald test at $p = .10$. LVCM—Lake Victoria crescent and Mbale; NAADS—National Agricultural Advisory Services; NM—northern moist; NRM—natural resource management; NW—northwestern; PMI—potential market integration; SW—southwestern; SWC—soil and water conservation; SWH—southwestern highlands; TLU—tropical livestock units; Ush—Ugandan shillings.

Table A.2   Factors associated with per capita household income

	Ordinary least squares	Reduced model	Instrumental variables
Natural capital			
ln(slope, %)	−0.004	−0.022	0.013
ln(soil depth, cm)	0.005	−0.001	0.006
ln(nitrogen stock, kg ha^{-1} year^{-1})	0.060	—	0.198**
ln(phosphorus stock, kg ha^{-1} year^{-1})	0.265***	—	0.289***
ln(potassium stock, kg ha^{-1} year^{-1})	−0.083	—	−0.129*
Practice agroforestry	0.180**	0.233**	0.121
Have SWC structures	0.474***	0.487***	0.455***
Perennial crops (cf. annual crops)	0.421***	0.366***	0.250**
Have other NRM investments	0.953**	1.044***	0.820*
ln(farm size in acres)	0.388***	0.371***	0.332***
Physical capital			
ln(TLU)	0.222***	0.205***	0.232***
ln(value of farm equipment, Ush/household)	0.025	0.032	0.042*
Human capital			
Proportion of female household members with: (cf. no education)			
Primary education	0.052	0.052	−0.021
Secondary education	−0.244	−0.206	−0.175
Postsecondary education	0.378	0.443	0.576*
Proportion of male household members with: (cf. no formal education)			
Primary education	0.168	0.195	0.072
Secondary education	0.404**	0.468**	0.238
Postsecondary education	0.369	0.491*	0.285
Sex of household head (cf. female)	0.228	0.304	0.180
ln(household size)	−0.206	−0.184	−0.144
Primary activity of household head (cf. crop production)			
Nonfarm activity	0.207*	0.226**	0.178*
Livestock	−0.516	−0.543	−0.545
Proportion of land area owned by women	0.100	0.245	0.127
Land tenure (cf. leasehold and freehold)			
Mailo	−0.053	0.004	0.038
Customary	0.204	0.181	0.277
Access to rural services			
ln(distance to residence + 1, km)	0.155*	0.201*	0.151*
PMI	0.001	0.001	0.000
ln(distance to all-weather road + 1, km)	−0.155**	−0.127*	−0.131*
Participates in NAADS	0.035	—	−0.077
ln(number of contact hours with extension agent + 1)	0.004	—	0.006
Has access to credit	0.449***	—	0.335***
Village-level factors			
ln(population density, persons/km^2)	0.013	0.026	−0.065
ln(wage rate in community, Ush/day)	0.078	0.074	0.023
Agroecological zone (cf. LVCM)			
NM farmlands	−0.354	−0.433	−0.560**
Northern moist farmlands	0.241	0.385	0.057
Mt. Elgon farmlands	0.066	0.387	0.219
SW grass-farmlands	0.651***	0.790***	0.663***
SWH	0.229	0.483*	0.206

Table A.2   Continued

	Ordinary least squares	Reduced model	Instrumental variables
Constant	2.180*	4.573***	2.737**
Hansen *J*-test of overidentification restrictions (*p*-value)	—	—	0.249
C-statistic (exogeneity/orthogonality) (*p*-value)	—	—	0.325
Relevance tests of excluded variables (*p*-value)			
Nitrogen stock	—	—	0.038
Phosphorus stock	—	—	0.010
Potassium stock	—	—	0.000
Contact hours with extension agent	—	—	0.000
NAADS	—	—	0.000
Access to credit	—	—	0.000
*R*²	0.303	0.264	0.269
Number of observations	759.000	789	749.000

Notes: *, **, *** indicate that the coefficient is statistically significant at the 10, 5, or 1 percent level, respectively. LVCM—Lake Victoria crescent and Mbale; NAADS—National Agricultural Advisory Services; NM—northern moist; NRM—natural resource management; NW—northwestern; PMI—potential market integration; SW—southwestern; SWC—soil and water conservation; SWH—southwestern highlands; TLU—tropical livestock units; Ush—Ugandan shillings.

References

Adams, W. M., and M. J. Mortimore. 1997. Agricultural intensification and flexibility in the Nigerian Sahel. *Geographical Journal* 163: 150–160.

Adhikari, B. 2003. Property rights and natural resources: Socio-economic heterogeneity and distributional implications of common property resource management. Working Paper 1-03. South Asian Network for Development and Environmental Economics (SANDEE), Kathmandu, Nepal.

Agrawal, A. 2001. Common property institutions and sustainable governance of resources. *World Development* 29 (10): 1649–1672.

Alderman, H., J. Hoddinott, L. Haddad, and C. Udry. 1995. Gender differentials in farm productivity: Implications for household efficiency and agricultural policy. Food Consumption and Nutrition Division Discussion Paper 6. International Food Policy Research Institute, Washington D.C.

Alemu, T. 1999. Land tenure and soil conservation: Evidence from Ethiopia. Ph.D. thesis, Department of Economics, Gothenburg University, Sweden.

Alston, L. J., G. D. Libecap, and R. Schneider. 1996. The determinants and impact of property rights: Land titles on the Brazilian frontier. *Journal of Law, Economics and Organization* 12 (1): 25–61.

Anderson, C. L., M. Dietz, A. Gordon, and M. Klawitter. 2004. Discount rates in Vietnam. *Economic Development and Cultural Change* 52: 873–887.

Angelsen, A., and D. Kaimowitz. 1999. Rethinking the causes of deforestation: Lessons from economic models. *World Bank Observer* 14 (1): 73–98.

Anonymous. 2007a. Strategic investment programme for sustainable land management in Sub-Saharan Africa. Unpublished report. Global Environmental Facility (Project Development Facility B), Pretoria, South Africa.

———. 2007b. Strategic investment programme for sustainable land management in Sub-Saharan Africa: Assessment of the nature and extent of barriers and bottlenecks to scaling-up sustainable land management investments in Uganda. Unpublished report. TerrAfrica, Pretoria, South Africa.

Appleton, S. 2001a. Poverty reduction during growth: The case of Uganda. Mimeo. Center for African Studies, Oxford University, U.K.

———. 2001b. What can we expect from universal primary education? In *Uganda's recovery: The role of farms, firms, and government,* ed. R. Reinikka and P. Collier. Washington, D.C.: World Bank.

Appleton, S., and S. Ssewanyana. 2003. Poverty analysis in Uganda, 2002/03. Mimeo. Economic Policy Research Center.

Atwood, D. A. 1990. Land registration in Africa: The impact on agricultural production. *World Development* 18 (5): 659–671.

Bai, Z., D. Dent, L. Olsson, and M. Schaepman. 2008. *Global assessment of land degradation and improvement 1: Identification by remote sensing.* Report 2008/01. Rome and Wageningen, Netherlands: Food and Agriculture Organization of the United Nations and World Soil Information (ISRIC).

Baland, J. M., and J. P. Platteau. 1996. *Halting degradation of natural resources: Is there a role for rural community?* Oxford, U.K.: Clarendon Press.

Banana, A., and W. Gombya-Sembajjwa. 2000. Successful forest management: The importance of security of tenure and rule enforcement in Ugandan forests. In *Forests, Trees and People Program,* ed. C. Gibson, A. McKean, and E. Ostrom, 73–82. Forest Department Working Paper 3. Rome: United Nations Food and Agriculture Organization.

Barbier, E. B., and J. C. Burgess. 1996. Economic analysis of deforestation in Mexico. *Environment and Development Economics* 1 (2): 203–239.

Barbier, E. B., Y. Joanne, and C. Burgess. 1997. The economics of forest land use. *Land Economics* 73 (2): 174–195.

Barrett, C. B. 1996. On price risk and the inverse farm size–productivity relationship. *Journal of Development Economics* 51: 193–215.

Barrett, C. B., F. Place, and A. Aboud. 2002. The challenges of stimulating adoption of improved natural resource management practices in African agriculture. In *Natural resources management in African agriculture,* ed. C. B. Barrett, F. Place, and A. A. Aboud. Nairobi, Kenya: World Agroforestry Centre (ICRAF) and CAB International.

Barrett, C. B., T. Reardon, and P. Webb. 2001. Non-income diversification and household livelihood strategies in rural Africa: Concepts, dynamics and policy implications. *Food Policy* 26 (4): 315–331.

Bassett, T. J., and D. Crummey. 2003. Contested images, contested realities: Environment and society in African savannas. In *African savannas: Global narratives and local knowledge of environmental change,* ed. T. J. Bassett and D. Crummey. Oxford, U.K.: James Currey.

Battese, G. E. 1997. A note on the estimation of Cobb-Douglas production functions when some explanatory variables have zero values. *Journal of Agricultural Economics* 48 (2): 250–252.

Baum, C. F., M. E. Schaffer, and S. Stillman. 2002. Instrumental variables and GMM: Estimation and testing. Unpublished working paper 545. Department of Economics, Boston College. <http://fmwww.bc.edu/ec-p/WP545.pdf>. Accessed February 2003.

Bekele, W. 2004. Economics of soil and water conservation: Theory and empirical application to subsistence farming in the eastern Ethiopian highlands. Ph.D. thesis, Swedish University of Agricultural Sciences, Uppsala.

Bekele, W., and L. Drake. 2003. Soil and water conservation decision behavior of subsistence farmers in the Eastern Highlands of Ethiopia: A case study of the Hunde-Lafto area. *Ecological Economics* 46: 437–451.

Bekunda, M. 1999. Farmers' responses to soil fertility decline in banana-based cropping systems of Uganda. *Managing African Soils* 4 (February): 1–20.

Benin, S. 2006. Policies and programs affecting land management practices, input use, and productivity in the highlands of Amhara Region, Ethiopia. In *Strategies for sustainable land management in the East African Highlands,* ed. J. Pender, F. Place, and S. Ehui. Washington, D.C.: International Food Policy Research Institute.

Benin, S., and J. Pender. 2006. Collective action in community management of grazing lands: The case of the highlands of northern Ethiopia. *Environment and Development Economics* 11: 127–149.

Bergametti, G., E. Remoudaki, R. Losno, E. Steiner, B. Chatenet, and P. Buat-Menard. 1992. Source, transport and deposition of atmospheric phosphorus over the northwestern Mediterranean. *Journal of Atmospheric Chemistry* 14 (1–4): 501–513.

Berry, R. A., and W. R. Cline. 1979. *Agrarian structure and productivity in developing countries.* Baltimore, Md., U.S.A.: Johns Hopkins University Press.

Bhalla, S. S. 1988. Does land quality matter? Theory and measurement. *Journal of Development Economics* 29: 45–62.

Binswanger, H. P. 1980. Attitudes towards risk: Experimental measurement in rural India. *American Journal of Agricultural Economics* 62 (3): 395–407.

Binswanger, H. P., and J. McIntire. 1987. Behavioral and material determinants of production relations in land abundant tropical agriculture. *Economic Development and Culture Change* 35 (1): 73–99.

Birdsall, N., and S. W. Sinding. 2001. How and why population matters: New findings, new issues. In *Population matters: Demographic change, economic growth, and poverty in the developing world,* ed. N. Birdsall, A. C. Kelley, and S. W. Sinding. Oxford, U.K.: Oxford University Press.

Bojö, J. 1996. The cost of land degradation in Sub-Saharan Africa. *Ecological Economics* 16 (2): 161–173.

Boserup, E. 1965. *The conditions of agricultural growth.* New York: Aldine.

Bound, J., D. A. Jaeger, and R. M. Baker. 1995. Problems with instrumental variables estimation when the correlation between the instruments and the exogenous explanatory variable is weak. *Journal of the American Statistical Association* 90: 443–450.

Boyd, C., and T. Slaymaker. 2000. Re-examining the "more people less erosion" hypothesis: Special case or wider trend? *Natural Resource Perspective* 63 (November): 1–6.

Breman, H., and J. J. Kessler. 1995. *Woody plants in agro-ecosystems of semi-arid regions.* Berlin: Springer-Verlag.

Bumb, B., C. Debrah, and L. Maene. 2006. Input subsidies and agricultural development: Issues and options for developing and transitional countries. Background paper for the Africa Fertilizer Summit, Abuja, Nigeria, June.

Cardenas, J. C., and J. P. Carpenter. 2005. Experiments and economic development: Lessons from field labs in the developing world. Economics Discussion Paper 05-05. Middlebury College, Middlebury, Vermont, U.S.A.

Carney, D. 1998. Implementing the sustainable rural livelihoods approach. In *Sustainable rural livelihoods: What contribution can we make?,* ed. D. Carney. London: U.K. Department for International Development.

Carter, M. R. 1984. Identification of the inverse relationship between farm size and productivity: An empirical analysis of peasant agricultural production. *Oxford Economic Papers* 36 (1): 131–145.

Carter, M. R., and C. B. Barrett. 2006. The economics of poverty traps and persistent poverty: An asset-based approach. *Journal of Development Studies* 42 (2): 178–199.

Cavendish, W. 2000. Empirical regularities in the poverty-environment relationship of rural households: Evidence from Zimbabwe. *World Development* 28 (11): 1979–2003.

Chayanov, A. 1966. *The theory of peasant economy.* Homewood, Ill., U.S.A.: Richard Irwin.

Chen, S., and M. Ravallion. 2000. *How did the poor fare in the 1990s?* Washington, D.C.: World Bank.

Chomitz, K. M., and D. A. Gray. 1996. Roads, land use, and deforestation: A spatial model applied to Belize. *World Bank Economic Review* 10 (3): 487–512.

Clay, D. C., T. Reardon, and J. Kangasniemi. 1998. Sustainable intensification in the highland tropics: Rwandan farmers' investments in land conservation and soil fertility. *Economic Development and Cultural Change* 46 (2): 351–378.

Cleaver, K. M., and G. A. Schreiber. 1994. *Reversing the spiral: The population, agriculture and environment nexus in Sub-Saharan Africa.* Washington, D.C.: World Bank.

Collier, P. 2002. The future of perennial crops. *African Development Review* 14 (2): 237–250.

Croppenstedt, A., M. Demeke, and M. M. Meschi. 2003. Technology adoption in the presence of constraints: The case of fertilizer demand in Ethiopia. *Review of Development Economics* 7 (1): 58–70.

Cuesta, M., G. Carlson, and E. Lutz. 1997. An empirical assessment of farmers' discount rates in Costa Rica. Environment Department, World Bank, Washington, D.C. (cited in Ekbom and Bojö 1999).

Dasgupta, P. 2000. Population and resources: An exploration of the reproductive and environmental externalities. *Population and Development Review* 26 (4): 643–689.

Davidson, R., and J. G. MacKinnon. 2004. *Econometric theory and methods.* Oxford, U.K.: Oxford University Press.

Deininger, K. 2003. *Land policies for growth and poverty reduction.* World Bank Policy Research Report. Washington, D.C., and Oxford, U.K.: World Bank and Oxford University Press.

Deininger, K., and J. S. Chamorro. 2004. Investment and income effects of land regularization: The case of Nicaragua. *Agricultural Economics* 30 (2): 101–116.

Deininger, K., and J. Okidi. 2001. Rural households: Incomes, productivity and non-farm enterprises. In *Uganda's recovery: The role of farms, firms and government,* ed. R. Reinikka and P. Collier. Washington, D.C.: World Bank.

Deininger K., S. Jin, B. Adenew, S. Gebre-Selassie, and B. Nega. 2003. Tenure security and land-related investment: Evidence from Ethiopia. World Bank Policy Research Working Paper 2991. World Bank, Washington, D.C.

Deininger, K., D. Ayalew, S. Holden, and J. Zevenbergen. 2007. Rural land certification in Ethiopia: Process, initial impact, and implications for other African countries. World Bank Policy Research Working Paper 4218. World Bank, Washington, D.C.

De Jager, A., I. Kariuki, F. M. Matiri, M. Odendo, and J. M. Wanyama. 1998. Monitoring nutrient flows and economic performance in African farming systems (NUTMON). IV. Linking nutrient balances and economic performance in three districts in Kenya. *Agriculture, Ecosystems and Environment* 71: 81–92.

De Janvry, A., M. Fafchamps, and E. Sadoulet. 1991. Peasant household behavior with missing markets: Some paradoxes explained. *Economic Journal* 101: 1400–1417.

Department for International Development (DFID). 1999. Sustainable livelihoods guidance sheets. <http://www.livelihoods.org/>.

Dercon, S. 1998. Wealth, risk and activity choice: Cattle in Western Tanzania. *Journal of Development Economics* 55: 1–42.

Der Pol, V. F. 1993. Analysis and evaluation options for sustainable agriculture with special reference to southern Mali. In *The role of plant nutrients for sustainable food crop production in Sub-Saharan Africa,* ed. H. Van Reuler and W. H. Prins. Leidschendam, Netherlands: VKP.

De Soto, H. 2000. *The mystery of capital: Why capitalism triumphs in the West and fails everywhere else.* New York: Basic Books.

Diagana, B. 2003. Land degradation in sub-Saharan Africa: What explains the widespread adoption of unsustainable farming practices? Mimeo. Montana State University, Bozeman.

Dorward, A., S. Fan, J. Kydd, H. Lofgren, J. Morrison, C. Poulton, N. Rao, L. Smith, H. Tchale, S. Thorat, I. Urey, and P. Wobst. 2004. Institutions and policies for pro-poor agricultural growth. *Development Policy Review* 22 (6): 611–622.

Dregne, H. E., and N. T. Chou. 1992. Global desertification dimensions and costs. In *Degradation and restoration of arid lands,* ed. H. E. Dregne. Lubbock, Tex., U.S.A.: Texas Tech University.

Durning, A. 1989. *Poverty and the environment: Reversing the downward spiral.* Worldwatch Paper 92. Washington, D.C.: Worldwatch Institute.

Ekbom, A., and J. Bojö. 1999. Poverty and environment: Evidence of links and integration into the Country Assistance Strategy process. Discussion Paper 4. Environment Group, Africa Region, World Bank, Washington, D.C.

Elias, E., and I. Scoones. 1999. Perspectives on soil fertility change: A case study from southern Ethiopia. *Land Degradation and Development* 10 (3): 195–206.

Ellis, F. 1998. Household strategies and rural livelihood diversification. *Journal of Development Studies* 35: 1–38.

Ersado, L., G. Amacher, and J. Alwang. 2003. *Productivity and land-enhancing technologies in northern Ethiopia: Health, public investments, and sequential adoption.* Environment and Production Technology Division Discussion Paper 102. Washington, D.C.: International Food Policy Research Institute.

Fafchamps, M., and J. L. Pender. 1997. Precautionary saving, credit constraints, and irreversible investment: Theory and evidence from semiarid India. *Journal of Business and Economic Statistics* 15 (2): 180–194.

Fairhead, J., and M. Leach. 1996. *Misreading the African landscape: Society and ecology in a forest-savanna mosaic.* Cambridge, U.K.: Cambridge University Press.

Fairhead, J., and I. Scoones. 2005. Local knowledge and the social shaping of soil investments: Critical perspectives on the assessment of soil degradation in Africa. *Land Use Policy* 22 (1): 33–42.

Fan, S., and C. Chan-Kang. 2004. Returns to investment in less-favored areas in developing countries: A synthesis of evidence and implications for Africa. *Food Policy* 29: 431–444.

Fan, S., and N. Rao. 2003. *Public spending in developing countries: Trends, determination and impact.* Environment and Production Technology Division Discussion Paper 99. Washington, D.C.: International Food Policy Research Institute.

Fan, S., X. Zhang, and N. Rao. 2004. *Public expenditure, growth, and poverty reduction in rural Uganda.* Development Strategy and Governance Division Discussion Paper 4. Washington, D.C.: International Food Policy Research Institute.

FAO (Food and Agriculture Organization). 1995. Land degradation and environmental degradation and desertification in Africa. <http://www.fao.org/docrep/x5318e/x5318e00.htm>.

Feder, G. 1985. The relation between farm size and farm productivity. *Journal of Development Economics* 18: 297–313.

Feder, G., R. E. Just, and D. Zilberman. 1985. Adoption of agricultural innovations in developing countries: A survey. *Economic Development and Cultural Change* 33: 255–297.

Feder, G., T. Onchan, Y. Chalamwong, and C. Hongladaron. 1988. *Land policies and farm productivity in Thailand.* Baltimore, Md., U.S.A.: Johns Hopkins University Press.

Foster, H. L. 1971. Rapid routine soil and plant analysis without automatic equipment. I. Routine soil analysis. *East African Agriculture and Forest Journal* 37: 160–170.

———. 1976. Soil fertility in Uganda. Ph.D. thesis, University of Newcastle upon Tyne, England.

———. 1978. The influence of soil fertility on crop performance in Uganda. I. Cotton. *Tropical Agriculture* 55: 255–268.

———. 1980a. The influence of soil fertility on crop performance in Uganda. II. Groundnut. *Tropical Agriculture* 57: 29–42.

———. 1980b. "The influence of soil fertility on crop performance in Uganda. III. Finger millet and maize. *Tropical Agriculture* 57: 123–132.

Freeman, H. A., and R. Coe. 2002. Smallholder farmers' use of integrated nutrient management strategies: Patterns and possibilities in Machakos District of Eastern Kenya. In *Natural resources management in African agriculture: Understanding and improving current practices,* ed. C. B. Barrett, F. Place, and A. Abdillahi. Wallingford, U.K.: CAB International.

Gebremedhin, B., and S. Swinton. 2002. Sustainable management of private and communal lands in northern Ethiopia. In *Natural resources management in African agriculture: Understanding and improving current practices,* ed. C. B. Barrett, F. Place, and A. Abdillahi. Wallingford, U.K.: CAB International.

Giller, K. E., J. F. McDonagh, and G. Cadish. 1994. Can biological nitrogen fixation sustain agriculture in the tropics? In *Soil science and sustainable land management in the tropics,* ed. J. K. Syers and D. L. Rimmer. Wallingford, U.K.: CAB International.

Gladwin, C. H. 1991. *Structural adjustment and African women farmers.* Gainesville: University of Florida Press.

Gladwin, C. H., and A. M. Thompson. 1999. Food or cash crops: Which is the key to food security? Report submitted to the U.S. Agency for International Development Collaborative Research Support Program on Gender and Soil Fertility in Africa, University of Florida, Gainesville. <http://www.fred.ifas.ufl.edu/CRSP/food.htm>. Accessed September 26, 2004.

GOU (Government of Uganda). 2007. The plan to achieve prosperity for all Ugandans understanding *bonna baggaggawale.* Unpublished. Kampala.

Gray, L. C., and W. G. Moseley. 2005. A geographical perspective on poverty-environment interactions. *Geographical Journal* 171: 9–23.

Grepperud, S. 1996. Population pressure and land degradation: The case of Ethiopia. *Journal of Environmental Economics and Management* 30 (1): 18–33.

———. 1997. Poverty, land degradation and climatic uncertainty. *Oxford Economic Papers* 49 (4): 586–608.

Haggblade, S., and G. Tembo. 2003. *Conservation farming in Zambia.* Environment and Production Technology Division Discussion Paper 108. Washington, D.C.: International Food Policy Research Institute.

Haggblade, S., P. Hazell, and J. Brown. 1989. Farm-nonfarm linkages in rural sub-Saharan Africa. *World Development* 17 (8): 1173–1201.

Hagos, F., and S. Holden. 2006. Tenure security, resource poverty, public programs, and household plot-level conservation investments in the highlands of northern Ethiopia. *Agricultural Economics* 34(2): 183–196.

Hamilton, K., and M. Clemens. 1999. Genuine savings rates in developing countries. *World Bank Economic Review* 13 (2): 333–356.

Hanna, S. 1995. Efficiency of user participation in natural resource management. In *Poverty rights and the environment,* ed. S. Hanna and M. Munasighe, 59–68. Stockholm and Washington, D.C.: Beijer International Institute of Ecological Economics and World Bank.

Hardin, G. 1968. The tragedy of the commons. In *Managing the commons,* ed. G. Hardin and J. Barden. San Francisco: W. H. Freeman.

Hartemink, A. E., R. J. Buresh, B. Jama, and B. H. Janssen. 1996. Soil nitrate and water dynamics in sesbania fallows, weed fallows, and maize. *Soil Science Society of America Journal* 60: 568–574.

Heltberg, R. 1998. Rural market imperfections and the farm size–productivity relationship: Evidence from Pakistan. *World Development* 26 (10): 1807–1826.

Henao, J., and C. Baanante. 2006. *Agricultural production and soil nutrient mining in Africa: Implications for resource conservation and policy development.* IFDC Technical Bulletin. Muscle Shoals, Ala., U.S.A.: International Fertilizer Development Center.

Holden, S. T., and B. Shiferaw. 2002. Poverty and land degradation: Peasants' willingness to pay to sustain land productivity. In *Natural resource management in African agriculture: Understanding and improving current practices,* ed. C. B. Barrett, F. M. Place, and A. A. Aboud. Oxon, U.K., and New York: CAB International and International Centre for Research in Agroforestry.

Holden, S. T., B. Shiferaw, and J. Pender. 2004. Off-farm income, household welfare and sustainable land management. *Food Policy* 29: 369–392.

————. 2005. *Policy analysis for sustainable land management and food security: A bio-economic model with market imperfections.* Research Report 140. Washington, D.C.: International Food Policy Research Institute

Holden, S., B. Shiferaw, and M. Wik. 1998. Poverty, credit constraints and time preference of relevance for environmental policy. *Environment and Development Economics* 3: 105–130.

Hunt, D. 2003. The debate on land privatization in Sub-Saharan Africa: Some outstanding issues. Discussion Paper in Economics 96. Sussex University, Brighton, U.K.

IAEA (International Atomic Energy Agency). 1975. *Root activity patterns of some tree crops.* Technical Report Series 170. Vienna.

IBSRAM (International Board for Soil Research and Management). 1994. *Strategies for the management of upland soils of humid and subhumid Africa.* Network Document 9. Bangkok.

IFAD (International Fund for Agricultural Development). 1999. *Assessment of rural poverty in west and central Africa.* Rome.

International Crisis Group. 2006. *Peace in northern Uganda?* Africa Briefing 41. Brussels.

Jagger, P., and J. Pender. 2006. Impacts of programs and organizations on the adoption of sustainable land management technologies in Uganda. In *Strategies for sustainable land management in the East African Highlands,* ed. J. Pender, F. Place, and S. Ehui. Washington, D.C.: International Food Policy Research Institute.

Jama, B., R. J. Buresh, J. K. Ndufa, and K. D. Shepherd. 1998. Vertical distribution of roots and soil nitrate: Tree species and phosphorus effects. *Soil Science Society of America Journal* 62: 280–286.

Jansen, H. G. P., J. Pender, A. Damon, and R. Schipper. 2006. *Rural development policies and sustainable land use in the hillside areas of Honduras: A quantitative livelihoods approach.* Research Report 147. Washington, D.C.: International Food Policy Research Institute.

Jansky, L., and R. Chandran. 2004. Climate change and sustainable land management: Focus on erosive land degradation. *Journal of the World Association of Soil and Water Conservation* 4: 17–29.

Jayne, T., and D. Boughton. 2006. Strategic options for achieving CAADP's agricultural growth targets. Paper presented at the SAKSS-SA regional workshop, Johannesburg, South Africa, October 4, 2006.

Jodha, N. S. 1986. Common property resources and rural poor in dry regions of India. *Economic and Political Weekly* 21 (27): 1169–1181.

Joliffe, D. 1997. *Whose education matters in the determination of household income? Evidence from a developing country.* Food Consumption and Nutrition Division Discussion Paper 39. Washington, D.C.: International Food Policy Research Institute.

Kaboré, D., and C. Reij. 2004. *The emergence and spreading of an improved traditional soil and water conservation practice in Burkina Faso.* Environment and Production Technology Division Discussion Paper 114. Washington, D.C.: International Food Policy Research Institute.

Kaizzi, C. K. 2002. The potential benefit of green manures and inorganic fertilizers in cereal production on contrasting soils in eastern Uganda. Ph.D. thesis, University of Bonn and German Center for Development Research (ZEF).

Kaizzi, K., J. Byalebeka, C. Wortmann, and M. Mamo. 2007. Low input approaches for soil fertility management in semiarid eastern Uganda. *Agronomy Journal* 99: 847–853.

Kates, R., and V. Haarmann. 1992. Where the poor live: Are the assumptions correct? *Environment* 34 (May): 4–28.

Kazianga, H., and W. A. Masters. 2002. Investing in soils: Field bunds and microcatchments in Burkina Faso. *Environment and Development Economics* 7: 571–591.

Keeley, J., and I. Scoones. 2003. *Understanding environmental policy processes: Cases from Africa.* London: Earthscan.

Kevane, M., and B. Widyck. 2001. Social norms and the time allocation of women's labor in Burkina Faso. *Review of Development Economics* 5 (1): 119–129.

Kirby, K., R. Godoy, V. Reyes-Garcia, E. Byron, L. Apaza, W. Leonard, E. Perez, V. Vadez, and D. Wilkie. 2002. Correlates of delay-discount rates: Evidence from Tsimane Amerindians of the Bolivian rain forest. *Journal of Economic Psychology* 23: 291–316.

Kochian, L. V., O. A. Hoekenga, and M. A. Piñeros. 2004. How do crop plants tolerate acid soils? Mechanisms of aluminum tolerance and phosphorus efficiency. *Annual Review of Plant Biology* 55: 459–493.

Koning, N., and E. Smaling. 2005. Environmental crisis or "lie of the land"? The debate on soil degradation in Africa. *Land Use Policy* 22 (1): 3–12.

Kunze, D., H. Waibel, and A. Runge-Metzger. 1998. Sustainable land use by women as agricultural producers? The case of Northern Burkina Faso. *Advances in Geoecology* 31: 1469–1477.

Kwesiga, F., S. Franzel, P. Mafongoya, O. Ajayi, D. Phiri, R. Katanga, E. Kuntashula, F. Place, and T. Chirwa. 2005. *Improved fallows in eastern Zambia: History, farmer practice and impacts.* Environment and Production Technology Division Discussion Paper 130. Washington, D.C.: International Food Policy Research Institute.

LaFrance, J. T. 1992. Do increased commodity prices lead to more or less soil degradation? *Australian Journal of Agricultural Economics* 36 (1): 57–82.

Lamb, R. L. 2003. Inverse productivity: Land quality, labor markets, and measurement error. *Journal of Development Economics* 71 (1): 71–95.

Lanjaouw, P. 2007. Does rural nonfarm economy contribute to poverty reduction? In *Transforming the rural nonfarm economy: Opportunities and threats in the developing world,* ed. S. Haggblade, P. Hazell, and T. Reardon, 55–82. Baltimore, Md., U.S.A.: Johns Hopkins University Press.

Leach, M., and R. Mearns. 1996. Environmental change and policy: Challenging received wisdom in Africa. In *The lie of the land: Challenging received wisdom on the African environment,* ed. M. Leach and R. Mearns. London: International African Institute and James Currey.

Leonard, H. J. 1989. *Environment and the poor: Development strategies for a common agenda.* New Brunswick, N.J., U.S.A.: Transaction.

Lindblade, K., J. Tumuhairwe, and G. Carswell. 1996. More people, more fallow: Environmentally favorable land-use changes in southwestern Uganda. Report to the Rockefeller Foundation and CARE International. Atlanta, Ga., U.S.A., and New York.

López, R. 1997. *Land titles and farm productivity in Honduras.* Washington, D.C.: World Bank.

———. 1998. Where development can or cannot go: The role of poverty-environment linkages. In *Annual World Bank Conference on Development Economics 1997.* Washington, D.C.

Lubwama, F. 2000. Gender issues in animal traction and rural transport in Uganda. In *Empowering farmers with animal traction,* ed. P. G. Kaumbutho, R. Pearson, and T. Simalenga. Proceedings of the workshop of the Animal Traction Network for Eastern and Southern Africa, September 20–24, 1999, Mpumalanga, South Africa. <http://www.atnesa.org>.

Lufafa A., A. M. Tenywa, M. Isabirye, M. J. G. Majaliwa, and P. L. Woomer. 2003. Prediction of soil erosion in a Lake Victoria basin catchment using a GIS-based universal soil loss model. *Agricultural Systems* 76: 883–894.

Lufumpa, C. 2005. The poverty-environment nexus in Africa. *African Development Review* 17 (3): 366–381.

Lynam, J. K., S. M. Nandwa, and E. M. A. Smaling. 1998. Introduction. *Agriculture, Ecosystems and Environment* 71: 1–4.

MAAIF (Ministry of Agriculture, Animal Industries and Fisheries). 2005. Operationalisation of the rural development strategy for increased agricultural productivity. Unpublished. Entebbe, Uganda.

MAAIF/MFPED (Ministry of Agriculture, Animal Industries and Fisheries, and Ministry of Finance, Planning and Economic Development). 2000. *Plan for modernization of agriculture (PMA): Eradicating poverty in Uganda.* Kampala, Uganda: Government Printer.

Maddala, G. S. 1983. *Limited-dependent and qualitative variables in econometrics.* Econometric Society Monographs 3. Cambridge, U.K.: Cambridge University Press.

Magunda, M. K., and M. M. Tenywa. 1999. Soil and water conservation. Mimeo. Uganda National Agricultural Research Organization (NARO), Kampala.

Majaliwa, J. G. M. 2003. Soil and plant nutrient losses from major agricultural land use types and associated pollution loading in selected micro-catchments of the Lake Victoria catchment. Ph.D. thesis, Department of Soil Science, Makerere University, Kampala, Uganda.

McCann, J. C. 1999. *Green land, brown land, black land: An environmental history of Africa, 1800–1990.* Oxford, U.K.: James Currey.

McCarthy, N., E. Sadoulet, and A. de Janvry. 2001. Common pool resource appropriation under costly cooperation. *Journal of Environmental Economics and Management* 42: 297–309.

Mekonnen, K., R. J. Buresh, and B. Jama. 1997. Root and inorganic nitrogen distributions in sesbania fallow, natural fallow and maize fields. *Plant and Soil* 188: 319–327.

Mekonnen, K., R. J. Buresh, R. Coe, and K. M. Kipleting. 1999. Root length and nitrate under *Sesbania sesban:* Vertical and horizontal distribution and variability. *Agroforestry Systems* 42: 265–282.

Mekuria, M., and S. Waddington. 2002. Initiatives to encourage farmer adoption of soil fertility technologies for maize-based cropping systems in Southern Africa. In *Natural resources management in African agriculture: Understanding and improving current practices,* ed. C. B. Barrett, F. Place, and A. Abdillahi, 219–234. Wallingford, U.K.: CAB International.

Mercer, D. 2004. Adoption of agroforestry innovations in the tropics: A review. *Agroforestry Systems* 61–62 (1–3): 311–328.

Mertens, B., and E. F. Lambin. 1997. Spatial modeling of deforestation in southern Cameroon. *Applied Geography* 17 (2): 143–162.

Meyer, L. D., S. M. Dabney, and W. D. Kemper. 2001. Designing research to improve runoff and erosion control practices: Example, grass hedges. In *Sustaining the global farm: Selected papers from the 10th International Soil Conservation Organization Meeting, May 24–29, 1999, Purdue University,* ed. D. E. Scott, R. H. Mohtar, and G. C. Steinhardt, 447–481. Lafayette, Ind., U.S.A.: Purdue University Press.

MFPED (Ministry of Finance, Planning and Economic Development). 2001. *Background to the budget, financial year 2001/02.* Kampala, Uganda.

————. 2003. *Background to the budget, financial year 2003/04.* Kampala, Uganda.

Migot-Adholla, S., P. Hazell, B. Blarel, and F. Place. 1991. Indigenous land right systems in sub-Saharan Africa: A constraint on productivity? *World Bank Economic Review* 5 (1): 155–175.

Ministry of Natural Resources. 1994. *State of the environment report for Uganda.* Kampala, Uganda: National Environment Information Centre.

Mink, S. 1993. *Poverty, population and the environment.* Discussion Paper 189. Washington, D.C.: World Bank.

Minten, B., and C. Barrett. 2008. Agricultural technology, productivity, and poverty in Madagascar. *World Development* 36 (5): 797–822.

Mock, P. 1976. The efficiency of farmers as farm managers: Kenya. *American Journal of Agricultural Economics* 58: 831–835.

Mokwunye, A., S. Chien, and E. Rhodes. 1986. Phosphorus reaction with tropical African soils. In *Management of nitrogen and phosphorus fertilizers in Sub-Saharan Africa,* ed. A. Mokwunye and P. Vlek, 253–281. Dordrecht, Netherlands: Martinus Nijhoff.

Moseley, W. G. 2001. African evidence on the relation of poverty, time preference and the environment. *Ecological Economics* 38: 317–326.

Muchena, F., D. Onduru, G. Gachini, and A. de Jager. 2005. Turning the tides of soil degradation in Africa: Capturing the reality and exploring opportunities. *Land Use Policy* 22: 23–31.

Mukherjee, C., H. White, and M. Wuyts. 1998. *Econometric and data analysis for developing countries.* London: Routledge.

Mulebeke, R. 2003. Validation of a GIS-USLE model in a banana-based micro-catchment of the Lake Victoria basin. M.Sc. thesis, Department of Soil Science, Makerere University, Kampala, Uganda.

NAADS Secretariat. 2000. *National Agricultural Advisory Services Programme (NAADS). Master document of the NAADS Task Force and joint donor groups.* Entebbe, Uganda: Ministry of Agriculture, Animal Industry and Fisheries.

Narain, U., S. Gupta, and K. van't Veld. 2005. Poverty and the environment: Exploring the relationship between household incomes, private assets, and natural assets. Resources for the Future Discussion Paper 05-18. Washington, D.C. <http://www.rff.org/Documents/RFF-DP-05-18-REV.pdf>.

NARO (National Agricultural Research Organization) and FAO (Food and Agriculture Organization of the United Nations). 1999. Uganda soil fertility initiative: Draft concept paper. Mimeo. Investment Centre Division, FAO. and World Bank Cooperative Programme, Rome.

NEAP (National Environmental Action Plan). 1992. *Land tenure and land management in Uganda: Report of task force on land management.* Kampala, Uganda: Ministry of Natural Resources.

Nelson, G. C., and D. Hellerstein. 1997. Do roads cause deforestation? Using satellite images in econometric analysis of land use. *American Journal of Agricultural Economics* 79 (1): 80–88.

NEMA (National Environment Management Authority). 2001. *State of the environment report for Uganda 2000.* Kampala.

Nerina, V., and K. Roy. 1998. *Poverty, female-headed households and sustainable development.* Westport, Conn., U.S.A.: Greenwood Press.

Nielsen, U. 2001. Poverty and attitudes towards time and risk: Experimental evidence from Madagascar. Mimeo. Department of Economics and Natural Resources, Royal Veterinary and Agricultural University, Frederiksberg, Denmark.

Nkonya, E., C. Kaizzi, and J. Pender. 2005. Determinants of nutrient balances in a maize farming system in eastern Uganda. *Agricultural Systems* 85: 155–182.

Nkonya, E., J. Pender, and E. Kato. 2008. Who knows, who cares? The determinants of enactment, awareness and compliance with community natural resource management regulations in Uganda. *Environment and Development Economics* 13 (1): 79–109.

Nkonya, E., J. Pender, P. Jagger, D. Sserunkuuma, C. Kaizzi, and H. Ssali. 2004. *Strategies for sustainable land management and poverty reduction in Uganda.* Research Report 133. Washington, D.C.: International Food Policy Research Institute.

Nkonya, E. M., D. Phillip, T. Mogues, M. Yahaya, G. Adebowale, J. Pender, T. Arokoyo, and E. Kato. 2008. *From the ground up: Impacts of a pro-poor community-driven development project in Nigeria.* Discussion Paper 756. Washington, D.C.: International Food Policy Research Institute.

NWDR (National Water Development Report). 2006. Case study Uganda: National Water Development Report—2005. Prepared for the Second United Nations World Water Development Report, Water: A shared responsibility. <http://unesdoc.unesco.org/images/0014/001467/146760e.pdf>.

Nziguheba, G., C. Palm, R. Buresh, and P. Smithson. 1998. Soil phosphorus fractions and adsorption as affected by organic and inorganic sources. *Plant and Soil* 198: 159–168.

Okurut, F., A. Schoombee, and S. van der Berg. 2005. Credit demand and credit rationing in the informal financial sector in Uganda. *South African Journal of Economics* 73 (3): 482–497.

Oldeman, L. R., R. T. A. Hakkeling, and W. G. Sombroek. 1991. *World map of the status of human-induced soil degradation: An explanatory note.* Wageningen, Netherlands, and Nairobi, Kenya: International Soil Reference and Information Centre and United Nations Environment Programme.

Olson, M. 1965. *The logic of collective action.* Cambridge, Mass., U.S.A.: Harvard University Press.

Omamo, W. 2002. Fertilizer trade and pricing in Uganda. Paper presented at the Association for Strengthening Agricultural Research in Eastern and Central Africa (ASARECA) workshop on the assessment of the fertilizer sub-sector in East Africa, Nairobi, Kenya, July 15–17, 2002.

Ostrom, E. 1990. *Governing the commons: The evolution of institutions for collection action. Political economy of institutions and decisions.* New York: Cambridge University Press.

Pagiola, S. 1996. Price policy and returns to soil conservation in semi-arid Kenya. *Environmental and Resource Economics* 8: 251–271.

———. 1999. The global environmental benefits of land degradation control on agricultural land. World Bank Environment Paper 16. Washington, D.C.

Palm, C. 1995. Contribution of agroforestry trees to nutrient requirements of intercropped plants. *Agroforestry Systems* 30: 105–124.

Palm, C. A., R. J. Myers, and S. M. Nandwa. 1997. Combined use of organic and inorganic nutrient sources for soil fertility maintenance and replenishment. In *Replenishing soil fertility in Africa,* ed. R. J. Buresh, A. Sanchez, and F. Calhoun, 192–216. Madison, Wisc., U.S.A.: American Society of Agronomy and Soil Science Society of America.

Pearce, D. W., and J. J. Warford. 1993. *World without end: Economics, environment and sustainable development.* New York: Oxford University Press.

Pender, J. 1996. Discount rates and credit constraints: Theory and evidence from rural India. *Journal of Development Economics* 50: 257–296.

———. 1998. Population growth, agricultural intensification, induced innovation and natural resource sustainability: An application of neoclassical growth theory. *Agricultural Economics* 19: 99–112.

———. 2001. Rural population growth, agricultural change and natural resource management in developing countries: A review of hypotheses and some evidence from Honduras. In *Population matters: Demographic change, poverty and economic growth in developing countries,* ed. N. Birdsall, S. Sinding, and A. Kelley. Oxford, U.K.: Oxford University Press.

Pender, J., and B. Gebremedhin. 2006. Land management, crop production, and household income in the highlands of Tigray, Northern Ethiopia: An economic analysis. In *Strategies for sustainable land management in the East African highlands,* ed. J. Pender, F. Place, and S. Ehui, 107–140. Washington, D.C.: International Food Policy Research Institute.

Pender, J., and J. Kerr. 1998. Determinants of farmers' indigenous soil and water conservation investments in India's semi-arid tropics. *Agricultural Economics* 19: 113–125.

———. 1999. The effects of land sales restrictions: Evidence from south India. *Agricultural Economics* 21: 279–294.

Pender, J., and O. Mertz. 2006. Soil fertility depletion in Sub-Saharan Africa: What is the role of organic agriculture? In *Global development of organic agriculture: Challenges and prospects,* ed. N. Halberg, H. F. Alrøe, M. T. Knudsen, and E. S. Kristensen, 215–240. Wallingford, U.K.: CAB International.

Pender, J., and S. J. Scherr. 2002. Organizational development and natural resource management: Evidence from Central Honduras. In *Property rights, collective action and technologies for natural resource management,* ed. R. Meinzen-Dick, A. Knox, F. Place, and B. Swallow. Baltimore, Md., U.S.A.: Johns Hopkins University Press.

Pender, J., S. Ehui, and F. Place. 2006. Conceptual framework and hypotheses. In *Strategies for sustainable land management in the East African highlands,* ed. J. Pender, F. Place, and S. Ehui. Washington, D.C.: International Food Policy Research Institute.

Pender, J., F. Place, and S. Ehui. 2006. Strategies for sustainable land management in the East African highlands: Conclusions and implications. In *Strategies for sustainable land management in the East African highlands,* ed. J. Pender, F. Place, and S. Ehui. Washington, D.C.: International Food Policy Research Institute.

Pender, J., B. Gebremedhin, S. Benin, and S. Ehui. 2001a. Strategies for sustainable development in the Ethiopian highlands. *American Journal of Agricultural Economics* 83 (5): 1231–1240.

Pender, J., P. Jagger, E. Nkonya, and D. Sserunkuuma. 2001b. *Development pathways and land management in Uganda: Causes and implications.* Environment and Production Technology Division Discussion Paper 85. Washington, D.C.: International Food Policy Research Institute.

Pender, J., P. Jagger, E. Nkonya, and E. Kato. 2004a. Livelihood and land use options in northwestern Uganda. Mimeo. International Food Policy Research Institute, Washington, D.C.

Pender, J., S. Ssewanyana, E. Kato, and E. Nkonya. 2004b. *Linkages between poverty and land management in rural Uganda: Evidence from the Uganda National Household Survey, 1999/2000.* Environment and Production Technology Division Discussion Paper 122. Washington, D.C.: International Food Policy Research Institute.

Pinstrup-Andersen, P., and R. Pandya-Lorch. 1994. *Alleviating poverty, intensifying agriculture, and effectively managing natural resources.* Food, Agriculture, and the Environment Discussion Paper 1. Washington, D.C.: International Food Policy Research Institute.

Place, F., and P. Hazell. 1993. Productivity effects of indigenous land tenure systems in sub-Saharan Africa. *American Journal of Agricultural Economics* 75 (1): 10–19.

Place, F., S. Franzel, J. Dewolf, R. Rommelse, F. Kwesiga, A. Niang, and B. Jama. 2002. Agroforestry for soil fertility replenishment: Evidence on adoption processes in Kenya and Zambia. In *Natural resources management in African agriculture: Understanding and improving current practices,* ed. C. B. Barrett, F. Place, and A. Abdillahi. Wallingford, U.K.: CAB International.

Place, F., M. Adato, P. Hebinck, and M. Omosa. 2005. *The impact of agroforestry-based soil fertility replenishment practices on the poor in western Kenya.* Research Report 142. Washington D.C.: International Food Policy Research Institute.

Platteau, J. P. 1996. The evolutionary theory of land rights as applied to sub-Saharan Africa: A critical assessment. *Development and Change* 27: 29–86.

Qamar, K. 2005. *Modernizing national agricultural extension systems: Practical guide for policy makers of developing countries.* Rome: United Nations Food and Agriculture Organization.

Quisumbing, A. R., and R. Meinzen-Dick. 2001. Overview. In *Empowering women to achieve food security,* ed. A. R. Quisumbing and R. Meinzen-Dick. 2020 Focus 6, Brief 01. Washington, D.C.: International Food Policy Research Institute.

Quisumbing, A. R., J. Estudillo, and K. Otsuka. 2004. *Land and schooling: Transferring wealth across generations.* Baltimore, Md., U.S.A.: Johns Hopkins University Press.

Ravnborg, H. M. 2003. Poverty and environmental degradation in the Nicaraguan hillsides. *World Development* 31 (11): 1933–1946.

Reardon, T. 1997. Using evidence of household income diversification to inform study of the rural nonfarm labor market in Africa. *World Development* 25 (5): 735–748.

Reardon, T., and S. Vosti. 1995. Links between rural poverty and the environment in developing countries: Asset categories and investment poverty. *World Development* 23 (9): 1495–1506.

Reddy, S. R. C., and S. P. Chakravarty. 1999. Forest dependence and income distribution in a subsistence economy: Evidence from India. *World Development* 27 (7): 1141–1149.

Renard, K. G., G. R. Foster, G. A. Weesies, and J. P. Porter. 1991. RUSLE: Revised universal soil loss equation. *Journal of Soil and Water Conservation* 46 (1): 30–33.

Renkow, M. 2000. Poverty, productivity and production environment: A review of the evidence. *Food Policy* 25: 463–478.

Republic of Uganda. 1998. *Land Act, 1998.* Kampala: Government Printer.

———. 2007. *Interministerial framework for cooperation on the development and implementation of a country program on sustainable land management in Uganda.* Kampala: Government Printer.

Ribot, J. 2002. *Democratic decentralization of natural resources: Institutionalizing popular participation.* Washington, D.C.: World Resources Institute.

Riedmiller, S. 2002. Primary school agriculture: What can it realistically achieve? *Entwicklung und Laendlicher Raum* 28 (3/94): 9–13.

Sachs, J. D., J. W. McArthur, G. Schmidt-Traub, M. Kruk, C. Bahadur, M. Faye, and G. McCord. 2004. Ending Africa's poverty trap. *Brookings Papers on Economic Activity* 1: 117–240.

Sanchez, P. 2002. Soil fertility and hunger in Africa. *Science* 295 (5562): 2019–2020.

Sanchez, P. A., K. D. Sheperd, M. J. Soule, F. M. Place, R. J. Buresh, A.-M. N. Izac, A. V. Mokwunye, F. R. Kwesiga, C. G. Ndiritu, and P. L. Woomer. 1997. Soil fertility replenishment in Africa: An investment in natural resource capital. In *Replenishing soil fertility in Africa,* ed. R. J. Buresh, A. Sanchez, and F. Calhoun, 1–46. Madison, Wisc., U.S.A.: American Society of Agronomy and Soil Science Society of America.

Scherr, S. 2000. A downward spiral? Research evidence on the relationship between poverty and natural resource degradation. *Food Policy* 25(4): 479–498.

Scherr, S., and P. Hazell. 1994. *Sustainable agricultural development strategies in fragile lands.* Environment and Production Technology Division Discussion Paper 1. Washington, D.C.: International Food Policy Research Institute.

Scoones, I., C. Chibudu, S. Chikura, P. Jeranyama, and B. Zirereza. 1996. *Hazards and opportunities: Farming livelihoods in dryland Africa—Lessons from Zimbabwe.* London: Zed.

Semana, A. R., and E. Adipala. 1993. Towards sustaining crop production in Uganda. *African Crop Science Conference Proceedings* 1: 19–22.

Sen, A. 1975. *Employment, technology, and development.* London: Oxford University Press.

Sender, J., and D. Johnston. 2004. Searching for a weapon of mass production in rural Africa: Unconvincing arguments for land reform. *Journal of Agrarian Change* 4 (1–2): 142–164.

Shiferaw, B., and S. T. Holden. 1998. Resource degradation and adoption of land conservation technologies in the Ethiopian highlands: A case study in Andit Tid, North Shewa. *Agricultural Economics* 18: 233–247.

———. 2000. Policy instruments for sustainable land management: The case of highland smallholders in Ethiopia. *Agricultural Economics* 22: 217–232.

———. 2001. Farm-level benefits to investments for mitigating land degradation: Empirical evidence for Ethiopia. *Environment and Development Economics* 6: 336–359.

Shipton, P. 1988. The Kenyan land tenure reform: Misunderstandings in the public creation of private property. In *Land and society in contemporary Africa,* ed. R. E. Downs and S. P. Reyna, 91–135. Hanover, N.H.: University Press of New England.

Singh, I., L. Squire, and J. Strauss. 1986. *Agricultural household models: Extensions, applications and policy.* Baltimore, Md., U.S.A.: Johns Hopkins University Press.

Smaling, E. M. A., S. M. Nandwa, and B. H. Janssen. 1997. Soil fertility is at stake. In *Replenishing soil fertility in Africa,* ed. R. J. Buresh, P. A. Sanchez, and F. Calhoun. SSSA Special Publication 51. Madison, Wisc., U.S.A.: Soil Science Society of America and American Society of Agronomy.

Smaling, E. M. A., J. J. Stoorvogel, and P. N. Windmeijer. 1993. Calculating soil nutrient balances in Africa at different scales. II. District scale. *Fertilizer Research* 35: 237–250.

Ssali, H. 2002. Soil organic matter in Uganda and its relationship to major farming systems. Resource paper submitted to the International Food Policy Research Institute, Washington D.C.

Ssewanyana, N., A. Okidi, D. Angemi, and V. Barungi. 2004. Understanding the determinants of income inequality in Uganda. Centre for the Study of African Economies Working Paper 229. <http://www.bepress.com/csae/paper229>.

Stocking, M. 1996. Soil erosion: Breaking new ground. In *The lie of the land: Challenging received wisdom on the African environment,* ed. M. Leach and R. Mearns, 140–154. Oxford, U.K.: International African Institute and James Currey.

Stokey, N. L., and R. E. Lucas. 1989. *Recursive methods in economic dynamics.* Cambridge, Mass.: Harvard University Press.

Stoorvogel, J. J., and E. M. A. Smaling. 1990. *Assessment of soil nutrient depletion in sub-Saharan Africa: 1983–2000.* Report 28. Wageningen, Netherlands: Winand Staring Centre for Integrated Land, Soil and Water Research.

Sumberg, J. 2002. Livestock nutrition and foodstuff research in Africa: When is a nutritional constraint not a priority research problem? *Animal Science* 75: 332–338.

Swinton, S. M., G. Escobar, and T. Reardon. 2003. Poverty and the environment in Latin America: Concepts, evidence and policy implications. *World Development* 20 (10): 1–8.

Teklewold, H. 2004. Risk and time preferences on soil conservation decisions in the central highlands of Ethiopia. M.Sc. thesis, Department of Economics, Addis Ababa University, Ethiopia.

Templeton, S. R., and S. J. Scherr. 1999. Effects of demographic and related microeconomic change on land quality in the hills and mountains of developing countries. *World Development* 27: 903–918.

Tesfay, G. 2006. Agriculture, resource management and institutions: A socioeconomic analysis of households in Tigray, Ethiopia. Ph.D. thesis, Institute of Development Economics, Wageningen University, Netherlands.

Thirtle, C., L. Lin, and J. Piesse. 2003. The impact of research-led agricultural productivity growth on poverty reduction in Africa, Asia and Latin America. *World Development* 31 (12): 1959–1975.

Tiffen, M., M. Mortimore, and F. Gichuki. 1994. *More people—less erosion: Environmental recovery in Kenya.* London: Wiley.

Toulmin, C., and J. Quan. 2000. Registering customary rights. In *Evolving land rights, policy and tenure in Africa,* ed. J. Toulmin and J. Quan, 207–228. London: International Institute for Environment and Development and Natural Resource Institute.

Tripp, R. 2006. *Self-sufficient agriculture: Labour and knowledge in small-scale farming.* London: Earthscan.

Tukahirwa, J. 1996. Measurement, prediction and social ecology of soil erosion in Kabale, Southwestern Uganda. Ph.D. thesis, Institute of Environment and Resource Management, Makerere University, Kampala, Uganda.

UBOS (Uganda Bureau of Statistics). 1999. National Household Survey dataset. <http://www.ubos.org>.

———. 2002. National Household Survey dataset. <http://www.ubos.org>.

———. 2003a. *Uganda National Household Survey 2002/2003: Report on the socio-economic survey.* Entebbe.

———. 2003b. *Statistical abstracts, 2003.* Entebbe.

———. 2005. National Household Survey dataset. <http://www.ubos.org>.

———. 2006. *Uganda National Household Survey 2005/2006: Report on the socio-economic survey.* Kampala.

Udry, C. 1996. Gender, agricultural production, and the theory of the household. *Journal of Political Economy* 104 (5): 1010–1046.

UNCCD (United Nations Convention to Combat Desertification). 2007. *Africa action programs.* <http://www.unccd.int/actionprogrammes/africa/africa.php>.

UNDP (United Nations Development Programme). 2004. *Human development report, 2004: Cultural liberty in today's diverse world.* New York.

UPPAP (Uganda Participatory Poverty Assessment Process). 2002. Uganda Participatory Poverty Assessment Process national report final draft. Kampala: Ministry of Finance, Economic Development and Planning.

Varugheese, G., and E. Ostrom. 2001. The contested role of heterogeneity in collective action: Some evidence from community forestry in Nepal. *World Devolvement* 28: 201–230.

Vlek, P. L. G. 1993. Strategies for sustaining agriculture in Sub-Saharan Africa. In *Technologies for sustaining agriculture in the tropics,* ed. J. Rogland and R. Lal, 265–277. ASA Special Publication 56. Madison, Wisc., U.S.A.: American Society of Agronomy (ASA), Crop Science Society of America (CSSA), and Soil Science Society of America (SSSA).

Voortman, R. L., B. G. Sonneveld, and M. A. Keyzer. 2000. African land ecology: Opportunities and constraints for agricultural development. Center for International Development Working Paper 37. Cambridge, Mass., U.S.A.: Harvard University.

Wade, R. 1987. The management of common property resources: Finding a cooperative solution. *World Bank Research Observer* 2 (2): 219–234.

WCED (World Commission on Environment and Development). 1987. *World Commission on Environment and Development: Our common future.* Oxford, U.K.: Oxford University Press.

Woelcke, J. 2003. *Bio-economics of sustainable land management in Uganda.* Frankfurt: Peter Lang.

Wood, S., K. Sebastian, F. Nachtergaele, D. Nielsen, and A. Dai. 1999. *Spatial aspects of the design and targeting of agricultural development strategies.* Environment and Production Technology Division Discussion Paper 44. Washington, D.C.: International Food Policy Research Institute.

Wooldridge, J. 2003. *Introduction to econometrics.* Mason, Ohio, U.S.A.: Thomson Southwestern.

World Bank. 1992. *World development report: Development and the environment.* Washington, D.C.

———. 2006. *Where is the wealth of nations? Measuring capital for the 21st century.* Washington, D.C.

———. 2007. *World development indicators.* Washington, D.C. <http://web.worldbank.org/WBSITE/EXTERNAL/DATASTATISTICS/>.

———. 2008. Uganda sustainable land management public expenditure review (SLM PER). Mimeo. Washington, D.C.

Wortmann, C. S., and C. A. Eledu. 1999. *Uganda's agroecological zones: A guide for planners and policy makers.* Kampala, Uganda: Centro Internacional de Agricultura Tropical.

Wortmann, C. S., and C. K. Kaizzi. 1998. Nutrient balances and expected effects of alternative practices in farming systems of Uganda. *Agriculture, Ecosystems and Environment* 71 (1–3): 115–130.

Yesuf, M. 2004. Risk, time and land management under market imperfection: Applications to Ethiopia. Ph.D. thesis, Department of Economics, Gothenburg University, Sweden.

Yesuf, M., A. Mekonnen, M. Kassie, and J. Pender. 2005. *Cost of land degradation in Ethiopia: A critical review of past studies.* Addis Ababa: Environmental Economics Policy Forum in Ethiopia.

Zimmerman, F. J., and M. R. Carter. 2003. Asset smoothing, consumption smoothing and the reproduction of inequality under risk and subsistence constraints. *Journal of Development Economics* 71: 233–260.